PRAISE FOR *RISK MATURITY MODELS*

'Risk management maturity models enable organizations to gauge the development and evolution of their risk management practices. Domenic Antonucci's *Risk Maturity Models* stands out from other risk management texts on this topic because it provides very practical guidance, supported by numerous case studies. The book brings to life the benefits of risk maturity models when effectively applied and is simple but effective in its approach.'
Nicola Crawford, IRM UK Board member

'We live and work in an increasingly complex, faster-moving and connected world. The risk landscape faced by organizations today and in the future is increasingly one made up of intangible risks: risks typically more difficult to assess and control than more "traditional" physical risks. Intangible risks demand an enterprise risk management (ERM) approach – archaic risk silos have no place in this world – cyber is not just an IT risk, people are not just an HR risk. Risk management is at the top of the boardroom agenda and organizations are seeking ways in which they can evaluate and benchmark their ERM maturity. This authoritative book by Domenic Antonucci, a recognized international thought leader in the space of risk maturity, is a welcome addition to every risk professional's toolkit. The book follows a logical approach and is packed with information designed to explain risk maturity and to help risk professionals use this technique in support of their position as risk leaders and trusted risk advisors.'
Julia Graham, Airmic Ltd

'For years Domenic Antonucci has been one of the leading thinkers on risk management maturity models. Now he's sharing his thoughts in a book that can help others use maturity models as a means to advance risk management maturity. *Risk Maturity Models* should be in the library of every risk mana
practitioner who's looking to advance their risk management capab
Paul Sobel, Vice President/Chief Audit Executive, Georg
and ex-Chairman of The IIA

'Risk maturity models are useful to organizations that want to compare their current state of risk management capability to an appropriate target level. With his book, Domenic Antonucci offers risk practitioners not only a comprehensive review of existing risk maturity models, but also a method to build one that will satisfy the specific needs of any organization.'
Ghislain Giroux Dufort, President, Baldwin Risk Strategies Inc

'Risk Maturity is currently a hot topic within the Risk Management discipline, being mentioned in various standards as well as being discussed at length in conferences across the globe. Up until this book however, there have been a lack of publications on the topic. Domenic Antonucci provides a detailed insight into the history of Risk Maturity Models and their benefits.

The book is relevant to all organizations implementing risk management who are seeking more information on risk maturity models, whether they believe themselves to be "best in class" and looking for a way to measure their risk maturity, or having only recently started their Risk Management Journey and looking for a roadmap to help guide them to increased levels of maturity.'
Alexander Larsen, BHRM, FIRM, Risk and Controls Co-ordinator, West Qurna Project, Pilot Camp, Iraq

Risk Maturity Models

How to assess risk management effectiveness

Domenic Antonucci

KoganPage

First published in Great Britain and the United States in 2016 by Kogan Page Limited

2nd Floor, 45 Gee Street
London EC1V 3RS
United Kingdom
www.koganpage.com

1518 Walnut Street, Suite 900
Philadelphia PA 19102
USA

4737/23 Ansari Road
Daryaganj
New Delhi 110002
India

ISBN 978 0 7494 7758 5
E-ISBN 978 0 7494 7759 2

British Library Cataloguing-in-Publication Data

A CIP record for this book is available from the British Library.

Library of Congress Cataloging-in-Publication Data

Names: Antonucci, Domenic, author.
Title: Risk maturity models : how to assess risk management effectiveness / Domenic Antonucci.
Description: London ; Philadelphia : Kogan Page Limited, [2016] | Includes bibliographical references and index.
Identifiers: LCCN 2016016341 (print) | LCCN 2016024355 (ebook) | ISBN 9780749477585 (alk. paper) | ISBN 9780749477592 (ebook)
Subjects: LCSH: Risk management. | Risk assessment.
Classification: LCC HD61 .A567 2016 (print) | LCC HD61 (ebook) | DDC 658.15/5–dc23

Typeset by Graphicraft Limited, Hong Kong
Print production managed by Jellyfish
Printed and bound by CPI Group (UK) Ltd, Croydon, CR0 4YY

CONTENTS

LIST OF CONTRIBUTORS

Ahmed Barakat
Alex Dali
Alex Sidorenko
Alexander Larsen
Arnold Schanfield
Barbara Monda
Beaulah Misrole
Dan Clayton
Eddie McLaughlin
Ghislain Giroux Dufort
Grant Purdy
Henry Ristuccia and team
Henry Ziff
Kevin Knight
Liz Taylor
Michael Herrinton and his team
Nick Wildgoose and his board
Nicola Crawford
Martin Davies
Norman D Marks
Paul Hopkins
Sandra Parkins
Steven Halliday
Stig Sunde
Tim Leech
Toby Shore

ABOUT THE AUTHOR

Domenic Antonucci

Domenic is a practising chief risk officer and senior strategic risk, governance and compliance specialist. An Australian expatriate based in Dubai UAE, Domenic specializes in bringing organizations 'up the risk maturity curve' and building risk practitioner tools for implementing ERM, ISO 31000:2009 and COSO ERM. Formerly with Marsh Risk Consulting, Shell and Red Cross, he enjoys over 30 years experience in risk, corporate strategic planning and business management across many sectors in Europe, Africa, the Middle East, Asia and Australia-Pacific. A regular international conference presenter and author, he is the content author for various risk maturity model software releases. These include *Benchmarker*™ risk maturity model, the first tool to self-assess risk management effectiveness through a set of capabilities expected to be delivered by a head of risk and 'cross-walked' to both ISO 31000 and COSO ERM.

FOREWORD
By Kevin Knight

The concept of risk management has been around for decades with respect to the buying and selling of insurance and managing loss-control activities. With the publication of *AS/NZS 4360 – Risk Management* by Standards Australian and Standards New Zealand in 1995 and its subsequent revisions in 1999 and 2004, it moved into how organizations made decisions with respect to uncertainty. The publication of *ISO 31000:2009 Risk management – Principles and guidelines* saw the risk management process being applied to the management of the effect of uncertainty on organizational objectives and how managerial decisions created the risk of 'Is this the right decision and can the organization manage the decision to a successful outcome?' Risk was seen as neutral and management was focused on maximizing the opportunity whilst minimizing the threat.

Importantly, organizations should develop strategies to improve their risk management maturity alongside all other aspects of their organization. Risk maturity models are powerful tools to effect such strategies.

A consequence of this focus on managing the effect of uncertainty on objectives within the organization is the need to measure its effectiveness in achieving organizational objectives, as well as the effectiveness of line-management decision making with respect to risks under their control.

Domenic Antonucci takes us on the journey from the initial modification of capability modelling in 1997 and its evolution into a risk maturity model through to the multitude of risk maturity models competing for attention in today's marketplace.

The author asserts quite rightly that the highest purpose behind risk maturity models is, amongst other uses, to assess risk management effectiveness tailored to your unique organization. In the chapter 'Tailoring and benchmarking a risk maturity model' he provides a wealth of practical advice and examples to enable the risk practitioner to develop a risk maturity model that is focused on the needs of their organization.

Domenic brings many years of knowledge, skills and practical experience in the management of risk and organizations and the measurement of its effectiveness within a wide range of organizations. He is especially focused on the role of the board and top management in providing the mandate and commitment to ensure risk is addressed and managed, along with the important role of internal audit in providing assurance to the board that policy is in place and reporting is accurate, timely and rigorous with respect to the management of risk within the organization.

As he points out, the board 'must give it [the risk maturity model] equal importance to the risks themselves [managing risks]. They must demand and compare independent risk maturity assessments from the three lines of defence/offence. In the context of risk maturity, they should oversee that appropriate risk management principles are in-effect or not in-breach, how the risk and business functions do their risk managing and how IA coordinates combined assurance of the risk maturity model process.'

I am delighted to recommend this most practical contribution to assisting risk practitioners in providing boards and top management with the tools and information needed for them to effectively manage risk within their organizations but also to make the management of risk an integral part of the way the organization is managed and risk owners' performance is measured.

Kevin W Knight, AM
Chairman, ISO/TC 262 – Risk Management

FOREWORD
By Norman Marks

Risk maturity models – useful or an illusion?

I have not only used a maturity model to discuss the current condition of risk management with executives when I was a chief risk officer, but suggested in my book, *World-Class Risk Management*, that they can serve a valuable purpose: 'Risk management maturity models are an excellent way for organizations to see where they are, compare their current state to where they want and need to be if they are to derive full benefit and discuss the value and cost of further investment in risk management.'

But, there are preconditions to this being a useful exercise. For a start, there has to be agreement among all affected parties, from the board and top management through the risk officer to operating management, on what constitutes *effective* or *mature* risk management. I attempt to explain my position on that in the book by saying that 'effective risk management enables more intelligent and informed decisions'.

While it is useful, as John Fraser points out, to take stock every so often of the more significant risks to the achievement of objectives, it is arguably more important to recognize that risk is created or modified with every decision – not only at the executive or board level, but by individuals across the extended enterprise.

The effective management of risk involves understanding what might happen as you strive to achieve your objectives, then acting to provide greater assurance that: 1) what you want to happen does; and 2) what you don't want to happen does not.

The management of risk is not limited to avoiding open manhole covers – hazards – but increasing the likelihood and extent of reward. It is about optimizing potential outcomes, which translates to performance over time. In other words, it translates to success.

This is a challenge that thoughtful managers have been addressing since the dawn of time. What might happen to me or the business? What if I do this? What if I do that? What if I do nothing?

In other words, the consideration of risk (aka the management of risk, or 'risk management') should be an integral part of every decision. I will come back to that in a moment.

A second precondition is agreement on where you want to be. What is the desired state? If risk management is seen as a compliance exercise, or as a way of avoiding open manhole covers, rather than as a way to make better decisions and deliver performance, executive management will be satisfied (perhaps *complacent* is a better word) with just 'getting by'. Check the box and move on.

I would argue that the desired state is achieved when operating management at every level, as well as at the executive and board levels, agree that risk management helps them to set and execute more successfully on strategies. It helps them to make more informed, intelligent decisions every day.

In other words, it is when they need and want effective risk management. And that brings me back to my main point.

Risk management should never be an isolated activity. It should not be performed by a siloed organization.

No, risk management is – or should be, in a mature, world-class organization – an essential skill and activity of every manager and decision-maker across the extended enterprise.

Perhaps we should stop talking about risk management and, instead, just talk about effective management. So what should be the top level, the world-class or fully mature level of the risk maturity model?

I believe that it should be the state where management of the organization is, overall, world-class. Risk management feeds information and provides a structure for decision-makers at all levels to collectively and individually make the decisions that are necessary for the organization to thrive.

A maturity model can help explain where you are. But it only has real value when it helps explain what you are missing. It has to be aspirational.

The final precondition is that everyone involved has to be committed to taking the actions required to move up the maturity curve.

There is no certainty that a maturity model will drive the leaders of an organization to embrace and leap towards mature risk management. But when a risk officer (or internal auditor) uses risk management principles to consider and address the potential obstacles, great reward is possible.

Norman D Marks, CPA, CRMA

ACKNOWLEDGEMENTS

This book is dedicated to all practitioners and students of risk management, risk assurance and corporate governance who are looking to improve and move up the risk management maturity curve.

A big thanks to my best man and mate Stig Sunde, a senior audit professional who never takes offence when I jokingly call auditors bad names. My bigger thanks go to my wife Jenni for her forbearance and support, as well as to my reviewers and Jenni and Anna, my editors, for their trust and enthusiasm. They have all inspired me to keep going after-hours from my day job and sunny weekends when I would have preferred that glass of red to facing the computer screen.

LIST OF ABBREVIATIONS

CMM	Capability maturity model.
COSO	Committee of Sponsoring Organizations of the Treadway Commission, approvers of the COSO ERM (2004) Enterprise Risk Management – Integrated Framework.
CRO	Chief risk officer.
CxO	Executive or senior management team or C-suite member.
DCRO	Directors and Chief Risk Officers Group and Governance Council.
ERM	Enterprise risk management.
EY	Ernst & Young.
FERMA	Federation of European Risk Management Associations.
GRC	Governance, risk and compliance.
IA	Internal Audit.
IIA	Institute of Internal Auditors.
IIARF	Institute of Internal Auditors Research Foundation.
IRM	Institute of Risk Management UK.
ISO 31000	ISO International Organization for Standardization ISO/IEC (2009a) ISO/IEC 31000:2009 Risk Management – Principles and Guidelines on Implementation, Switzerland.
King III	'King Report on Governance for South Africa 2009' also known as 'The King Code of Governance Principles' by Institute of Directors in Southern Africa (IoDSA).
PwC	PricewaterhouseCoopers.
RIMS	Risk and Insurance Management Society, also known as RIMS, the Risk Management Society.
RMM	Risk maturity model.
SCRLC	Supply Chain Risk Leadership Council.
SEC	US Securities and Exchange Commission.
SEI	Software Engineering Institute at Carnegie Mellon University.
S&P	Standard & Poor's.

Introduction

Megan is sitting at her desk feeling lost and stressed. Her boss has just told her that she now has to present monthly to the Executive Committee and board on risk management, including an assessment of how effective the risk management is at her non-government organization (NGO). Megan has never before presented to the board. She has no budget and no staff. She has never been trained to be an enterprise risk manager and is not even sure what that role means. Megan is a quality manager.

Noting the dazed look on Megan's face, her boss did give her one tip: 'Megan, as a quality manager you know that the principle behind Six Sigma is to close our service defect gap to higher "sigma" levels of quality. You're a smart cookie. You know where Six Sigma came from, right? From capability maturity models. So, there is a version of these called *risk maturity models* where you gap-improve the capabilities needed for risk management. I suggest you check out risk maturity models and start using one. The board expects to see our first dashboard slide in six months. You won't need good luck, Megan, just a bit of application.'

Megan is one of four practitioners we shall return to shortly, with introductions to each of them. All four practitioners will contribute at various points throughout the book to provide alternative perspectives on issues and approaches to designing and managing a risk maturity model. Of the four, Megan's developing story has been chosen to start each chapter in order to demonstrate how easy it is for even a novice – with no enterprise risk management training, and no budget or initial internal support – to implement a risk maturity model and meet the demands of modern boards and senior management to assess enterprise risk management (ERM) effectiveness. Of all our four practitioners, Megan proves that nothing should be stopping your organization moving up the risk maturity curve.

Capabilities and risk management effectiveness

A *risk maturity model* is more correctly and fully termed a *risk management system capability maturity model*. For ease of use, we just call it a *risk maturity model* and we call the concept *risk maturity*. As Megan has discovered, it is a process-biased *capability maturity model* from the 1980s that has been evolving and has become specialized to an expanded set of *risk management system capabilities*. It represents a diagnostic tool using levels of *maturity* to track gap-improvement of the right set of organization capabilities designed to deliver risk management effectiveness.

When I worked in national security intelligence, we assessed the credibility of every bit of information from any source. But we also separately assessed and constantly reassessed the reliability of the source itself. The two ratings worked together to strengthen each other. The same principle should apply to the reporting of risks to boards and management. If a cartoon publisher took over the *New York Times* this month, would your level of confidence in the future quality of that newspaper drop? Would you wonder if the capabilities driving that newspaper would change with new editorial policy, new editorial staff and new objectives?

This question can be put another way: how confident are stakeholders (such as Megan's board and Executive Committee) in your organization's *capabilities specific to risk management* (as represented by the risk management system)? Do they support in practice the intent of the organization to report and take the right risks? A tailored risk maturity model is a powerful solution to assessing and improving risk management system capabilities over time and thereby assessing risk management effectiveness. It is probably the best tool of this type we have at hand. The challenge for the risk discipline is to unlock the full potential of the risk maturity model – a potential that is not even close to being realized as yet.

Our purpose

This book tries to do a few things. At the very least it is the first reference book and guide written for risk practitioners and management that is devoted to the specific subject or domain of ERM risk maturity. It is also written by a practising head of risk with experience in balancing the needs that are lower on the risk maturity curve for developing/emerging organizations (like Megan's) with those of 'higher maturity' developed organizations. In fact, my focus is less on what is *at the top* of the risk maturity curve and more on *what it takes to move up* the curve. That is why this book contains resource directories and other mechanisms as reference guides. As to personal bias, I freely declare I am Australian with my own risk maturity software in the market and my own set of views within my profession. I have tried hard, however, to remain as unbiased as possible throughout the book.

This book hopefully represents a few other things as well. It is a thought-piece to inspire researchers and scholars to do more to quantitatively and qualitatively measure risk maturity models. This research should not just suit the developed-level elites but the developing world and still-developing organizations. This book is a challenge to old or fixed mindsets to open up and get tailored to what is a best-fit to their organization's needs over slavish standardization. It is a call to arms for the risk profession to continue on the road to professional recognition by at least agreeing on a core set of enterprise-wide risk management capabilities (yes, some standardization). Put more simply: what are the *capabilities* needed for risk management effectiveness? What are those *right things* to do (ie effectiveness-enhancing capabilities)? It is a pointer to the future where boards, chief executive officers (CEOs) and auditors will ask for the risk maturity rating of their organization as naturally as they now ask for how it treats significant risks.

Above all, this book is a declaration of how relatively easy it is to just get going with a simple spreadsheet. This is because all the reference information that is needed is at hand at no or low cost and now this book can guide you to it. I would like to show people how – and get them on their way. Being a practising chief risk officer helps, as I know a thing or two about the practice and have the inclination to share it.

I recall in Shell Downstream in the 1980s we informally applied some of the principles behind risk maturity levels to assist how much support we gave to resellers and distributors to improve their capabilities. I was later introduced to my first *formal* risk maturity model in 2008 in Melbourne, Australia. The board at that time effectively wanted a benchmark rating as to '*How bad are we at risk management compared to everyone else?*' This was the first year that the organization was implementing ERM to the ASNZ 4360:2004 standard (the precursor to ISO 31000:2009). Marsh was our insurance broker and Marsh Australasia used a new tool that at the time they called Risk Focus. It rated my organization as about average. This met with some board relief. But then an interesting thing happened: all further interest died. This struck me as a great shame and rather odd. Here was something begging the organization to continue to self-improve its capability in risk management, yet it was treated as a tick-box or check-box and... we just left it at that.

I also moved on, but in a different way. I saw the potential for me to continue to develop that rather raw tool of the day as an ongoing self-improvement tool for organizations. I wished I had been using it in a formal way back in my Shell days, where we did a lot of excellent if informal risk management. So, in short, I have been working through one improved version after another since 2008, reading and researching widely, discussing it with working peers, testing it within – or on – one organization after another and from one country or region to another.

Whilst doing so, I noted other risk maturity models (RMMs). I noted that they came in all sorts of shapes, colours and sizes. The idea solidified that if the ERM discipline practitioners could agree on what capabilities we are supposed to be improving then it must help the ERM discipline to become a recognized profession.

Risk maturity models still climbing up their own risk maturity curve

The other point of interest for me about risk maturity models is the irony. As a tool approaching 20 years of age, risk maturity models still remain relatively immature. They still have a long way to develop and grow in usage across the world, especially the developing world with huge numbers of organizations. I question some voices saying that risk maturity models are outdated and ask: how so – when we have not been maturing and applying them correctly as yet? I modestly admit that even after so many years of improving my own model, it is still developing and heading up the elusive maturity curve.

Global potential

The global potential for risk maturity models is ambitious, but why not? Every time you read a media headline, is it not talking about yesterday's risk that has now been realized? When the highest regulator in the United States (the SEC) blames the 2008–09 global financial crisis on bad risk management, but does not even suggest one practical remedy – as I think they should have – don't you want to cry out, 'but where is the guidance on the capabilities that organizations need in order to do better risk management?'

Introduction to our practitioner representatives

I also hope to spice up your reading by introducing differing practitioner perspectives. This promotes the importance of tailoring by introducing some fictional character devices. May I introduce our four fictional character avatars: Asha, Chris, Alan and, of course, you have already met Megan at the opening to this Introduction. They represent a mix of risk-related roles and types of organization sectors and risk cultures. They will offer different ways of approaching the opportunity to create and adapt your own tailored risk maturity model. This is to enhance the applicability of the content as well as reinforcing the concept of tailoring a risk maturity model as a best fit to each organization.

Each of these characters is fictional but they are very real composite types that the author has worked alongside or known. Hopefully you may recognize some of their personal traits and work cultures from where you yourself work. They are also meant to represent an interesting mix of differing needs from an effective risk maturity model in the hope that more readers may relate to them.

Introducing Asha

Asha is a new hire but an experienced head of ERM for a very large multinational listed recruitment firm. Their culture is summed up in their brand tagline 'People mean business'. The company is headed up by an entrepreneur and supports every progressive 'employer of choice' mantra. They enjoy the highest levels of technology available and a budget is always found for a reasonable business case. Asha is catching up with how a people-oriented commercial business should be run but is keen to demonstrate how ERM can add value.

Introducing Chris

Chris is a young risk and insurance manager for a small to medium-size private construction and contracting company. Their culture is 'blokey', hands-on, directive and a proud 'family-style business' and 'small/lean/mean' manufacturer. Profit is project-driven. They rely on staff experience; project or risk plans, registers or other sophisticated tools are not used. Technology is to them 'what the kids do at home' and the organization only uses basic e-mail, mobile phones and non-connected PCs. Chris knows he needs to 'KISS' (keep it simple, stupid) in order to get risk management going at this 'old-style' business.

Introducing Alan

Alan is a switched-on member of the internal audit team for a medium-sized government-owned power utility. Their culture is businesslike, cool, professional, technical and ordered. The engineers like their process maps. The organization deploys mixed levels of technology – modern office technology, basic in-field technologies and advanced technologies for product maintenance and customer billing/services. Alan gets on well with the new ERM manager heading up the ERM programme – that includes a tool called a risk maturity model – and is interested in collaborating with this fast-growing new discipline and tool. Alan assures and acts as an independent assessor for an existing risk maturity model that the ERM manager stewards.

Introducing Megan

Megan is a quality manager for an NGO running government-funded welfare, mental health and education programmes. She is effectively a risk manager, but her company culture avoids even using the word 'risk' because lawsuits and other external pressures from clients have made both management and staff wary of formalizing 'risk'. Her work environment is full of proud and caring professionals who are strong on standards and procedures (SOPs) and incident reporting/compliance using basic office technology. Many of the programmes involve long-term and complex projects with many stakeholders. Budgets are tight. She wants to move into ERM, where she hopes to add value to her organization.

Starting with the background to risk maturity models

Our four practitioners will undertake their own journeys throughout this book. We start with a background chapter clarifying the basic concepts and definitions behind risk maturity models and how they are connected to the organization's need to assess risk management effectiveness.

Our practitioners weave in and out of the narrative. In our final summary their individual stories will be pulled together to see how they have grown from no or limited experience with risk maturity models to being positive and capable risk maturity modellers.

Background to risk maturity models

01

This chapter covers:

- Concepts and definitions
- Capability not competency or capacity
- *Tailored risk maturity model* meaning
- *Assessing risk management effectiveness* meaning
- Origins of capability maturity models
- Risk maturity model offshoot
- Misunderstandings:
  - All models are born equal
  - Global best practice
  - Progression without regression or stasis
  - Just a tool
- Summary

Introduction

Megan, a quality manager at an NGO, had been given a formidable task and felt lost. Using the information contained in this chapter, Megan learnt to understand the way that *risk* maturity models evolved away from the *capability* maturity models that lead to Six Sigma and other concepts in quality management that she was more familiar with. She did not feel lost anymore but understood the direction she needed to take with risk maturity. She even had a few misconceptions cleared up along the way.

The purpose for this background chapter is to start by clarifying the basic concepts and definitions behind risk maturity models and how they are connected to the organization's need to assess risk management effectiveness. We trace how, since 1997, risk maturity models have evolved away from their parent, the capability maturity model. We learn how risk maturity models have expanded to cover multiple risk-related capabilities other than just process. We clear up some common misunderstandings to clarify language and to avoid things that should not deter organizations from 'moving up the risk maturity curve'. This enables us to understand the benefits and potential in these models, which is covered in Chapter 2.

Concepts and definitions

A *risk maturity model* is a *capability maturity model* adapted to the needs of risk management. It serves, amongst other benefits, as a powerful tool to *assess risk management effectiveness*. Understanding each of these terms one step at a time will help to compare, tailor, design and enhance your risk maturity model in our later chapters.

The meaning of capability maturity model

The meaning of *maturity*

A dictionary definition for *maturity* and to be *mature* takes in several perspectives that are a mosaic of several notions (COED, 2011). The economic, industry or organization perspective defines it as developing to a point where substantial expansion no longer takes place. A people or organisms perspective defines it as becoming or being fully developed, full-grown, having reached a stage of mental or emotional development, characteristic of an adult, or to be grown-up. A process perspective means reaching the most fully developed stage for that process. A thought and planning perspective takes in being of a careful and thorough nature. A food and drink perspective means becoming ready for consumption, or in a ripe state. Finally, a bill, insurance policy or security perspective involves becoming due for payment having reached the end of its term.

The *maturity* concept relates to the current or future state, fact or period of being mature. For organizations, this concept relates to the current or future state, fact or period of evolving development, quality, sophistication and effectiveness of attributes characteristic of that organization. Of course, this is not necessarily age-dependent. For example, New York University (NYU) reported recently that their ERM global programme and risk management at their newest campus operation in China was more mature than the parent operation founded in 1831.

In other words, maturity is a path or direction ascending from low to more highly developed capability state or states. This ascending direction implies increasing effectiveness over various time periods. However, progression states are always subject to periods of stasis (where progress stays still or travels sideways) and regression (where progress goes backwards).

The meaning of *maturity model*

A *model* represents a simplified description of a system or process to assist evaluation, calculations or predictions. It is typically repeatable and testable over time.

A *maturity model* uses a model of some sort to order its subject matter content into maturity-related structures. A *maturity model* conceptualizes a systemic or organized way to follow a path of organization actions. It normally applies a mix of theory, practice, experience, wisdom, 'perfection' assumptions or acculturation. It assumes that the working answer to the common question 'what is effective/what works?' for an organization lies in some form of progression over time, rather than a creation event at one point in time. It harks back to the adage 'Rome was not built in a day'.

In process terms, a *maturity model* involves some type of repeatable construct with content representing inputs and outputs leading to outcomes. The model often takes the form of a ladder, continuum or set of structured ascending levels or classes describing content that is evolving, developing or adding more sophisticated qualities over time. The content subject area can vary and may represent almost anything. It may be actions, objects or things but it typically includes progressive ways of doing something, characteristics of something, initiatives, practices and processes.

Maturity models are often dubbed 'road maps' for planning and implementation purposes. This signifies that maturity models attempt to transform content that may be complex and difficult into a more simplified actionable system to 'road map' improving, desired, anticipated, typical or logical evolutionary paths for organization actions.

It is important to note that whilst maturity model evaluations may outline anticipated, typical, logical and desired evolutionary paths, these paths need not necessarily lead to 'perfection' or 'best practice' for an organization within any given time period. For example, a simple maturity model could define a path of successively improved tools for doing maths to track finances: using fingers, using an abacus, using an adding machine, using a slide rule, using a computer, or using a hand-held calculator. Using a hand-held calculator may be viewed as a more mature tool than a slide rule but you may not be willing and able to use one if you are a hunter-gatherer tribe in Highland New Guinea where one's fingers may still be effective at the lowest cost.

Our working definition, then, is that a *maturity model* is a simplified system that 'road maps' improving, desired, anticipated, typical or logical evolutionary paths of organization actions. This ascending direction implies increasing effectiveness over time but need not necessarily lead to 'perfection' or 'best practice' for an organization (albeit subject to stasis and regression).

The meaning of *capability maturity model*

Capabilities are the specific abilities, faculties or powers of an *organization*, enabling it to collectively deliver organization objectives in the face of threats and to leverage opportunities. Capabilities may include unused and undeveloped or still-developing abilities that lend themselves to assessment as to how complete they are at any current point in time (as-is) or can be at a targeted period of time (to-be).

For organizations, capabilities can be represented or evidenced by the interaction of many tangibles. These may change over time and may be qualitatively and/or quantitatively measured. Capabilities include but are not limited to: processes, technologies, assets, people, decision-related behaviours, practices, attitudes, competencies, disciplines and approaches of an organization to achieve or exceed their objectives. Another way to think of a capability is to think of a specific ability as a flow diagram, being inputs-to-outputs-to-outcomes where the end outcome is the achievement of specific organization objectives and strategies. For example, a sales training programme (an input) can improve customer relationship management (output) leading to organization growth targets being met (outcome). Put more simply, the key challenge for an organization is: is it capable of 'doing the right things' to achieve objectives? Those 'right things' are likely to represent capabilities when correctly framed and prioritized.

Capability levels are indicators, positions or stages on a scale of quantity, extent, rank or quality of organization capability. These are typically achieved by visible and verifiable evidence for the implementation of each capability and its attributes or subcomponents.

A *capability maturity model* at its simplest focuses a maturity model on the maturation of one specific organization process capability. A typical example is software engineering development where 'maturity' measures the degree of formality and optimization of processes, typically ascending in maturity levels from ad hoc practices to formally defined steps, to managed result metrics, to active optimization of the processes.

The term *capability maturity model* started becoming popular in the 1980s within the US software engineering sector. The term developed with several permutations over time within this sector. Early on, *maturity* was seen more simply as 'the state of being complete, perfect or ready' (Simpson and Weiner, 1989). By 2005 within the information systems (IS) discipline, *maturity* was seen more pragmatically as 'a measure to evaluate the capabilities of an organization' (Rosemann *et al*, 2005). By 2009, *capability maturity models* were seen to be facilitating 'evaluation by outlining anticipated, typical, logical and desired evolution paths' (Röglinger, Pöppelbuß and Becker, 2012). By 2011, it implied an evolutionary progress from an initial to a desired target or naturally existing end-stage (Marx, 2011).

Modern-day researchers are still refining the capability maturity model. This is yielding increasingly clearer descriptions of the model elements, classification schemes for models and construction methods. However, what commonly defines the shared components for all modern capability maturity models is that they share, as a minimum: process maturity levels, different process dimensions and a process assessment instrument (Rosemann *et al*, 2005).

We return to this point later, but what is important to note here is that the original software sector and its followers have a quite narrow definition of a capability maturity model as modelling the maturity capabilities of a *specific organization process* to deliver the defined objectives of that process to its process owners. It focuses on a set of organizing capabilities for a process rated to a maturity level or dimension (being the degree to which processes are institutionalized) and the degree to which the organization demonstrates process maturity. It does not focus on non-process capabilities.

Capability does not mean competency or capacity

Capability does not mean competency

Competency and capability are not the same. The two terms have become confused by some over the years and are sometimes used as synonyms when in fact this confusion should be avoided and the terms need to stay completely separate.

A *competency* is the underlying ability of an *individual* to perform a job or task properly or excel at it, by combining a set of observable knowledge, skill and attitude that often results in work behaviours. In order for a competency to be considered a competency it must have all of these elements in play, according to the IIA Global Internal Audit Competency Framework 2012. As basic definitions, *knowledge* is application at work of content or material obtained through the use of experience, books or any other medium. *Skill*, on the other hand, is the ability to execute a certain task. *Attitude* demonstrates a person's willingness and/or intent.

By this definition, a *competency* therefore is an applied knowledge that a person is willing to use to excel at a certain task. Some prefer to think of it in the form of a common sequence as in 'apply knowledge then attitude then skill equals task done'. Competency professionals test and assess for competencies using observable indicators that may answer the following types of questions: 'Given a few minutes or hours sitting beside an employee at work, would I be able to quantify (count) and qualify (rate) these behaviours?' For the sake of clarity, competencies should not be ascribed to an organization, albeit the similar language and techniques used may confuse.

Capability on the other hand, within our context here, involves the ability or power of an *organization* to *collectively* deliver organization objectives. Capability is not confined to just individual people and people-related knowledge, skills and behaviour (even to risk-informed decision making). It is escalated and widened to teams, units, divisions and projects evoking an organization culture, technology, process, reputation and so forth. Capabilities represent what the organization is good at and known for. These capabilities outlive the performance or behaviour of any individual manager or single management system. For, say, the human relations/culture domain, such capabilities might include innovation, speed, customer focus and efficiency so that the *capability* of the organization reflects not just the amalgam of speed, efficiency and so forth, but the deeper values of the employees and the organization.

In our sense, then, a competency is a subset or part of one or more capabilities but not the other way around. So if a capability maturity model or risk maturity model contains many capabilities, one or a few of these may relate to competencies. For example, one capability that may be designed into your risk maturity model may be described as: 'Appropriate competencies of all risk owners to manage a risk management plan evidenced in part by risk training, risk knowledge and appropriate application of risk-informed management decision making.'

Capability does not mean capacity

Capacity and capability are not the same. This confusion should also be avoided. *Capacity* commonly refers to the maximum amount that something can contain or produce (COED, 2011). For organizations, this is typically expressed in terms of metrics for the use or build-up of resources to a desired or measured level, optimum or maximum. For example, in a capacity-planning context, it is a process for sizing the operational demand for a technology or other asset over a variable range of operational needs. In financial and actuarial circles, it can refer to *material risk-bearing capacity* to financially measure the capacity of the organization to take a financial 'hit' on the books, or to invest in a new opportunity (implied by capital and funding constraints). Like *competency*, *capacity* is best considered a subset or part of one or more capabilities. For example, one capability may be described as: 'A flexible organization capacity to provide appropriate resources to enable risk owners to effect risk action plans to which they are accountable and responsible.'

The meaning of a tailored risk maturity model

The meaning of *risk maturity model*

A *risk maturity model* is a capability maturity model specialized to an expanded set of *risk management system* capabilities. It is expanded because it is not just concerned with process maturity, like a standard capability maturity model, but a wider range of organization capabilities, as we previously noted and will continue to note throughout this book.

System commonly means a set of things working together as a mechanism or interconnecting network at the organization level. This should not be confused with an information technology system (albeit a risk management system may include risk management information systems).

Risk is the 'effect of uncertainty on [organization] objectives where the effect is a deviation from the expected – positive and/or negative' (ISO, 2009b: 1.1). *Risk management* means the coordinated activities that direct and control an organization in pursuit of its objectives with regard to risk, according to the ISO 31000:2009 risk management standard (ISO, 2009a) and its associated vocabulary guide (ISO, 2009b: 2.1). *Risk management* for our purposes is synonymous with such terms as *enterprise risk management* (ERM), *integrated risk management* or *strategic risk management*.

Risk management for ISO 31000 involves the architecture (principles, framework and process) for managing risk effectively. In other words, the risk principles, risk management framework (policies, mandate, standards, the organization resources, systems, culture and so forth to enable it), a common risk management process and their desired objectives or outputs-to-outcomes. These are ideally integrated or aligned by the different operating units and functions to existing management systems. A *risk management plan* refers to a scheme within the risk management framework specifying the approach, the management components and resources to be applied to the management of risk.

All these things may be considered *risk management capabilities* suitable for tracking with a *risk maturity model*. Whilst ISO 31000 does not use the collective term *risk management system*, this is common parlance and is promoted by King III (2009), the leading corporate governance standard. Therefore, we will use it for the purposes of this book as a useful and accurate term of convenience. We take the elements cited by what ISO 31000 calls *architecture* as representing desired capabilities within a risk management system and suitable content for a risk maturity model.

Risk maturity model is a shortened term that is sometimes reduced further to *risk maturity* (but assumed to be tracked by a *risk maturity model*). The more correct full term should be: a *risk management system capability maturity model*. That is, a *maturity model* focusing on the *capabilities* characterizing the *risk management system*, being the interconnected mechanisms organizing the right organization capabilities to deliver risk management effectiveness. However, this is cumbersome parlance for all, so the popular term for convenience of use is *risk maturity model*.

Risk maturity must not be confused with the 'maturity' of a risk, as in the maturation or realization of specific risks per se within the risk assessment process. For example, it should not be confused with risks moving from a watch-list status to a 'closed/archived/treated' status; or, moving from the so-called 'unknown-unknown risk' to a 'known-unknown' status.

Risk management maturity is cited by ISO 31000:2009 in strategic terms. It states that organizations should develop and implement *strategies to improve their risk management maturity* alongside all other aspects of their organization (Principle k). These strategies involve the planning and deployment of deliberately coordinated and resourced initiatives to improve organization capabilities specific to the *risk management system* – including its outcomes – in order to achieve maturity targets aligned to organization objectives.

The meaning of a *tailored risk maturity model*

A *tailored* risk maturity model means it represents a best fit or optimal fit to your unique organization. Following the ISO 31000 approach, 'tailoring' your risk maturity model means it becomes bespoke and as customized as possible to three elements:

- your organization **objectives**;
- the changing internal, and the internal and external, **context** in which it operates;
- the changing **risk profile** it adopts.

For *risk maturity models*, tailoring is driven primarily by choice and quality of the *capabilities* content and *scales*, and influenced by external and internal *benchmarking*, model design of *components*, and other techniques and methods.

In summary, a *risk maturity model* is a capability maturity model specialized to an expanded set of *risk management system* capabilities. It represents a diagnostic tool using levels of *maturity* to track gap-improvement of the right organization capabilities designed to deliver risk management effectiveness. More correctly: a *risk management system capability maturity model*.

The meaning of assessing risk management effectiveness

Assessing is to evaluate and/or to use a diagnostic. The aim is to arrive at an estimate of a nature, value and quality.

Effectiveness is to produce a desired or intended result (COED, 2011). For organizations, this equates to a focus or mantra on 'doing the right things' such as planning and delivering the right organization objectives and the capabilities needed to do so. This may be applied for the risk maturity domain by simply substituting the word 'things' with the more specific word 'capabilities' – as in 'doing the right capabilities'.

Practitioner Chris separates effective from efficient systems

Chris's new boss came from an investment bank. The boss is fond of expensive computer risk software and high-end financial risk and quantification techniques and he introduces them to the construction firm. These produce some novel and faster risk reports that seem to initially improve the risk analysis and reporting steps in the risk process. However, there is a lot of passive resistance from most of the line managers who are not ready for such technology at this 'small/lean/mean' outfit. This passive resistance has a GIGO-effect (garbage-in-garbage-out). This means the overall rate of risk treatment effectiveness fell rather than rose. Chris feels that the new boss has confused efficiency with effectiveness, to the detriment of the latter.

Assessing risk management effectiveness is to evaluate 'doing the right things' in terms of the risk management system capabilities that include the desired risk management outputs-to-outcomes. For our purposes, this means evaluating the capability improvement gaps between the current 'as-is' state and targeted future 'to-be' states of the risk management system over planned budget periods. 'Doing the right capabilities' must be able to be evidenced and reasonably assured for their adequacy and effectiveness (as per ISO Guide 73: 3.8.2.6; ISO, 2009b). This is opposed to 'doing things right', which defines *efficiency*, not *effectiveness*. Risk management ineffectiveness (ie the risk of ineffective risk management) is arguably the greatest risk of all to organization success.

Assessing risk management effectiveness from an internal audit/board perspective typically means an objective written assessment of the effectiveness of the system of risk management and the internal control framework to the board (King III, 2009). Assessment typically includes monitoring, review and assessment techniques applied towards the effectiveness of the *risk management system*, its issues and constraints, and the need for improvements. Results should be shared with executive management and board.

Origins of capability maturity models

It is difficult to appreciate the power of risk maturity models without understanding their history and provenance (a record of ownership of where a work came from to establish trust). We defined the *risk* maturity model as an evolutionary offshoot of the *capability* maturity model (often dubbed CMM) that is adapted to the specific domain of risk management capabilities. Here, we quickly trace the origin of the risk maturity model since 1997, starting with its parent, the capability maturity model. In this way, we appreciate the history of the risk maturity model as a proven but still evolving tool that is still underutilized around the world and yet to release its full potential in widespread global practice from developed to developing countries.

We also appreciate that we can expect cross-fertilization to the enterprise risk management (ERM) umbrella domain to continue into the future. Therefore, if we want to design and improve our risk maturity models we need to understand where to look. ERM practitioners will continue to draw from new capability maturity models as the latter will continue to represent a sister body of knowledge for inspiration and for potential submodels feeding their own ERM-level models.

Capability maturity models (CMMs)

Capability maturity models began as a process maturity framework with origins in 1920s industrial quality control. The first pioneering work to assess how managers could improve a single process originated with Walter Stewart at Western Electric in 1924 where he became known as the father of statistical quality control. The second pioneer was Watts S. Humphrey and his 1989 book *Managing the Software Process*. The model was focused in this 1980s era in evaluating the ability of government and US Department of Defence military contractors to perform software projects. It was only concerned with the software engineering process.

The capability maturity model has diversified since the 1990s into an internationally recognized model with broader domain applications than software engineering. Over time, the theory behind the capability maturity model has inspired other like-models. It has been applied to most corporate functions and a variety of large and small organizations across many industries/sectors. These include: software development, systems engineering, project management, defence, business development and human resources.

SEI-style capability maturity model

The work by the earliest pioneers of the capability maturity model (CMM) were further developed at Carnegie Mellon University in the late 1980s.

This still forms the foundation of most maturity models today. By 1991, the Carnegie Mellon University Software Engineering Institute (SEI) released the Software Capability Maturity Model (commonly referred to as the 'SEI CMM').

The SEI model increments process development from one level to the next along a theoretical continuum of process maturity. It is process-centric and the focus is on single-process capability improvement. The predictability, effectiveness and control of an organization's software processes are believed to improve as the organization moves up five maturity levels. Within each of these maturity levels are key process areas, which characterize that level. Skipping levels is regarded as either not allowed or not feasible.

A typical SEI CMM has five Likert scale levels with titles and short descriptors:

- ***Initial (Chaotic) – level 1*** title describes undocumented or dynamically changing processes, tending to be driven in an ad hoc, uncontrolled and reactive manner by users or events.
- ***Repeatable – level 2*** describes some repeatable processes with some consistent results but process discipline is unlikely to be rigorous, especially under stress.
- ***Defined – level 3*** describes sets of defined and documented standard processes that are established, provide consistent process performance and are subject to some degree of improvement over time.
- ***Managed – level 4*** refers to the use of process metrics and other ways to manage, adjust and adapt processes to ensure effective control without measurable losses of quality or deviations from specifications.
- ***Optimizing – level 5*** refers to a focus on continually improving process performance through both incremental and innovative technological changes/improvements.

SEI capability maturity model components

As the SEI style of capability maturity models developed over time, the number of hierarchical components grew:

- ***Maturity level*** components are organized on a five-level process maturity continuum where the uppermost (fifth) level is a notional ideal state where processes would be systematically managed by a combination of process optimization and continuous process improvement.

- ***Key process areas*** appear under each level; these identify a cluster of related activities that, when performed together, achieve a set of goals considered important.
- ***Goals*** for each key process area summarize the states that must exist for that key process area to have been implemented in an effective and lasting way. The extent to which the goals have been accomplished is an indicator of how much capability the organization has established at that maturity level. The goals signify the scope, boundaries and intent of each key process area. The goals are of two types, either specific goals leading to specific practices, or generic goals sharing common features (see below) and leading to general practices.
- ***Common features*** include practices that implement and institutionalize a key process area. There are five types of common features: commitment to perform, ability to perform, activities performed, measurement and analysis, and verifying implementation.
- ***Key practices*** are the key practices to describe the elements of infrastructure and practice that contribute most effectively to the implementation and institutionalization of the area.

SEI CMM competition, constraints and growth

The major competitor to the SEI Capability Maturity Model (CMM) is *ISO/IEC 33001:2015 Information technology – Process assessment – Concepts and terminology.* This replaced its predecessor the ISO/IEC 15504 Capability Maturity Model, as of March 2015. ISO/IEC 33001 supporters prefer their model for a number of reasons. Supporters claim it is publicly accessible through national standards bodies (rather than through one 'expensive' private source), that it therefore has more international support through these national standards bodies and that it and ISO/IEC 15504 have proven themselves through over 4,000 assessments conducted to date over a range of industries. These industries include automotive, space and medical systems with industry-relevant variants.

Capability maturity models have constraints. We have already seen how they have a maturity-of-process bias. Further, this maturity-of-process methodology is not mandatory for commercial success. This is demonstrated by some of the better-known software development firms, including 'shrink-wrap' companies (also called commercial-off-the-shelf or 'COTS' firms or software package firms). Such firms have included Claris, Apple, Symantec, Microsoft and Lotus. Critics claim that these companies have successfully developed their software, without having considered or managed their processes as a capability maturity model. Moreover, if they had done so, they would be better rated as a typical SEI CMM lower level 1 or 2 (as described above).

Despite their limitations, capability maturity models have evolved since the early 1980s and have successfully branched out. The original aim of CMM to improve existing software development processes has now been applied to many other business processes, including business development, supply chain, human resource, work culture, project management, business intelligence, information security, corporate reputation, health sector management, business resiliency and record keeping. CMMs are sector-extensive across the world, especially in government offices, commerce, industry and software development organizations. They have even been combined with other methodologies such as the ISO 9001 standard, extreme programming (XP) computer programming methodology and Six Sigma (as we saw with our practitioner Megan).

Risk maturity model *offshoot to capability maturity model*

The risk maturity model offshoot

The SEI-style of capability maturity model has been adapted to the risk management discipline since 1997 with *risk maturity model* offshoots. Sometimes the same SEI-style labels and descriptors as we outlined earlier have been slavishly copied by the risk management discipline with little thought to tailoring.

As we mentioned earlier, the risk management discipline and the remit for risk maturity models is wider than just a set of processes. A risk maturity model is a set of structured levels that integrate a mix of *multiple capabilities*. These capabilities do not just involve processes but include how the behaviours, practices, attitudes, competencies, disciplines and approaches of an organization interact to produce organization *outcomes*. These represent a *risk management system*. There are many components that make up a set of organization capabilities, far more than just the sort of processes most people think when they see a process map on a process chart, or the risk process diagram in ISO 31000:2009.

Practitioner Alan looks beyond a single capability model approach to multiple capabilities

Alan understands that the utility company he works for is very process-driven and relies on information technology (IT). For this reason, he had checked out both the *ISO/IEC 33001:2015 Information technology – Process assessment* standard and the SEI capability maturity models as they too are quite process-driven. He thought they might function well as reference material to independently assure by an annual audit the existing risk maturity model that the ERM manager was stewarding. He decides that his IT people might be interested in a capability maturity model for assessing their own process effectiveness as an IT function. But he also feels that the ERM manager is quite correct in saying that a capability maturity model is too narrow for ERM purposes and that the maturity levels are not a great fit to their utility. Alan also found support for the need for a multi-capability risk maturity model when he read McKinsey & Co for more guidance (Pergler, 2012).

Risk management maturity evolves from a process bias to capabilities

Alan's preferred solution goes to the need for a multiplicity of capabilities to make up a risk management system. Alan found an interesting article from McKinsey & Co with a particular take on the evolution of modern risk management that Alan did not agree with (Pergler, 2012).

McKinsey sees modern risk management origins in a set of disciplines, as well as processes, cradled within financial institutions since the 1980s. There was some cross-industry transfer from financial institutions to the non-financial sector. This was beneficial but differences between the two sectors developed in terms of expectations, challenges, language and many other *capabilities*. The non-financial sector evolved from an initial health and safety focus – especially in heavy industrial and natural-resource companies – and developed a 'risk register-bias'. McKinsey believes that this capability bias meant that the non-financial sector 'routinely miss or woefully miss-estimate the risks that end up really mattering to the achievement of their overall objectives or even fundamental health'. McKinsey goes on to say that 'these differences in maturity are neither accidental, nor irrelevant. Rather they reflect underlying differences in drivers of value creation, including assets and exposures, but also strategic capabilities; risk management can be one of these.'

McKinsey sees ERM as a journey for all business sectors over several stages of a maturity spectrum. As of 2012, McKinsey believed that certain sectors could be attributed to certain ascending maturity stages:

- The average retail and telecommunication corporates represented an intermediate ***Stage 0 to 1***.
- Financial institutions such as smaller regional banks represented ***Stage 1***.
- Strong natural resources exposures and important technical/research and development (R&D) risk sectors such as pharmaceutical corporates represented an intermediate ***Stage 1 to 2***.
- The average financial institutions represented ***Stage 2***.
- Energy corporates (using increasingly mature liquid commodity markets), conglomerates and asset managers/investors (juggling diverse portfolios of assets) all seeking competitive advantage in a crowded competitive arena represented an intermediate ***Stage 2 to 3***.
- Only a handful of investment banks represented ***Stage 3***.

Why McKinsey avoided the simpler maturity stage numbering from 1 to 4 or 5 is not known. The article (Pergler, 2012) does highlight our key point as to how far risk maturity models moved to expand from one to multiple capabilities. For McKinsey, then, key maturity-rating criteria are not just 'processes' but a diverse range of *organization capabilities* (such as asset management, competitive intensity and strategy, including risk management but also touching on risk registers, expectations, challenges and language).

Practitioner Alan feels risk management predates the 1980s

Practitioner Alan has one correction to the McKinsey view. He feels that the risk management discipline predates the adoption by financial institutions in the 1980s, not the other way around. Risk management draws on roots in the legal, insurance, project management as well as health and safety disciplines that predate the 1980s and were not sector specific. Alan had learnt a lot from an older mentor at his utility who, as an internal auditor, had lots of experience assuring these specialty risk disciplines that were important to utilities (and energy/oil and gas sectors) from the 1960s and 1970s.

FIGURE 1.1 Value contributed by evolving risk management

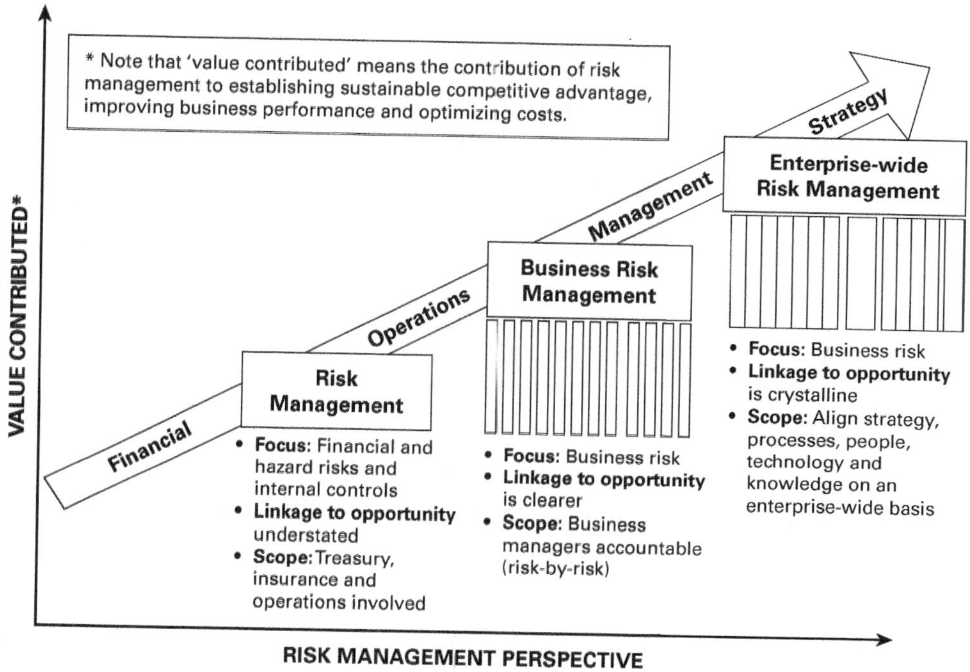

SOURCE: Reprinted with the kind permission of Dr Steven Halliday

One way of visualizing such evolution is to look at how risk management has value-added to the organization over time. Figure 1.1 (Halliday, 2012) summarizes this value-add evolution, which was not solely dependent on the financial sector.

Early risk management maturity model trends

The first risk management maturity model offshoot from an already-evolving line of capability maturity models came in 1997 with a groundbreaking paper from David Hillson (Hillson, 1997). Hillson dubbed his offshoot a 'risk maturity model' (or 'RMM'). He aggregated organization-level risk management maturity capabilities into four domains or themes: culture, process, experience and application. This represented a watershed for the risk discipline.

After an initial five-year hiatus, the Hillson risk maturity model of 1997 has been followed by a steady release of risk management-related models to the present day. The initial trend was for the release of various risk management subdomains such as project risk management. Over time, other content was blended into risk maturity models. Content often benefited from cross-fertilization from related disciplines. The European Foundation for Quality Management (EFQM) excellence programme and approaches is one notable example.

Later variations added domain-specific risk maturity models. The most notable of these was the enterprise risk management (ERM) domain, which has flourished. ERM risk maturity models were tailored to various industries or sectors and geography, such as those specific to Canadian national health services and even to Dutch municipalities. Some prominent dates and early risk maturity models included a mix of ERM and sub-ERM domains as follows:

- 2002 saw the release of a project risk-focused model called risk management maturity models (RMMM) by INCOSE.
- 2003 saw the release of a business continuity-focused model called BCCM® and a HR risk-culture-focused model by HRDC.
- 2006 saw an enterprise risk management (ERM)-focused model (Chapman, 2006) and a sophisticated project-focused model called the project risk maturity model (Hopkinson, 2011).

This rich evolutionary 'bush' of risk maturity models is represented in Figure 1.2. This summarizes how capability maturity models have continued

FIGURE 1.2 Maturity model evolution

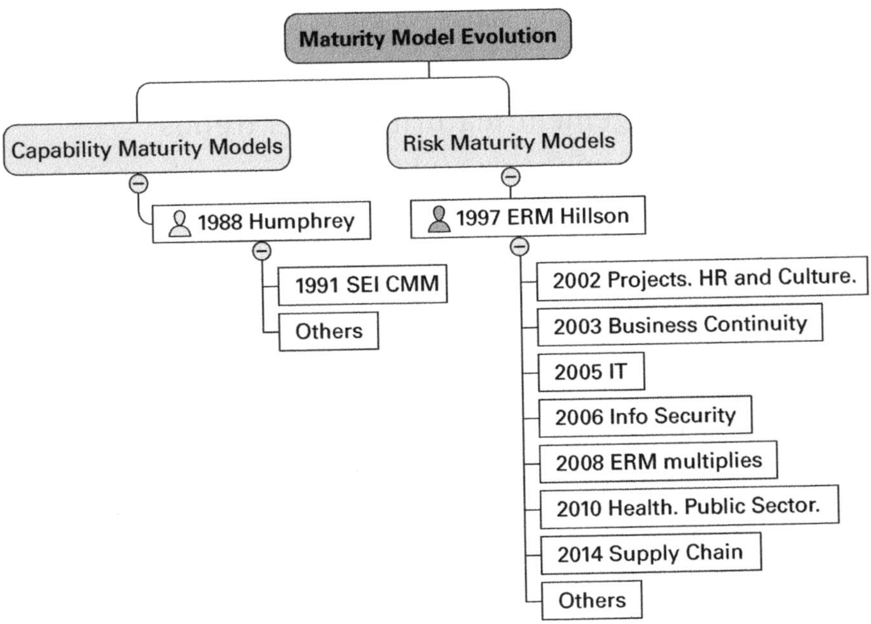

evolving whilst risk maturity models branched off in 1997 into ERM and ever-more risk-specialized offshoots to the modern day.

As in nature and biology, such evolutionary diversity is a most beneficial aid for maturity modellers wanting to tailor their own risk maturity model to their organization's internal and external context. Continuous improvement drives evolving risk maturity models akin to how biological evolutionary forces such as natural selection do the same for speciation. The diversity in model approaches provides a rich range of source material for tailoring. These sources continue to grow.

Now that we have some clearer vocabulary, let us turn our attention to some important misunderstandings that need to be clarified before closing this background chapter.

Misunderstanding 1: all models are born equal

All risk maturity models are not born equal. As in nature and biology, individuals of the same species may appear superficially equal and/or the same but their DNA and behaviour differ. If the highest purpose for a risk maturity model is to be tailored or fit-for-purpose to the unique organization, then logic declares that at least some or a number of models are never going to fit every organization. Some models will naturally be a better-fit-for-purpose for the unique organization than others.

From an organizational macro-perspective, all risk maturity models are valuable for at least three reasons. First, starting your risk management system somewhere and building on it over time is far better than doing nothing at all and especially so for early or low maturity organizations. Second, parts or attributes from any risk maturity model – even for one capability or a level description – can be put to use or influence the tailoring of your own model. Some part or whole of any model can be tailored and adapted to suit your organization. As many models are conceptual in nature, this lends itself to tailoring. Third, this inclusive attitude to content is a positive. It helps drive continuous improvement for the risk discipline/profession and for the common good.

In the end, you will find that you can tailor parts or the whole of some risk maturity models far more appropriately to your organization than others. Finding the right mix for you and your organization is the trick.

Misunderstanding 2: global best practice

There is a common search for what is termed *global best practice* in ERM and risk maturity models. Unfortunately, there is no such thing – at the time of writing – as an internationally agreed absolute or ideal. There are models that are 'good' or 'better' relative to each other in terms of tailoring and those that are better fit-for-purpose for a specific organization than others. However, there is no current 'best' model in either absolute quality or global reach terms, nor is one a mandatory requirement for risk maturity modelling. There is no 'silver bullet' model or one-size-fits-all.

What does *best* mean anyway – best at what, compared to who? Why do you need a model? Who is going to decide on it? Where will it apply? How can you prove it to senior stakeholders? Those brave risk management consultants who may have gone down the mistaken path of initially agreeing to work to a client brief clamouring for 'best practice' have often rued that agreement. We need to be cautious if we recall what has happened to all those Tom Peters lauded companies of the 1980s. We must not forget that Enron was held up by McKinsey & Co and others as 'global best practice' before it crashed. For a sobering Enron post-analysis do not go to Wall Street, read Malcolm Gladwell's account (Gladwell, 2009). Gladwell summarizes that the McKinsey-led 'very best and brightest talent' culture mindset that was the vogue at the turn of the century led to the Enron collapse in a mire of so-called brilliant mathematical models, twisted special-purpose vehicles and complex accounting.

The 'global best' misconception probably stems from how relatively naive and immature the enterprise risk management discipline is – ERM as a discipline is still feeling its way, is somewhat naive and playing 'catch-up' to far more mature professions such as the internal audit, project management or insurance professions. These related professions enjoy well-established tools, techniques, trade media sponsorship, deep coffers from large professional memberships and bodies of knowledge that spell out their capabilities to boards and executive or senior management (CxOs). The Project Management Institute's 'Project Management – Body Of Knowledge' (PM-BOK®) is one example of this. Other professions understand and have a common agreement as to the set of core capabilities they bring to the table. As yet, the risk 'profession' does not.

The claim to being 'global' is overused and needs to be used very carefully. Standards that are ISO-designated through accredited national bodies may legitimately claim to be 'global'. However, most other so-called frameworks or voluntary reference codes are not *global*. No matter how good they are – or they can be – they are national or at best semi-regional and usually support narrow commercial interests.

If a tag or label is required then *global best practice* may be attractive but it is unnecessary. The risk profession should be confident using a range of quite adequate terms as alternatives. *Striving towards global best practice* reflects the true reality and a better way to approach the matter. *World-class* is debatable but acceptable, as it does not imply an absolute and allows for more than one class or level. *Industry best practice* is a popular term that overcomes the challenges by the term global best practice and can be referenced by external evidence by researchers and organizations sharing data and approaches. *Global practice, good practice, better practice, appropriate practice, relevant practice, recommended practice* (by leading authorities and practitioners), *leading practice* or *best-fit–to-standards* are all acceptable. These can be substantiated by transparent criteria (ie be evidence-based) that garners stakeholder buy-in and they can be sustained over time.

Misunderstanding 3: progression without regression or stasis

The natural science process of evolution is not one of continuous smooth progress. Rather, it involves fits and starts and adaptations with readaptations and shorter or longer periods of stasis depending on the external environment and competition. Think of the various species such as whales that evolved from land to pond to sea then back again over time. The evolution lesson is that progression-regression-stasis are inseparable processes and not a smooth transition.

This lesson applies equally to the risk maturity domain. Organizations rarely progress smoothly or with any 'big bang'. Progressing from a lower phase of development or sophistication (maturity) to a higher phase rarely goes perfectly or evenly across all fronts. For some organizations the cost in investment, time and management distraction means that uniform progression on all capability fronts without stasis – or occasional regression – is neither an option, nor reality, nor even perhaps an ideal target.

In fact, an organization getting on in age probably leads to various forms of natural stasis – even fits and starts. Moreover, changes in environment and competition sometimes lead to organization regression. BP, for example, used to rate itself right up there on the maturity curve with the best.

Practitioner Megan reflects on BP and regression

Megan was interested in learning from the largest accidental marine oil spill in history, the BP Gulf of Mexico 2010 disaster, when the Deepwater Horizon offshore oil platform exploded. It caused 11 fatalities, reputation loss, a share price cliff-fall and at least US $65 billion in damages and reparations. She guessed that the oil giant rated its risk maturity level very highly at close to 90% Level Index after 100+ years of safety and risk management operations. Megan was shocked to discover when she looked into the causes that the BP subcontractor involved in the blowout had a nonsense risk register. This register was such a bad 'copy-and-paste check-the-box job' that it registered icebergs and whale risks in the Gulf of Mexico! Megan doubted that the cause could be swept under the carpet as just individual human error and oversight by a few individuals intent on taking safety and quality shortcuts. She is convinced this was not just one capability deficiency in, say, supplier management. She feels that the CEO comment that led to his forced resignation ('You know, I'd like my life back') corroborates her conclusion that Deepwater Horizon represented a very costly form of risk maturity regression when a highly risk mature organization's culture becomes too arrogant and complacent from the top-down and at any point in-between. She understands now that risk maturity is not only about managing progression, but regression and stasis as well.

CASE STUDY Regression case study: INFRACO, infrastructure firm

A real infrastructure company (name withheld, dubbed INFRACO) in the Middle East was newly established with a small permanent organization of up to 650 staff. In turn, it had to manage a multi-billion infrastructure mega-project via 1,500 external programme management company (PMC) staff. The PMC in turn, managed up to 16,000 workers. The project ran for six years over a large footprint size (equal to a quarter of Rhode Island in the United States or half of Singapore island). In effect, a two-track risk maturity developed: the new CEO ramped up the project and project-risk management maturity on the mega-project to a level he believed to be 'world class'. However, the associated resource constraints, executive management focus on the mega-project and cultural barriers between 'project' and 'corporate' staff meant that INFRACO itself remained way back on the risk maturity curve. When the mega-project successfully opened, the CEO moved on, the skilled ex-pat workforce were retrenched to improve the 'nationalization quota percentage' and both the PMC risk function and the ERM corporate risk function were demobilized. The organization, which had improved its overall risk maturity index from 6% to 40% over two years, had on rerating, regressed back to 32% with significant shortfalls in capability modules for managing the risk management process, treatment, monitoring, culture and embedding, and communication. The overall outcome was that the board and senior management had reduced confidence in the remaining organization's ability to manage risk effectively and needed to reinvest more money and at least two years of ERM programme work to recover to their previous level. Three years later, a brand new internal audit team is trying to restart an ERM programme for the third time in the organization's short nine-year history by 'incubating' it without dedicated ERM officers. See Chapter 5 on Designing a tailored risk maturity model, Figure 5.12 – INFRACO Benchmarker™ bar-chart sample.

Regression is uncommon, at least in each corporate memory. When it may occur, the risk function must be alert and warn in advance of its potential or advent. Typical lead indicators or triggers for regression include:

- major change in organization operations;
- merger or acquisition;
- new senior management or board;
- reorganization;
- major resource reallocation or cost-cutting programmes (most often in response to external economic or internal financial crisis).

Misunderstanding 4: just a tool

There is a famous adage that 'Essentially, all models are wrong, but some are useful' (Box, 1976). This excellent adage is true for risk maturity models as well. Is a risk maturity model just a tool, in a pejorative sense? The answer is both yes, and... no.

For the 'yes' case, no matter how well the risk maturity model is applied, the risk and audit functions still need the right mix of people competencies to apply their hand to the tool. People still remain the ERM drivers and process the 'hand-rail' (meaning an inert guide of no use unless put to its designed use by people). Any tool or technology will never make up for this. For example, look at the demanding combination of qualities or competencies that a risk director, chief risk officer (CRO) and risk function need to have according to the Directors and Chief Risk Officers Group (DCRO) and Governance Council (DCRO, 2013). They include multiple competencies categorized under: risk management acumen, personal attributes, business acumen, education, and experience. Tool-use does not at face value figure prominently here.

For the 'no' case, a risk maturity model tool is a powerful enabler – if not an ERM driver. This is not to say that a risk maturity or any model will guarantee organization success – no single model will guarantee this. However, it is a powerful tool to assess risk management system effectiveness. Look at the huge number of tools cited in ISO/IEC 31010:2009 (ISO, 2009c). If the risk and management disciplines accept such a brilliant range of tools just for the risk assessment process alone then there surely is no issue with adding a tool to road map a wider range of capabilities (including that risk assessment process). Practical risk managers and professionals generally want what is useful and works today – perfection can wait for tomorrow. Risk maturity models work.

In Chapter 2 we start to see how such a powerful tool is useful by understanding the many benefits of using a risk maturity model.

Summary

This background chapter clarifies the basic concepts and definitions behind risk maturity models and how they are connected to the organization's need to assess risk management effectiveness. We trace how risk maturity models have, since 1997, evolved away from their parent, the capability maturity model and the SEI CMM. We learn how risk maturity models have expanded to cover multiple risk-related capabilities other than just process. We clear up some common misunderstandings regarding risk maturity models: being treated equally, so-called 'global best practice', progression without regression or stasis states, and their status as a tool.

The case for a risk maturity model

02

This chapter covers:

- Benefits delivered
- Benefit in assessing risk management effectiveness
- Alternatives that complement risk maturity
- Limitations of the model
- Summary

Introduction

Megan no longer felt at a loss because she now understood what risk maturity models are and how they can be used. She saw her way was clear now that she had a grasp of the risk maturity model concept and held no misconceptions that might deter her or her organization from 'moving up the risk maturity curve'. Now she wanted to understand the effectiveness of a risk maturity model and how to mount her investment case backed by numbers and strong research.

ERM and a risk maturity model both deliver measurable benefits

In an increasingly changing and competitive world, organization management is under constant pressure to justify investment in doing the right sets of things needed to achieve or exceed objectives. Many organization disciplines and their tools – ranging from financial management to quality management to internal audit – have matured over the last century or more in such a way that they are now well accepted by boards and CxOs as worthy of ongoing investment.

In this context, the enterprise risk management (ERM) discipline is a recent arrival and the risk maturity model as a powerful ERM tool is an even more recent arrival. Both are still gaining acceptance and need to justify investment in order to create or protect organization value. Both work in tandem with each other and are the stronger for this. Both enjoy clear and proven benefits but these need clarity and better communication and promotion to stakeholders. For our purposes, we use ERM as synonymous with 'risk management' as the research we cite commonly does so.

If you are to design and implement a tailored risk maturity model, you will need to communicate the range of 'soft' and 'hard' benefits that both ERM and the risk maturity model bring to an organization in order to justify investment and the required top-management mandate and commitment. By 'hard' benefits we use the parlance of many CxOs at for-profit organizations. They expect to see from risk management and risk maturity models the tangible measures and success metrics of the sort they are familiar with as key performance indicators (KPIs) – as well as the intangible, generic or qualitative 'soft' benefits. We separate 'hard' from 'soft' benefits here as these CxOs often expect a case for investment to separate or balance both types.

You will also need to address the common problem that even when that investment and mandate from the top is granted, ERM and risk maturity management often breaks down in practice at the middle- and front-line management levels. According to the CEB Risk Management Leadership Council website, this assertion is supported by two-thirds of their surveyed ERM chief risk officers and ERM team leaders who believe line management lack the necessary accountability and capability to become part of the process and therefore cannot address significant risk to their organizations (CEB, 2016). I believe the CEB figure is wrong. The figure is probably closer to 90%+ globally (taking into account the non-US developing world and small to medium-size organizations).

Another reason why understanding these benefits is important is that – contrary to the advantage that boards and auditors enjoy – there is no specific regulation known anywhere in the world mandating the existence of ERM or a risk maturity model. This places a harsh burden of proof on the latter, which is ironic.

Practitioner Asha ponders ERM and maturity success metrics

Asha is an experienced head of ERM for a very large multinational listed recruitment firm that is open to any reasonable business case. She is keen to demonstrate how ERM can add value, and knew of some research behind strong bottom-line and top-line returns that support the use of a risk maturity model in particular and ERM in general.

Asha found it ironic, however, that some sort of double standard was at work. Her research failed to find any 'hard' evidence in the way of success metrics for both corporate governance/boards and internal audit, so why the constant pressure on risk management? She found a quote from Standard & Poor's (S&P), who reviewed the governance literature and, from their own experience of rating more than 3,000 corporate enterprises, summed up as follows:

> *Precisely determining what actually constitutes positive, strong (or good) governance has proven to be elusive even for the most experienced and seasoned thinkers on the subject... However... governance deficiencies at rated enterprises can, and on occasion have, led to both sudden and sharp deterioration in credit quality and that is why we have 'neutral' options for governance subfactors.' (S&P, 2012)*

Asha also found that the Institute of Internal Auditors (IIA) as the peak professional body admits it has very little in the way of organization metrics to demonstrate that internal audit (IA) adds value (IIA Austin Chapter Research Project 2008–09).

Of course, Asha would never suggest that boards and IA should or can be dispensed with but she was left feeling a combination of both resignation that the double-standard may not be adequately explained but also a sense of pride that ERM and risk maturity models do work – and that the risk discipline could do better to demonstrate their benefits. Her pride was based on not only the proven benefits and metrics for overall ERM programmes but specific to higher over lesser risk-mature organizations. She saw ample proof of this in the benefits section (see over) which was then reinforced by how risk maturity models contribute to assessing risk management effectiveness and how they complement alternative solutions to the latter within natural constraints. Asha made use of these success metrics to justify her investment case in risk maturity models.

Benefits delivered by ERM and a risk maturity model

Answering past ERM detractors

There will always be doubters as to the benefits for ERM and for assessing ERM effectiveness using a risk maturity model. Take McKinsey as one detractor, at least in the past. They referred back in 2012 to the 'absence of robust statistical evidence that "more mature risk management", however defined, would necessarily translate into better performance' (Pergler, 2012).

Supporters and practitioner-users of the risk maturity model strongly refute such detractor claims as either underinformed or outdated. So let us now look at the positive evidence, first for the benefits of ERM then for using a risk maturity model. The two are in natural synergy and work in tandem with each other.

ERM delivers 'soft' benefits

As we noted earlier, not-for-profit organizations have a different benefits focus. They focus more on stakeholder rather than shareholder value and cost-effective operations with the best allocation of resources to deliver service and other objectives (as outputs to outcomes). Much of the value here is qualitative and some quantitative in nature, especially in terms of budget efficiencies in delivering services and cost-control improvement results.

The story is different for for-profit organizations, where effective ERM benefits are well researched and available. ERM optimizes risks with positive consequences for organizations (ie the opportunities that create enterprise value). ERM controls or reduces the risks with negative consequences (ie that which protects enterprise value). In both these ways it reduces the level of uncertainty (ie risk) as to achievement of objectives.

KPMG see these ERM benefits in terms of business improvement strategic imperatives. These are to improve financial and operational performance, reduce losses and enhance competitive advantage (KPMG, 2008). KPMG states that ERM offers organizations a way to:

- reduce cash-flow volatility using derivatives, insurance or improved controls;
- allocate and evaluate capital based on risk-based performance;

- integrate risk and business planning, investment, and mergers and acquisitions (M&A);
- reduce costs through risk consolidation and cross-functional efficiencies;
- reduce losses through coordinated enterprise risk monitoring and reporting.

The above generic benefits represent a shortlist. One global ISO training body provides a *long list* of ERM benefits, as below. This long list is worth referring to for maturity modellers when designing and improving their models or assessing their risk management effectiveness by representing desired outputs of the risk management system and thereby acting as design question 'prompters'. That is: *Which specific capabilities are the right ones that should deliver x and y (chosen benefits)?* The tailored answers for your organization will most likely deliver the most benefit:

1 Improve overall management (create value). For example:
   - increase likelihood of achieving objectives;
   - improve performance;
   - improve competitive advantage;
   - treat opportunity as well as threat;
   - informed and reliable decision making;
   - improve operational effectiveness and efficiency;
   - effective allocation of resources;
   - encourage proactive management;
   - assess and treat/respond to risks;
   - improve controls.

2 Better financial performance (create value). For example:
   - reduce financial losses;
   - better return on capital;
   - better credit rating;
   - better conditions for corporate loans;
   - reduce long-term cost of risk.

3 Enhance reputation (create value). For example:
   - can be explicit part of brand value (eg Volvo, Mercedes, Qantas);
   - to bounce back or avoid crisis or reputation-damaging events or states (resilient, adaptive organization);

- to investors as secure sustainable investment;
- to supply chain for sustainability;
- as best-employer to attract and retain talent.

4 Respect laws and regulations (protect value). For example:
  - better compliance;
  - better health, safety and security for staff and supply chain;
  - respect environment and sustainability;
  - improve mandatory and voluntary reporting.
5 Reducing losses. For example:
  - improve loss prevention;
  - minimize losses, waste, frauds;
  - improve organization resilience;
  - better business continuity and maintenance management;
  - improve incident management.
6 Improve governance and internal controls. For example:
  - improve stakeholder confidence and trust;
  - improve corporate governance;
  - provide sound system of internal controls;
  - provide better accountability and audit;
  - improve protection for shareholders.

  Note: The public sector may focus more on stakeholder rather than shareholder value and cost-effective operations with the best allocation of resources to deliver the objectives (as outputs to outcomes).
  (Adapted with permission from C31000 Certification Foundation Training by G31000 Global Institute for 31000, 2013.)

The long list above may be summarized in one presentation slide for the benefit of presenting to senior management and stakeholders. This may help garner the investment and mandate and commitment needed to implement your risk maturity model over long periods of years. Figure 2.1 shows one example of such a summary slide.

The above reference to competitive advantage is worth noting. Accenture has correctly pointed to the natural link to strategic planning and how risk

FIGURE 2.1 Presentation slide: ERM pays at many levels to create not just protect value

ERM pays at many levels to create not just protect value

Create value	Protect value
• **Improve overall management** eg Improve performance and competitive advantage • **Better financial performance** eg Better return on capital • **Enhance reputation** eg part of brand value (eg Qantas)	• **Respect laws and regulations** eg Better health, safety and security for staff and supply chain • **Reducing losses** eg Improve loss prevention • **Improve governance and internal controls** eg Improve stakeholder confidence and trust

NB: Public sector may focus more on stakeholder rather than shareholder value and cost-effective operations with the best allocation of resources to deliver the objectives (as outputs to outcomes).
Acknowledgement: Adapted from C31000 Certification Foundation Training (Global Institute for 31000, 2013)

SOURCE: C31000 Certification Foundation Training by G31000 Global Institute for 31000, 2013

management capabilities can drive competitive advantage and not just present boards with 'risk lists':

> [There is] a growing recognition that companies have an opportunity to drive competitive advantage from their risk management capabilities, enabling long-term profitable growth and sustained future profitability. This means that risk management at the top-performing companies is now more closely aligned with strategic planning and is conducted proactively, with an eye on how such capabilities might help a company to move into new markets faster or pursue other evolving growth strategies. (Accenture, 2011)

ERM delivers 'hard' quantitative benefits

ERM offers for-profit organizations a range of 'hard' benefits. These include benefits in terms of key performance indicators such as market capitalization gains, stock price fall protection and certain financial returns. We summarize below the surveyed results since 2000 from a variety of sources ranging from consulting firms to economists. The results demonstrate tangible benefits from ERM enabling risk-smart decision making over time.

Market capitalization post-incident gains

ERM can provide a 23% difference by driving a +7% value gain (value creation) and avoid a 15% drop (value protection) in market capitalization due to better responses to a crisis or major incident threatening the share price (Knight and Pretty, 2000). Economists Knight and Pretty found that a realized risk that results in a 'crisis or incident' has a severe negative impact on financial results, brand, reputation or relationships with employees, customers or suppliers. The ability to respond effectively will have a major immediate impact on shareholder value and long-term impact on reputation/brand and therefore market share.

Major stock-fall recovery and stock price protection

The largest risk management consultant firm in the world, Marsh Risk Consulting, reported that 87% of major stock price falls are triggered by strategic risks rather than financial (9%), operational (2%) or hazard (1%) risks (Marsh, 2008). That is, by those risks holistically attended to by ERM rather than traditional risk management. Marsh studied 129 of the FTSE 250 companies in 26 sectors between 2003–07 and found that 50% never recovered their share price to the previous months' closing levels after witnessing their biggest fall. Marsh determined the primary cause of the trigger event(s), categorized causes and analysed that implications were strategic risks and that they represented the major contributors to stockholder wealth (de)generation.

Rajeev Peshawaria has worked in leadership development for leading corporations. Peshawaria attributes 65% of stock price to intangible value, promises of future economic benefits based on the quality of leadership and management, ability to innovate, the depth of talent and employee engagement (Peshawaria, 2012). Again, that is by those risks holistically attended to by ERM rather than traditional risk management.

Other financial returns improved

KPMG assert from their experience with thousands of clients worldwide that ERM directly contributes to a variety of improved returns. These include: better credit rating, cost of capital, investment returns, hedging costs and insurance costs (KPMG, 2008).

Risk management process improved return on investment

Some managers may view ERM primarily in process-centric terms as an organization or business process enabler. If so, then ERM process improvement may be assumed to be a contributor – amongst others – to overall business process management. Business process management research studies by the EFQM (formerly known as the European Foundation for Quality

Management) and McKinsey client survey reports (Luyckx, 2009a) claim a return on investment (ROI) in business process management (BPM). BPM is a systematic approach to improving a company's business processes, usually involving IT solutions. They claim returns in the order of:

- increased revenue of up to +35%;
- reduced costs of up to –30%;
- an agile organization that is able to quickly adapt to changed market situations.

Risk maturity models deliver a variety of 'soft' benefits

ERM-domain risk maturity models offer a stunning variety of 'soft' benefits. The key qualitative benefit and highest application is as a powerful tool to assess risk management effectiveness. We will cover this benefit in further detail shortly.

From a strategic perspective, a risk maturity model tracks how well the organization is doing the 'right things' to deliver its targeted outcomes in terms of organization objectives and strategies affected by uncertainty (risk). It provides a 'road map' of the right capabilities to support short-term and long-term planning by clearly identifying next steps and related resources to cover gaps (CEB, 2016). The road map of improvement activities supports a shift from compliance to business performance through effective risk management over several-year rolling periods and encourages integration of maturity targets into long-term strategic and business plans. It assists alignment of strategy and resources with business needs and improves performance and executive-enhanced strategies.

From a methodology perspective, risk maturity models are multipurpose. Depending on their design and use, they can represent a diagnostic, audit tool, benchmarking tool, model for creating a plan of action or road map.

From the perspective of the existing array of ERM maturity models in the public marketplace, their benefit statements have been surveyed. These are summarized below to serve as a useful reference for an investment or business case, as we may assume that their originators have already successfully used these benefits for their internal business cases. The study uses the data from the sample of 49 ERM maturity models from our directory set out in Chapter 3. We summarize key points and some sample sources from the study; not-for-profits are separated in order for better tailoring by readers from that sector.

Benefits cited from the not-for-profit sector

The not-for-profit sector perceives risk maturity model 'soft' benefits as focused on improving discrete organization success indicators using maturity capabilities (NSW Treasury). These are to be embedded 'at all levels of the organization... to inform a discussion [by government departments] whether resources need to be allocated or diverted to fill gaps to improve capability in key areas of risk management excellence' (Treasury Board of Canada, 2015). Others saw benefits in annual reporting and public statements about the review of risk management and internal control (HM Treasury, 2004) and in securing leadership buy-in and informing ERM implementation strategy (Parkins, 2010).

Benefits cited from the for-profit sector

The for-profit sector perceived a wide variety of risk maturity model 'soft' benefits. The broadest benefit is increasing stakeholder value (RIMS, 2014). A risk maturity model is a maturity profile 'route map' to improved corporate performance that addresses the challenges of strategy and growth across all sectors and establishes a value-measurement culture for management initiatives to ensure that the long-term interests of all their stakeholders are taken into account (Murphy, 2009). It helps turn risk into results and tracks specific risk practices that are consistently present in the top performers for revenue; earnings before interest, tax and depreciation and amortization (EBITDA); and EBITDA/EV, where EV represents enterprise value (FERMA, 2012). It offers an organization a holistic view and management of the financial risk profile according to McKinsey (Pergler, 2012). It offers itself as both a key performance indicator (KPI) and key risk indicator (KRI), integrated into the organization KPIs, business strategy scorecard and performance management system. It provides early warning capability linked to strategic planning and a 'dependable road map... to develop sustainable ERM programmes and infrastructure reflecting their organizations' strategies and business objectives' (RIMS, 2015a).

From an ERM programme perspective, a consistently cited theme is how a risk maturity model sustainably improves risk management capability (FERMA, 2015). It systemically integrates risk management into organization processes and decision making (EY, 2012). Hillson in 1997 originally saw the benefits as benchmarking current versus 'best practice', identifying realistic targets for improvement and developing action plans for developing or enhancing organization risk capability.

From an organization culture perspective, a risk maturity model helps cultivate an ERM mindset (Parkins, 2010). It identifies the next step in the process of implementing an effective ERM culture in any organization (Genius Methods Software, 2014). It helps to approach risk appetite at ERM level (IRM, 2012).

From an operational function perspective, a risk maturity model helps process effectiveness and efficiency. It can optimize the use of a risk management information system (Riskonnect, 2012). It can help in separating insurable risks (to buy insurance cover) from non-insurable risks (for management to focus on operationally); plus provide ideas for separating insurable from non-insurable capabilities (Zurich Insurance, 2012; Marsh McLellan, 2013). For key projects, it can improve the effectiveness of project risk management implementation and improvement (Hopkinson, 2011).

From a corporate governance and board perspective, a risk maturity model can promote the right sort of behaviours in the board and top management (Arguden, 2010). The model's outputs can act as the inputs to the risk-based audit plan and drive the risk management plan. It tracks continuous improvement for internal audit and for the board by providing a road map of sustainable change to enable an organization to mature their risk management approach by steadily increasing alignment with the principles, framework and process proposed in ISO 31000 (IIARF, 2012).

ISO 31000 supporters see the benefit of a risk maturity model as promoting continuous improvement. It does so by providing a road map of sustainable change to enable an organization to mature their risk management approach by steadily increasing alignment with the principles, framework and process proposed in ISO 31000 (G31000, 2013). A risk maturity model serves as a robust tool not only to implement a risk maturity strategy as required by Principle (k) but to carry out a critical review of an organization's existing practices and processes in the light of ISO 31000 standard.

Influential risk thought-leader Norman Marks summarizes the 'soft' benefits well (Marks, 2015). He agrees with Aon and Ernst & Young that once an organization achieves the highest level of risk maturity development then the latter is almost certainly contributing to the success of the organization. He agrees with Deloitte that risk maturity contributes to the successful execution of strategies. He affirms that organizations with mature risk management benefit by outperforming their peers when it comes to revenue growth and earnings. Higher capabilities create additional value because the higher level of maturity enables better decisions every day and will have a significant long-term effect on both selection of strategy and its execution.

Risk maturity models deliver many 'hard' quantitative benefits

A risk maturity model offers a variety of 'hard' measurable and tangible benefits to an organization. Of these, probably the one that meets the most surprise on initial exposure is that it can triple the bottom line! Here are 10 sets of researched and measured benefits.

Benefit 1: EBITDA profit tripled

Ernst & Young's (EY) global risk report survey of February 2012 reported the compound annual corporate performance growth rates over an extensive period from 2004 to November 2011 for a large sample of clients. EY reported that the top 20% risk maturity firms enjoy *triple* EBITDA levels to comparable firms in the bottom 20% of risk maturity (Ernst & Young, 2012). The top 20% averaged 20.3% EBITDA and outperformed their peers, with the middle 60% at 9.5% and the bottom 20% at 7.4%. See Figure 2.2.

FIGURE 2.2 Risk maturity triples the bottom line and improves revenue and EBITDA/EV

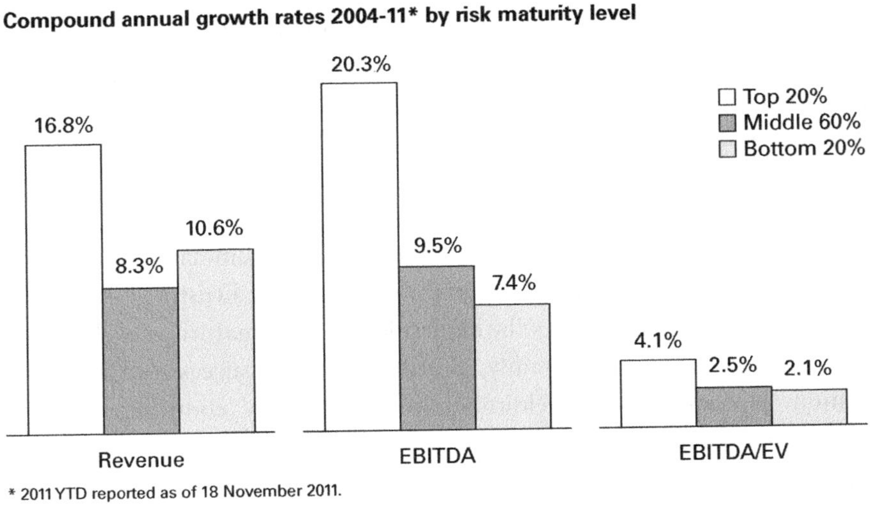

SOURCE: Michael Herrinton at http://blogs.hbr.org/2012/06/how-mature-is-your-risk-manage/ quoting Ernst & Young report, 2012. Reprinted with permission of EYGM Limited. Copyright 2012 EYGM Limited. All rights reserved. EYG no. AU1082.

EY summarized that:

> The top-performing companies (from a risk maturity perspective) implemented on average twice as many of the key risk capabilities as those in the lowest-performing group. Companies in the top 20% of risk maturity generated three times the level of EBITDA as those in the bottom 20%. Financial performance is highly correlated with the level of integration and coordination across risk, control and compliance functions. (Ernst & Young, 2012)

EBITDA is a profit indicator of a company's financial performance, which is calculated as: EBITDA = revenue – expenses (excluding tax, interest, depreciation and amortization).

FERMA augmented the above results with their own survey. FERMA reported that: '28% of companies with risk management advanced practices have an EBITDA growth over 10% whereas only 16% of companies with emerging practices present such growth', from a survey of n=809 firms across 20 European countries (FERMA, 2012). See Figure 2.3.

Benefit 2: higher revenue growth

The same FERMA report as above reported that '29% of companies with risk management advanced practices have a revenue growth over 10% whereas only 18% of companies with emerging practices present such growth' (FERMA, 2012). See Figure 2.4.

FIGURE 2.3 Maturity improves EBITDA (FERMA, 2012)

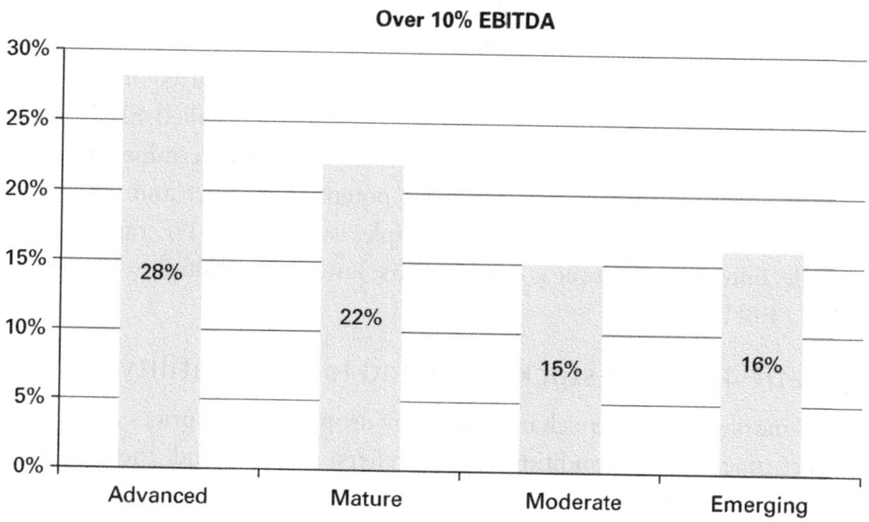

FIGURE 2.4 Maturity improves revenue growth (FERMA, 2012)

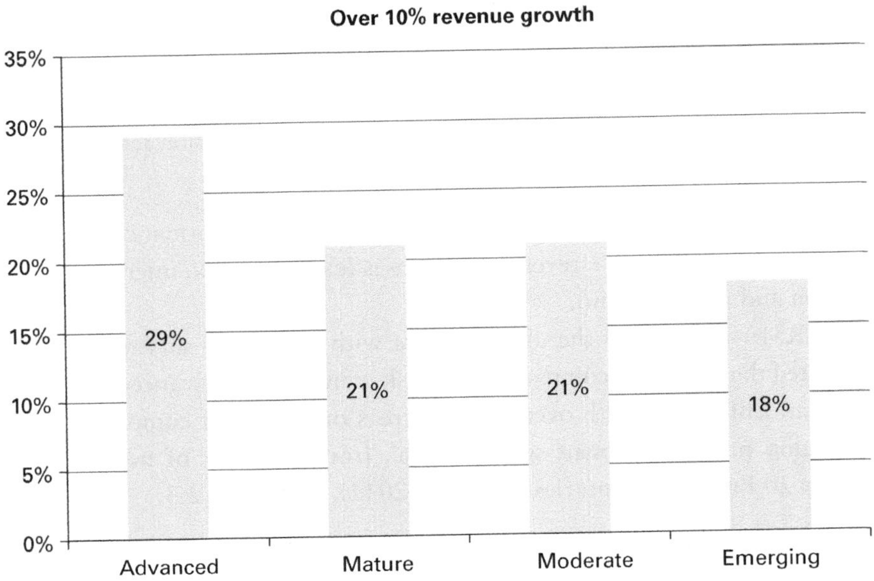

The EY prior report shown in Figure 2.2 also reported higher revenue for the top 20%.

Benefit 3: increase of 25% in firm valuations

Tobin Q ratio is a method to value a firm and is defined as the market capital value of the company divided by the replacement value of its assets. Higher-risk maturity firms enjoy a Tobin's Q firm valuation improvement of over 25% (Farrell and Gallagher, 2014).

The EY prior report shown in Figure 2.1 also reported higher firm valuation for the top 20% using a different valuation called EBITDA/EV (also called EBITDA Multiple). This ratio is used to determine the value of a company by looking at a firm as a potential acquirer and takes debt into account – an item that other multiples such as the P/E ratio do not include. Enterprise multiple is calculated as: Enterprise Multiple = Enterprise Value / EBITDA.

Benefit 4: better stock price and lower volatility

'Bear' market periods are characterized by dropping stock prices and higher market uncertainty conditions. Researchers at Aon and the Wharton Business School at the University of Pennsylvania conducted analysis of data collected by the Aon Risk Maturity Index Report and the annual financial results for more than 100 global public-traded companies across more than 25 industries. During a Bear market, the top 40% risk maturity firms enjoy stock price gains whilst the bottom 60% firms suffer falls (Aon-Wharton, 2013).

Benefit 5: stock price volatility cut by 34%

The same researchers as above reported that during a two-year period from 2010 to 2012 stock price volatility (up and down price movement) was 50% lower for surveyed organizations with high-risk maturity ratings than those with lower ratings. Between 2011 and 2012, when markets were marginally down and particularly volatile, organizations with more advanced risk management practices performed significantly stronger. Only organizations in the 'top 40%' closed the year with a positive return while lower-rated 60% of organizations ended the year within a 17–30% loss range (Aon-Wharton, 2013).

Benefit 6: return on equity (ROE) performance improved

The same researchers as above reported a 42% average ROE performance versus negative 23% for higher over lowest maturity programmes for organization risk management systems rated by the Aon risk maturity model (Aon-Wharton, 2013). That is an amazing 65% differential. ROE performance is a measure of how well a company has used reinvested earnings to generate additional earnings, equal to a fiscal year's earnings divided by book value, expressed as a percentage.

Benefit 7: return on asset (ROA) performance improved

The same researchers as above reported an 11% average ROA performance versus negative 10% for higher over lowest maturity programmes for organization risk management systems rated by the Aon risk maturity model (Aon-Wharton, 2013). That is a considerable 21% differential. ROA performance is a measure of a company's profitability, equal to a fiscal year's earnings divided by its total assets, expressed as a percentage.

Benefit 8: key project budget and schedule savings

Using long-term data from the UK Department of Defence and other major projects, Martin Hopkinson reported a series of benefits from applying project-level risk maturity models (Hopkinson, 2011). These results show savings of 23% in costs/budget and 48% in scheduling for key projects.

If your organization thinks of ERM as an 'ERM programme' and therefore as a collection of projects with extended or no deadlines, then the above benefits will be most relevant.

Benefit 9: credit ratings, business performance and operational risk improvements

Better-managed companies tend to have higher credit rating as well as higher ERM capability, according to a study released by the Risk and Insurance Management Society and LogicManager software (RIMS, 2008). The RIMS State of ERM Report 2008 was based on risk maturity assessments collected over a 14-month period for 564 organizations, commencing December 2006. The study claims validity to a 95% or greater confidence level, with the following positive correlations. Organizations with formalized ERM have higher risk maturity model (RMM) scores. Organizations without formalized ERM have lower RMM scores. Organizations with higher RMM scores have higher credit ratings. Organizations without formalized ERM have lower credit ratings. Moreover, the authors claim that organizations with higher RMM scores enjoy higher business performance scores, higher operational risk improvement metrics, higher cost-savings, increased efficiencies and higher revenue (RIMS, 2015b).

Benefit 10: better operational results

The Aberdeen Group published an impressive set of operational risk maturity benefits from a primary research benchmarking survey (Aberdeen Group, 2014). A sample n=147 manufacturing, utilities and other sector firms with a focus on operational risk (OpRisk) were surveyed by November 2013. They used four KPIs for their OpRisk maturity class framework to arrive at a set of metrics to measure operational benefits in absolute differential percentage-gap terms between the best-in-class top 20% mature firms and the laggard bottom 30% of aggregate performance scorers. These are cited below:

- +27% (top 20%) versus –1% (bottom 30%) = 28% better operating margin against corporate plan;
- –13% versus +4% = 17% better compliance costs past two years;
- 3% versus 15% = 12% better for unscheduled asset downtime;
- 90% versus 70% = 20% better for overall equipment effectiveness (OEE).

Assessing risk management effectiveness

We said earlier, as we build our case for using an ERM-domain risk maturity model, that it offers a great variety of benefits. The highest benefit is to use it as a powerful tool to assess risk management effectiveness across the board. Here, we strengthen our investment case by clarifying why this assessment is necessary and how it is connected to the risk maturity model as a solution.

Internal audit mandates assessing risk management effectiveness

Whilst the practice of 'assessing risk management effectiveness' is widely recognized by the risk management discipline, it is also a mandate by the peak professional body Institute of Internal Auditors (IIA). The IIA regard this assessment as an independent and at least annual exercise. The traditional internal IA solution took an audit binary judgement approach in the past. That is, it based the IA assessment on either a yes/effective or no/ineffective IA judgement on the effectiveness of risk management.

IIA thought-leaders have cast doubt on the subjectivity involved in the traditional binary judgement approach. The IA profession has been moving away from this approach for some years. Binary judgement opinions are based on subjective criteria, questionable results and are difficult to put into practice with repeatable and supported conclusions (Leech, 2012). They face practical resistance from the risk- and business-line functions for similar reasons.

The IIA has now most pointedly connected the dots between assessing effectiveness and using the risk maturity model to do so. Various IIA publications flag a risk maturity model as a solution. The IIA IPPF Mandatory Practice Guidelines (IIA, IPPF, 2010) state explicitly that a risk maturity model is one solution and links it to ISO 31000 for capability content for that model. It states that the maturity-model approach can assess the level of risk maturity or where the risk management process rests on the maturity curve so management and board can decide if it meets current and future targeted needs. The *IIA CRMA® Certificate in Risk Management Assurance™ Exam Study Guide 1st Edition* (IIARF, 2013: 126) states correctly that: 'Clearly, internal auditing plays a very important role in improving the maturity of risk management... championing risk and advocating enhanced risk maturity.' The intent of the following IIA title is obvious: *Selecting, Using, and Creating Maturity Models: A Tool For Assurance and Consulting Engagements* (July 2013).

Investment case backed by other key influencers

Any investment case may be bolstered by the fact that many key influencers in the corporate governance and risk management space actively use or support a risk maturity model. Apart from the IIA, the model is supported and promoted by some of the world's largest risk management institutes such as the Risk and Insurance Management Society (RIMS) and FERMA. All the leading insurance broking and accounting firms' risk-consulting arms use them as tools (see Chapter 3). Some government treasury departments even issue guides to using them (Canada, United Kingdom, NSW Australia). It rates mentions on online risk-discipline blogs, including the popular 'Marks on Governance'.

However, risk maturity model support is not confined to only the above space. The credit-rating agencies are powerful influencers on modern organizations not just for their ratings affecting finance raising but the wider reputation of the organizations and government regulators. Standard & Poor's (S&P) expects an annual report on risk management effectiveness that feeds into the strategic planning process (S&P, 2012).

The Organization for Economic Co-operation and Development (OECD) is a respected international body helping leading governments to stimulate economic progress and world trade. It supports risk maturity models. For example, it sponsored a report that all banking institutions should periodically assess their risk management maturity and that they should 'identify what steps they need to take in order to develop into risk intelligent organizations' (OECD, 2010).

Risk management system maturity and risk management effectiveness work in tandem

To reduce uncertainty, the board and stakeholders need to feel confident that management are delivering effective enterprise risk management (ERM). Two ERM programme outputs that are critical to ERM success – and by implication organization success – are:

1. Assessing the maturity and performance of the risk management system that then delivers an...
2. Understanding of risks, reporting the risk profiles (as a description of any set of risks (ISO, 2009b) Guide 73: 3.8.2.5) and how/why the risk profile(s) have changed (Knight, 2009). These can be considered as part of the risk management system as its outputs. Marks adds

that the risks should be multiple reported to help to understand the likelihood to achieve objectives, mixing risk and performance metrics and to highlight risk where the aggregated level is unacceptable (Marks, 2015).

The risk profile at (2) above is weakened without higher-risk maturity at (1). Why would you trust the quality and credibility of information at (2) without the confidence in the reliability of the *source* of that information at (1)? In other words, risk management system maturity at (1) gives the organization the reliability level to be confident that it is treating, reporting and taking the right risks and understands its risk profile at (2). How many boards, senior management, auditors and risk managers realize that if all they are preoccupied with is the risk profile at (2) then they are only doing half the job required?

As we mentioned in the Introduction for the security intelligence world, the credibility rating of information at (2) is typically cross-assessed by the reliability rating of the source at (1). If the source organization is moving towards a higher-risk maturity level at (1) and assuring the board and CEO that all their risks are managed effectively at (2), then that board will probably be more reasonably assured of (2).

Risk management effectiveness as reasonable assurance

An effective ERM maturity model provides a reasonable assurance on the achievement of the entity's objectives as far as risk management can ever do so. It can improve the ERM programme over the long term that contributes to more effective corporate governance.

This is the common theme from a wide range of authorities, including the leading corporate governance code King III, leading management consultants such as McKinsey, banker-academics such as Ciorciari and leading risk thought-leaders such as Norman Marks. Marks summarizes this well by tying in the imperative of top-level buy-in:

> The more 'mature' the risk management system, the more effective it will be in enabling better decisions and better outcomes for the organization... Using the term 'mature' instead of labelling the current state of risk management as 'ineffective' is less discouraging for its leaders, who often struggled to implement risk management without the support from and investment by senior management it merits. (Marks, 2015)

The working assumption underlying this is relatively simple and intuitive. The higher the level of risk management system maturity, the higher the level of confidence organization stakeholders enjoy that it is managing its risks effectively. That confidence may be shared with a positive knock-on effect for all key stakeholders, including the board, customers, supply chain, investors, credit-rating agencies and market analysts. This is probabilistic rather than deterministic in nature.

Risk management effectiveness as taking the right risks to achieve objectives

A risk maturity model improving the right mix of capabilities in the risk management system will be more likely to deliver effective risk management that gives an organization the confidence to take the right risks. For Norman Marks, effective risk management is not just about effecting risk principles, 'lucking it out' when your risk assessments work out, or just avoiding or treating risks (Marks, 2015). He correctly states:

> It's about taking the right risks... when you have confidence in your risk management system you can run the business at the desired speed and take the right risks... My belief, which the surveys support, is that effective risk management enables more intelligent and informed decisions. Over the longer term, better decisions should result in better performance. (Marks, 2015)

Alternatives complement using a risk maturity model

The case for using a risk maturity model is bolstered by the lack of competition for powerful and practical tools and solutions or options to assess risk management effectiveness. More correctly rephrased, alternative solutions are not considered here as competitors but as options that complement the use of a risk maturity model. Nearly all can be designed in, or be integrated with, a tailored model. We now shortlist a range of some eight alternatives/options by title and originator and add our comments as to how a risk maturity model can accommodate them.

Internal audit binary opinion – by IIA Standard Practice Advisory 2120–1 (2010)

Binary opinion is a dated and risky approach that is now passing out of favour even within the IA profession, as we previously discussed. Nevertheless, it may be used in conjunction with a risk maturity model if, for example, the board and senior management agree to use a certain maturity index score or rating as the 'effective/not effective' threshold.

General binary opinion – various sources

A minority of risk professionals take a binary-opinion approach to assessing risk management effectiveness by arguing that it is either 'effective or not' in entirely meeting a set of outputs or outcomes, with nothing in-between. If this seems logical to a specific organization then, as above, a binary opinion may be used in conjunction with a risk maturity model if, for example, the board and senior management agree to use a certain maturity index score or rating as the 'effective/not effective' threshold.

Control effectiveness assessment – a traditional approach by internal audit

Assessing control effectiveness remains a valid traditional and popular assurance mechanism. It complements any risk maturity model. It may be used as part of a risk maturity model if, for example, it is designed into one of the capabilities in the tailored risk maturity model related to combined assurance.

Comprehensive assessment approach and/or maturity assessment approach using ISO 31000-based audits – IIA IPPF 2012

This IPPF represents progressive approaches leveraging the well-respected and growing international standard ISO 31000:2009 for risk management. It complements any risk maturity model or it may be used to define capabilities to design your own risk maturity model. The danger is if it is deployed as a tick-box audit approach.

Residual status report to the board by internal audit – Tim Leech (2012), auditor

This is a valid approach as an assurance mechanism. It complements any risk maturity model. It may be used as part of a risk maturity model if, for example, it is designed into one of the capabilities in the tailored risk maturity model related to combined assurance.

Rigour/risk oversight using demand-driven assurance – Tim Leech (2012), auditor

Again, this is a valid approach as an assurance mechanism. A risk maturity model may design in capabilities that are consistent with a combination of IIA guidance and end-result objectives that boards are expected to meet, set by equivalent regulators and accounting peak bodies to the Financial Stability Board (FSB), National Association of Corporate Directors (NACD), Canadian Standards Association (CSA) or Canadian Institute of Chartered Accountants (CICA). This includes risk oversight committees and the boards making conscious decisions on the appropriate level of risk assessment rigour.

Elements of organizational maturity – Dan Clayton (2011), auditor

The organizational maturity 'elements' referenced can be taken to be capabilities (such as maturities in strategic/business objectives, management control and process control) and are certainly valid. In fact, the caption 'Others' in Figure 1.2: Maturity model evolution, Chapter 1, indicates such capability maturity models for such domains. They may either be designed happily into a tailored risk maturity model, or their total rating or score may be carried over and integrated into that for the risk maturity model.

Checklists, questionnaires and flow-charting techniques, surveys, facilitated sessions etc – PwC-authored COSO ERM 2004, audit and accounting bodies

These are perennial tools and techniques valid for any risk management or management activity. They do not compete with a risk maturity model but are useful as ways of arriving at and improving such a model.

Limitations to using a risk maturity model

Of course, there are natural limitations to using a risk maturity model. It is important to keep these in mind when constructing any investment case, when tailoring the design of your model and to avoid 'overselling' it to stakeholders as some form of perfection or absolute science. We have already covered in Chapter 1 ('Just a tool') certain natural limitations to a risk maturity model. Here we look at other minor limitations.

Risk maturity model still moving up its own maturity curve

Ironically, risk maturity models in themselves are at an early stage of maturity in terms of their usage and spread. They still have a long way to go. The ERM profession is relatively young (a twentysomething-year-old?) and not that much farther up the maturity curve, so risk maturity models as 'teenagers' naturally lag the spread and acceptance of ERM.

One indication of this is a recent joint survey by a leading risk management institute, RIMS, and the largest ERM consulting firm in the world, Marsh Risk Consulting (RIMS, 2014). They concluded that whilst risk management maturity certainly adds value, only 20% of the C-suite and 25% of the remainder believe their organizations are using risk management functions to their fullest capabilities. They surveyed 600 C-suite executives, risk managers and risk-related functionaries.

It is fair to concede that risk maturity models are still 'emerging' and are yet to gain widespread popularity. A risk maturity model is rarely a risk conference or risk media subject. In one of the most authoritative and popular-selling books on ERM case studies it represents only a side-mention and barely two pages of the book's 671 pages (Fraser, Simkins and Narvaev, 2015). The world's two most popular ERM voluntary reference codes are ISO 31000:2009 and COSO ERM 2004. ISO 31000 mentions the need for a risk maturity strategy but with no attendant detail as to how to execute the strategy, which was not on the international agenda in the years leading up to its release in 2009. COSO ERM 2004 refers to ERM *effectiveness* but not risk maturity.

It is unfair to say that risk maturity models are outdated or a confection. In fact, they are yet to reach their potential in terms of both micro-technical robustness and macro-widespread application. They are on the rise and still moving up the risk maturity curve. They absorb and complement would-be 'competing' alternative tools and techniques to assess risk management effectiveness.

One indication of growth is the wider spread and higher maturity-ratings of organizations in the OECD countries that are at the forefront of risk management standards and practice such as Australia. A landmark Australian survey by Dr Steven Halliday enjoyed a surprisingly high two-thirds response rate from the ASX Top 200 Listed Australian companies. The latter self-assessed an average level 3+ maturity level out of 5 levels (Halliday, 2013b). This is a surprisingly high result for this period in the evolution of the risk maturity model.

Another indication of growth can be inferred from two reputable survey providers – assuming that the risk maturity model lags ERM spread. They have longitudinally tracked ERM adoption rates in North America over time to their own consistent criteria and survey participants. These both show movement in the right positive direction. First, the *RIMS Enterprise Risk Management Survey 2013* reported that fully integrated ERM for its North American members rose from 12% over the four years to 21% in 2013. Partially integrated ERM programmes have nearly doubled in the same period to 42%.

Second, the latest results from the *Deloitte Global Risk Management Survey Series* are shown in Figure 2.5. The results show a steady growth over the period 2008–14 in the in-full and in-part adoption of an ERM programme for a US-dominated client sample answering the question: does your organization have an ERM programme or equivalent? It is assumed because of the lag-effect that the adoption of risk maturity models must be lower and are still emerging by trend.

FIGURE 2.5 Does your organization have an ERM programme in place? 2008–14 (Deloitte, 2015)

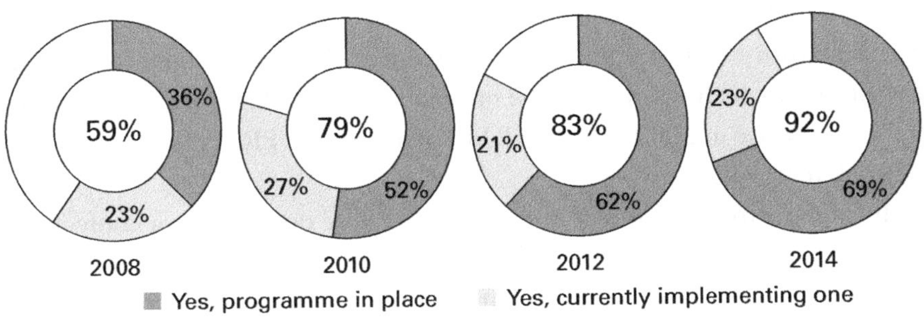

SOURCE: Reprinted with kind permission and Copyright © 2015 Deloitte International LLC

Risk maturity model not one-size-fits-all

No risk maturity model is a 'silver bullet' be-all and end-all methodology that is 'one-size-fits-all' for every organization. It may do a crucial job but not a complete job. In terms of methodology, all risk maturity models tend to be archetypal, akin to a road map or GPS where you have the stepped directions but you still have to manage the timing/schedule, read the local signs and local conditions, change directions along the way for road constraints and changing circumstances. These in-year adjustments have a place in the risk management plan and how each organization adapts its maturity strategy alongside all other organization components. The latter keep changing, of course, requiring adjustment to the risk maturity strategy, the model and its associated risk management system.

A typical risk maturity model aims to systematically document and guide the development of organizations using archetypal risk management capability levels (or described capabilities with levels of completion representing maturity). The model may lag behind practices and changing internal and external organization context within a specific organization. Whilst a model serves as a framework, a path and a guide for process improvements in business development it cannot prescribe an entire best practice, processes, assessment methodologies or implementation requirements, or cover every single one as if they are set in stone for ever. For example, an organization's actual processes depend on many factors, including organizational structure and size.

A model can describe to a certain degree but does not prescribe how capabilities are to be implemented by a specific organization within each maturity level and the specific means for getting there. For example, it may take several years for an organization to move from one maturity level to the next or to prioritize one capability over another. Models do not advocate any specific technology or other tools to use. Professional judgement is critical in using a model, and implementation decisions are left up to each organization, its history, culture(s) and the experience of its staff and environment, which may lead to human error.

Continuous improvement also applies to a risk maturity model itself and its associated design and redesign. The model is expected to continue to evolve as experience and expertise grows across both the developed and developing worlds. The shifting influence of adopters, alliance partners, providers, non-certified or future-certified assessors, government, industry, competition and academia will continue this evolution but this may mean that any one model or its user organization may be outdated quickly.

Success not guaranteed

A risk maturity model cannot guarantee organization success. A risk maturity model in the right hands can certainly provide reasonable assurance, improve organization confidence levels in terms of the probability of success, and measure improvement to agreed criteria to assess risk management effectiveness. In fact, since a robust model accepts regression and status as well as progression it takes a realistic approach to 'success' as a journey rather than a destination.

Many reputable sources agree on this matter. McKinsey notes the dilemma that any two like organizations may be seemingly rated at the same risk maturity level but operate at two very different performance levels. McKinsey cites lack of homogeneity even within sectors in the same market as the root cause (Pergler, 2012).

Research suggests that 80% of corporate financial and compliance collapses are the result of strategic and operational failures (Clayton, 2012). One banker who designed her own risk maturity model states that reasonable assurance on the achievement of the entity's objectives 'does not mean absolute assurance. Even an effective enterprise risk management can experience a failure. A failure can be due to judgement mistakes, collusive and illegitimate activities... Even when all information and resources are available, faulty judgements can be made in decision making. This is because there is always a possibility that even the most improbable event can occur.' Norman Marks posits that even 'world-class' risk management is imperfect, but ends on a positive note that 'when you have the best risk management possible, designed to deliver the information you need to make intelligent and informed decisions, you should consider it world-class. Mistakes will still be made, but the likelihood of the risk management system failing is minimized' (Marks, 2015).

Summary

A risk maturity model improves risk management system capabilities in a disciplined and consistent way but cannot guarantee that all organization initiatives will be successful. All models have natural limitations. Risk maturity models are still an emerging methodology and moving up their own maturity curve in technical and popularity terms. They do not claim to be one-size-fits-all organization solutions. There is no regulation specifically mandating either the use of ERM or related maturity models and they face the dual challenge of competing for top management investment, mandate and commitment, and overcoming middle- and front-line management-level resistance.

Nevertheless, ERM and risk maturity models rise to meet these challenges and present a robust case for organization investment. Research proves that both ERM and risk maturity deliver not only 'soft' but 'hard' measurable benefits that even the corporate governance and internal audit sectors cannot match. The headline 'hard' benefit is that higher-risk maturity organizations triple their bottom line over their opposite numbers. The long list of other quantifiable benefits range from higher revenues and firm valuations to project cost and schedule savings.

The headline qualitative benefit to an organization is that a risk maturity model is a powerful tool to assess risk management effectiveness. This is a convincing reason for investment in a model in its own right and this is backed by key influencer bodies such as the IIA. Risk management system maturity and risk management effectiveness work in tandem to provide reasonable assurance that an organization is taking the right risks to achieve objectives. The case for using a risk maturity model is bolstered by the fact that alternative solutions (such as binary judgement) are not competitors but can be designed into a tailored model.

Comparing risk maturity models against each other

03

This chapter covers:

- Dealing with biases
- Approach to comparing models
- Tiering the models
- Directory of 77 models compared
- Results and analysis
- Summary

Introduction

Megan's confidence was growing. She wanted the right information at hand to either select the risk maturity model most suited to her organization, or, if she was going to design her own, to survey the field and understand what type of models were out there. This would also back her investment case as long as she avoided overbias.

There is no better way to understand existing working risk maturity models than by comparing the field against each other to some standard criteria and quickly analysing the results. The intention here is not to rate one better than another but to illuminate their features, benefits, claimed advantages, potential disadvantages and tier them into style types.

The directory of maturity models in this chapter also acts as excellent reference material. It can help the reader to define their needs and select one or more existing models, define capabilities and approaches to start your first risk maturity model design or upgrade the design of an existing model. But before we start, let us understand how to look out for potential bias in the marketplace.

Dealing with biases when comparing risk maturity models

Dealing with bias when comparing, selecting, tailoring or designing your own risk maturity model will be a challenge. Bias becomes an issue for risk practitioners when they are pressured to understand and defend the investment case and why one model or aspect of a model is favoured over another.

Biases are tendencies with negative or positive consequences. Whilst *bias* can be an emotive and pejorative word, this is just something to be managed and not an insurmountable issue. Almost without exception, all risk and capability maturity models exhibit varying degrees of natural bias. The sources or root causes of this bias usually relate back to who designed the model and for what purpose (commercial, scholastic, educational and so forth).

Recognizing bias can be difficult. Biases are mostly helpful but can be an issue if they result in a negative consequence by not being a 'fit' to the organization. They are rarely explicit and can be all too subtle. Content quality, purpose and biases are often intertwined. Spot the biases in this introduction by one technology vendor: 'Technology is not the only component of developing an effective ERM process, but without good technology the process will never mature beyond a very basic approach' (vendor name and website withheld, 2013).

It is easy to miss the misleading assumptions in just this one sentence above. The vendor makes three false assumptions: ERM is just a 'process'; technology primarily delivers effectiveness; and that technology can be an absolute maturity progress-blocker ('never mature'). Whilst technology may deliver *efficiency* and *speed* benefits, it is not necessarily a key driver of *effectiveness*. Think of your family car – it might get you to A from B quicker and in more comfort today (efficiency) as a later model than the 'beat-up' VW you used to drive but that VW still got you to B (effectiveness).

Bias can also be difficult to spot because it typically involves underlying factors and historical legacies removed from day-to-day activities. Let us revisit the McKinsey historical view we began with in Chapter 1 when McKinsey pointed to how different sets of *capabilities* between the financial and non-financial sectors naturally developed (Pergler, 2012). McKinsey believes that the *non-financial sector* takes both a linear and discrete (eg oil price-tipping points) risk approach; that it is dominated by data-poor risks (eg strategic, reputation, operations, supply chain); and, its risk management system focus is on risk-related decision making and processes combined with risk appetite and strategy. McKinsey contrasts this with the *financial sector* that has a solely linear approach; feeds on data richness to drive quantitative analysis; and its risk management system focus is on IT and other infrastructure fundamentals. So, if your organization is an NGO, for example where our Megan works, you will have a natural bias to models with the sort of strong capabilities described above for the *non-financial sector*.

We also saw in Chapter 1 how bias to software engineering process/IT started with SEI and other capability maturity models in the 1980s. This IT bias seems to be continuing through the 21st century with the continuing rise in power within organizations of the IT function, the chief information officer (CIO), expensive business enterprise technology platforms and their IT vendors. At the time of writing, for example, risk-related conferences and professional media are still dominated by the sponsorship offered by the IT services as well as the finance/insurance sectors with their deep pockets.

Scratch the surface content when comparing the variety of risk maturity models currently available and you will probably find several forms of bias in their content and methodology. Some of the negative consequences of bias to be aware of include decision making based on misleading assumptions, presumed or wrong associations and misconceptions about risk maturity. For example, take what is called the 'halo effect' where people often cannot help associating success in one endeavour with an overall tendency for success in general. Risk consultants, insurance brokers and other bodies publish marketing material as risk management-related white papers, surveys and the like – including benchmarking studies with thousands of participants – which can create an aura of overall success for their brand. Some maturity-model buyers will tend to be positively biased towards one or other brand by this general marketing but, from a rational point of view, there is no reason to expect that if they are selling their own brand of maturity model that the latter warrants the same regard as their marketing efforts. I attend conferences organized by software vendors and meet attendees exiting with excitement that X-brand of well-reputed ERP system not only integrates ISO 31000:20009 risk management but integrates a full risk maturity model as well. I know X-brand has neither of the latter two capabilities but the halo effect is there.

Below are the five most common forms of bias in the risk management and maturity space to take into account when comparing or tailoring and designing your own risk maturity model. At the end of the day, the best criteria to keep in the mind's eye as to bias is likely to be: is this a reasonable or good fit to my organization context and risk profile(s)?

1. Bias to insurable risk

If the risk maturity model originates with an insurer or insurance broker then watch for a tendency to focus on insurable risks and organization capabilities that are involved in buying transfer products, especially the latest 'hot' product such as cyber risk. Be aware that the *risk* consulting arms within insurance brokers are far less powerful or influential within their firms than the insurance arms, where most of their money is generated.

2. Bias to information and technology-related systems

If the risk maturity model originates with the emerging Governance Risk and Compliance (GRC) fraternity, accounting firms and IT implementation providers chasing technology implementation billing, or a risk institute partnering with an IT vendor (eg RIMMS and LogicManager), then watch for a tendency to exaggerate the importance of automating risk-related information and the robustness of risk-related modules attached to enterprise resource platforms (ERP), systems and databases.

Many overstate effectiveness benefits when their system strengths rest more with efficiencies. Many overstate claims to 'comply' with standards and codes such as ISO 31000 or COSO ERM, with no transparency as to how they even align with these. Some software versions of risk maturity models are not purpose-built but originate from a different space (eg taxonomy systems) and bring technical restraints with them to their newly adapted risk maturity application.

3. Bias to process-related capabilities

If the risk maturity model originates with audit-assurance or compliance providers or in the early days of evolution away from process-biased capability models then they may tend to be overly process-of-risk biased at the expense of non-process capabilities such as people and culture. For example, the early Protiviti risk maturity model of 2008 that was still recently being used with clients was overly preoccupied with process and IT capabilities.

4. Bias to a 'door-opener' or 'check-the-box' approach

If the risk maturity model originates with consulting firms with a desire to avoid giving away intellectual property or to use their proprietary maturity model only as a 'door-opener' or 'check-the-box' exercise to sell their outsourced and consulting services, then there may not be enough quality in the model to satisfy clients in the long term. Such exercises effectively avoid capability self-improvement and position the answer to the issue as to 'how do we assess risk management effectiveness' as some sort of 'black box' that only the consultant can fathom on behalf of the client.

5. Bias to external benchmarking

If the risk maturity model originates with consulting firms then they may overemphasize expensive and lengthy external benchmarking (over internal self-improvement benchmarking) in order to win repeat business or to get paid to make contact with more potential clients.

Approach to comparing risk maturity models

Overview

The following directory section surveys the field of all public risk maturity models and a sample of capability maturity models. It provides comparison information on a range of maturity models, including ERM and other risk maturity models. It is formatted in tables as matrices or vignettes. The standard format is: Title Name/ERM or other Domain/Country of Origin/Year of Origin – Features – Benefits – Advantages – Disadvantages – Tier style. My subjective notes and comments that may assist the reader follow each table.

The vignette information contained is taken wherever possible directly from the maturity model provider or marketer with quotation marks shown. Most of this information is publicly provided or self-claimed by the model provider ('modellers') and some privately provided to me. Information contained in the 'Advantages' and 'Disadvantages' sections that may reflect my personal bias are *italicized* in order to alert the reader to potential bias.

The order in the directory below is alphabetical and not ranked in any way. The information provided is current at the time of writing but obviously subject to change and is non-exhaustive. Following many of the vignettes are my notes of interest relating to that model, including quotes from the modeller or their marketers.

Disclaimers and disclosures

At the risk of generalizing, the above rationale and classification is intended to help risk maturity model users to know where to start or where to refer to sources of information that can improve their own risk maturity model by understanding what is available in the market from existing modellers. Some disclaimers are in order here.

The information provided is current at time of writing but obviously subject to change and update. Readers should always independently validate the current information. Most of the information is as good or bad as what is publicly provided or self-claimed by the modellers. It is not intended to be rigid or scientific, nor pejorative or offensive to the modellers. Readers must expect that proprietary information will be missing but they may find here where to go to in order to follow this up of their own accord.

Italics in the tables and text sections below denote my subjective comments and information provided by me that may be subject to my personal bias. This is especially so for the 'Weaknesses' and 'Tier' classification sections. I declare that I am a content author for risk maturity models. This includes ones branded Benchmarker™ and ones co-branded or rebranded as modules in GRC or other software that are or may become commercially available.

I may not agree with any of the modeller or marketer claims. I may not agree with any of the practitioner or case study claims. Any subjective comments from our team of fictional practitioners (Asha, Chris, Alan and Megan) throughout this book obviously originate with me but I may not personally agree with all of the comments. The practitioner comments are meant to encourage the tailoring theme by demonstrating how quite different users of a risk maturity model and the organization they represent will have different perspectives on their usage needs and solutions.

Tiering the models

Tiering the risk maturity models will help readers and maturity modellers to compare more easily those types of models of most interest to them for reference purposes. It may stimulate more research to road-map maturity model references to user needs. It may also help one day to arrive at agreement within the ERM profession as what those core risk management capabilities are that define the ERM profession. It is expected that the following tiering criteria will change over time. It will mature and, with feedback, will continue to be refined, corrected and adjusted.

Approach to tiering explained

Our tiering or classification format is totally subjective. Each model in the following section is classed as one of six tiers that appear at the bottom of each vignette. The rationale for each of these six tiers is explained in Table 3.1. These are not 'ratings', nor meant to suggest any form of ascending or descending maturity order or to imply that one tier is 'better' than another. The latter depends on individual organization context and risk profile(s).

TABLE 3.1 Rationale for six-tier comparison of risk maturity models

Tier	Style and focus of maturity model methodology
Certifiable	Specialized sub-ERM domains with robust if prescriptive content and approach – geared to commercial certification eg BCCM®, PMI OPM3.
Benchmark-able	ERM domain with a measurement focus. Ratings encourage internal or external benchmarking by tracking specific targeted progress per maturity capability. Strong integration with risk management plan and organization management systems. Evidence-based ratings reduce optimism bias by separation from maturity levels. May encourage tailoring as fit-to-organization if focus is improvement measured against self. May be specifically cross-walked to standards or external reference codes to increase objectivity but not for certification eg Benchmarker™, LogicManager.
Intermediate	ERM domain broader than the Specialized tier and may share some attributes of Benchmark-able tier. Rating based on robust but often prescriptive and proprietary content, format and components such as standardized risk taxonomies. Mostly not amenable to tailoring to organization. Mostly 'pick-a-box' style and open to optimism bias as user can see maturity level as they rate eg RIMS, Willis.
Specialized	Content largely specialized or ready-tailored as ERM for a specific sector or as a subdomain of ERM eg Aberdeen Group, Health Care Canada.

TABLE 3.1 *Continued*

Tier	Style and focus of maturity model methodology
Basic	ERM domain simple content and components such as matrix grid or questionnaire. Not very elaborated or formal. Lacks detailed dimensions. Often intuitive rating. Sometimes acting as a marketing 'teaser'. Provenance may be unclear eg Zurich, Active Risk™.
Conceptual	Mainly conceptual rather than a working model. Typically white paper, academic paper or survey-based material. CMM or RMM. Often authored by non-risk practitioners eg Monda, S&P.

Practitioner needs met by referencing how models are tiered

Each tier may appeal to different risk maturity model creators and users. So let us reintroduce our practitioners and pick up their differing perspectives and needs that tiering the models may meet.

Practitioner Asha needs the 'best' ERM model

Asha is with a listed multinational recruiting firm and feels confident. She wants to go with the best single ERM risk maturity model provider first. She is attracted to referencing the Benchmark-able and Intermediary tiers and to explore her options in the Specialized tier of risk maturity models available out there. She would prefer if the provider is ISO 31000-aligned because she recognizes ISO 31000 as the freshest and most internationally recognized standard.

Practitioner Chris needs to keep it simple

Chris with the private construction firm wants to keep it simple. He thinks he will get some grounding in the Conceptual tier that will help him when looking at the Basic ERM tier.

Practitioner Alan needs a certifiable continuity submodel to score up to his ERM maturity model

Alan is becoming a rather advanced risk maturity modeller and thinker. He went to the trouble of researching all the key proponents of the four-point scale (such as ISO/IEC 15504 information technology – process assessment, Marsh, HR-sector Capability-to-Competencies, Projects, COBIT4.1 and the Protiviti Six ERM Infrastructure Elements). His utility company ERM manager and the chief operating officer are concerned over business continuity threats so Alan thinks they both might be interested in certification. So Alan goes straight to the Certifiable tier and compares the CERT® Resiliency and BCCM® business continuity models as submodels to his ERM model. He likes how detailed and systematic they seem. He chuckles to himself that the chief operations officer (COO) and the engineering personnel might take to either submodel. If so, he could easily convert the overall score from the submodel straight into his capability covering resilience on his ERM risk maturity model.

Practitioner Megan needs to explore first

Megan as a quality manager still rates herself a novice at enterprise risk management (ERM). She prefers to design her own model rather than buy one at this stage. So she thought it best to start on designing her own risk maturity model by exploring some ideas for tailored capabilities from the Conceptual tier. She intends to then check with the Basic tier and maybe, in time, augment her tailored risk maturity model by referring to the Specialized tier.

Directory comparing 77 maturity models

A directory of 77 risk maturity models and capability maturity models follows. If a table of contents is needed in order to search the directory then refer to Table 3.2. This segments all the directory entries by alpha-order within their tier classification.

TABLE 3.2 Comparison of maturity models in the directory by six tiers

Tier	Alpha order listing of *n* = 77
Certifiable *n = 6 = 8%*	Axelos P3M3.* BCCM®. *CERT® Resiliency. OCEG 2.1®. OGC M_o_R®. *PMI OPM3.
Benchmark-able *n = 7 = 9%*	Benchmarker™. G31000. IIARF-Sobell. LogicManager™. Marsh ERM. Marsh Risk Focus. RIMS.
Intermediate *n = 9 = 12%*	Aon-Wharton. CEB. Deloitte. EY. KPMG. LTRC/EFQM. NSW Treasury. Risk Academy. Willis.
Specialized *n = 33 = 43%*	Aberdeen OpRisk. *Aho Corporate Performance Management (CPM). ALARM government. *BD-CMM business development. Capgemini Sigma Map™. Causal Capital Credit and OpRisk. Ciorciari banking. CIPS supply chain. *COBIT IT. *Elmaallam info security. Fraser Health. Genius Methods culture. Hopkinson projects. HRDC human relations. *IBM business value. INCOSE projects. Influence regulatory. INSEAD-Arguden corporate governance. IRM risk appetite. IRM risk software. ISACA IT risk. *ITI IT reliability. Kerzner projects. *Lederman record keeping. *Luyckx business process. Marsh insurance.*McGraw BSIMM-V IT. MMGRSeg info security. Murphy 4e. Riskonnect risk technology. S&P for Insurers. SCRLC supply chain. Syntex OpRisk.
Basic *n = 6 = 8%*	Active Risk™. Booz. KPMG.Treasury Board Canada. PwC. Zurich.
Conceptual *n =16 = 21%*	Accenture. CIRANO. COSO ERM:2004. Economist Intelligence Unit. FERMA. *Gartner. Hillson. HM Treasury. ISO 31000:2009. Kaplan-Mikes. *Marx. Monda ERMi. Pergler-McKinsey. S & P for Corporates. Tiel. CRMS.

Based on publicly available information, so proprietary information is missing.
* Represents a capability maturity model rather than a risk maturity model

The directory starts here.

TABLE 3.3 Aberdeen Group OpRisk maturity model, UK 2014

Features:	Three operational risk maturity levels (best in class 20%, average 50%, laggard bottom 30%) with various capabilities quantified as KPIs from a benchmarking survey n=142 in Nov 2013. Consulting firm gratis white paper. Promotes ISO 31000 / 27000.
Benefits:	Excellent quantification of the differences and four KPI benefits between maturity levels as defined by authors. For example, the top 20% enjoy a net 28% better operating margin versus corporate plan (being +27% versus laggard 30%–1%).
Advantages:	'Hard' benefit metrics. Great source of proven and measured capabilities for tailoring own model especially for OpRisk-focused and manufacturing organizations.
Disadvantages:	*OpRisk focus.*
Rated Tier:	*Specialized to OpRisk.*

A robust model specialized to operational risk well suited to manufacturing organizations (Table 3.3). Offers a superb set of 'hard' success metrics to promote operational risk maturity as quoted in Chapter 2.

TABLE 3.4 Accenture ERM maturity assessment, United States 2013

Features:	Unknown number of levels to 22 capabilities under 4 themes of strategy and governance, process excellence and integration, regulatory reform and performance, and insight and execution. Proprietary consulting model (website). Accenture 2011 Survey claims x8 'advanced capabilities': 'The large sample size of the Accenture 2011 Global Risk Management Study enabled the identification, with statistical validity, of a subset of companies deemed to be "Risk Masters" – companies whose practices and capabilities across a set of factors include existing ERM programmes, analytics and integration with decision-making processes. Mastery is multidimensional. It requires a mix of governance, process, technology and talent, and it also requires commitment to improvement and consistency over time.'

TABLE 3.4 *Continued*

Benefits:	Claim no single road map to risk management mastery but that the 'Risk Mastery' by a top 10% of those surveyed can exemplify eight 'advanced risk capabilities'.
Advantages:	Advanced risk management capabilities are high on the executive agenda and now seen as a critical business driver and source of sustained growth and long-term competitive advantage.
Disadvantages:	*IT vendor implementer bias to process and compliance.*
Rated Tier:	*Conceptual.*

Currently regarded as a Conceptual tier classification as the only public evidence is one study with some contradictory public information (Table 3.4). However, it may belong to the Intermediate tier assuming a paid consulting engagement with Accenture will provide clients with a proprietary working risk maturity model.

TABLE 3.5 Active Risk™ risk maturity, UK 2012

Features:	Active Risk™ Enterprise Risk Management Readiness Guide includes short questionnaire 'teaser' (go to info@activerisk.com). Five levels with six questions. A brief, self-guided risk maturity assessment. Compute your maturity index by adding together the values at the end of each of your selected responses.
Benefits:	Understanding Your Risk Maturity.
Advantages:	Crunchy quick format. Balanced content.
Disadvantages:	*A risk maturity model is not part of the ERM application software.*
Rated Tier:	*Basic.*

This seems to be a marketing 'teaser' for a popular ERM risk register software with a small number of capabilities that are quite pithy (Table 3.5). Good for novices.

TABLE 3.6 Aho capability maturity model for corporate performance management (CPM) maturity, Finland 2013

Features:	Six levels with 16 key components to assess the maturity of the corporate performance management (CPM) in an organization. PhD student paper for a conceptual model. Literature study and five case-study companies where the author participated in CPM development projects in various consultation roles. Constructive and action-oriented research approaches were used with different methods for data collection and analysis.
Benefits:	Balanced view of technology and processes as they only represent half of the capability categories. Avoids being process-centric.
Advantages:	Corporate performance management specialist capability maturity model offering some potential ERM capabilities.
Disadvantages:	*Academic.*
Rated Tier:	*Part-specialist to corporate performance and part-conceptual.*

This risk maturity model is difficult to tier (Table 3.6). Certainly a conceptual academic paper but also part-specialized to corporate performance management. It is commendable that it avoids being dominated by process and technology.

TABLE 3.7 ALARM Public Risk Management Association National Performance Model for Risk Management in the Public Services, UK 2010

Features:	Five levels with 58 capabilities under seven 'strands', two focused on results and five enablers. Adapted by UK public service ALARM's Benchmarking Special Interest Group 2010 from HM Treasury RMAF and the EFQM Excellence Model. Paper-based unrated matrix tool and 5+ year survey benchmarking statistics published on their website.
Benefits:	Assessing the ERM maturity of public sector organizations.

TABLE 3.7 *Continued*

Advantages:	Specialized public sector capability 'quick health check' guide. Focus on evidence-based behavioural progress indicators. Easy 10p guide. Link to quality and performance management.
Disadvantages:	
Rated Tier:	*Specialist to public sector ERM.*

Do not be put off by the long-winded title, ie the ALARM Public Risk Management Association National Performance Model for Risk Management in the Public Services (Table 3.7). This is one of the first places to go to for risk maturity model ideas specialized to public-sector ERM. Enjoys an excellent pedigree. Claims to be the only public service-focused risk management benchmarking group in the UK (ALARM, 2015).

TABLE 3.8 Aon-Wharton Risk Maturity Index (RMI), United States 2011

Features:	40 questions (down from original 126) underlie 10 characteristics rated to five levels. Online self-assessment questionnaire of risk management practices. Tool co-developed by Wharton Business School Uni of Penn, United States, with Aon Risk Solutions, Aon Global Risk Consulting and Aon Hewitt.
Benefits:	Greater understanding of their organization's ERM capabilities. Benchmarking index to a total organization base of growing size.
Advantages:	Wharton Business School's reputation. Free assessment report, risk maturity rating, comments for improvement and benchmark index. Good for external benchmarking as tracks growing database of responders n=?. Suitable for all organizations. Claims Wharton Business School receives no compensation from Aon. Overall satisfactory quality of content and sizable quantity. Includes 'soft' capabilities: eg people, decision making.
Disadvantages:	No links to codes or a recognized reference set. *Bias to an insurance, compliance and quantification-financial services mindset?*
Rated Tier:	*Intermediate.*

Well worth a look as this is a sophisticated ERM model (Table 3.8). It also acts as a 'door-opener' to insurance sales. The website offers downloadable annual white papers called the Risk Maturity Index Whitepaper and the Risk Maturity Index Insight Report 2015. The Aon website positions their model as: 'a... tool... to assess an organization's risk management practices and provide... an easy-to-understand questionnaire on risk management processes, corporate governance and risk understanding... Upon completion of the Index questions, you will receive an immediate risk maturity rating as well as comments designed to offer general guidance for enhancing the organization's level of risk maturity.'

TABLE 3.9 Axelos P3M3 Management, UK 2014

Features:	Five levels of process maturity (awareness, repeatable, defined, managed and optimized). Seven 'process perspectives' (themes): management control, benefit management, financial management, stakeholder engagement, risk management, organizational governance and resource management. Multiple 'attributes' (capabilities) are divided into specific and generic. Certifiable. '3' in brand name stands for portfolio, programme and project risk. P3M3 is owned by Axelos, a JV between the UK Government and Capita, which took ownership of the materials in January 2014. Prior to this, P3M3 was owned by the Office of Government Commerce (OGC), a department within the UK Government with a remit to help public sector organizations improve their efficiency, gain better value for money from procurements and deliver improved success from programmes and projects.
Benefits:	Assessing project and programme risk maturity of organizations.
Advantages:	Robust heritage and UK practice.
Disadvantages:	Focus on process improvement rather than behaviour (see Kerzner, 2005). *Complex 5 x 7 x 3 portfolio, programme and project perspectives.*
Rated Tier:	*Certifiable.*

P3M3 (Table 3.9) is owned by Axelos, a joint venture between the UK Government and Capita, which in January 2014 took ownership of the material that was originally owned by the Office of Government Commerce (OGC), a department within the UK Government with a remit to help public-sector organizations improve their efficiency, gain better value for money from procurements and deliver improved success from programmes and projects.

An interesting approach in many ways starting with the split between what it calls general and specific capabilities. Interesting because it can also be classified in the Specialist (projects) tier. Also because of the contrast between the P3M3 focus on process improvement versus that on behaviour (see Kerzner following Table 3.48; Kerzner, 2005).

TABLE 3.10 BCMM® Business Continuity Maturity Model by VirtualCorp, United States 2003

Features:	Six levels with 11 competencies (sic capabilities) theming many business continuity (BC) organizational attributes (capabilities) and associated BC programme performance requirements. Free initial on ine 'open-access' self-assessment acts as teaser to buy a spreadsheet-based system, assessor ICOR training and consulting. Claims users in over 50 countries. Multiple versions with add-on resources, eg mini-deck, white paper, glossary. Proprietary model includes comparative data and enhanced reporting. Certifiable.
Benefits:	Identify your business continuity programme strengths and weaknesses.
Advantages:	Business-continuity specialized. Highly technical. Robust and detailed 35pp reference cross-walk to BS25999, ASIS, NFPA and ISO 22301 standards showing where BCMM matches or exceeds (bias?). Standardized methodology generates benchmarking-to-other data.
Disadvantages:	*Highly technical – over 370 questions must receive a 0–100% score to complete. Prescriptive content trade-off for benchmarking against external organizations. Spreadsheet constraints. Shallow risk management plan. Confuses competencies for capabilities. Dated?*
Rated Tier:	*Certifiable and specialized for business continuity.*

A leading certifiable risk maturity model tool for business continuity specialists (Table 3.10). Lends itself to becoming a submodel for any business continuity-driven organization feeding its rating there up to an umbrella ERM model. Probably the most technical and detailed model I have seen.

TABLE 3.11 BD-CMM Business Development Capability Maturity Model® V1.0 BDI, United States 2005

Features:	Four key process areas (KPAs customer, focus, people, capabilities) with five levels as per SEI CMM staged-representation model matrix, ie matrices of BD-CMM goals against key process categories (KPCs). The BD Institute's book chapters 2–5 present detailed characterizations for each of the growth levels of the BD-CMM (ie levels 2–5) (BD Institute, 2005). These descriptions address the four key process areas that comprise each level, including extensive examples. A capability maturity model.
Benefits:	Excellence and major gains in business development process effectiveness and efficiency. Designed to guide BD organizations in selecting high-priority improvement actions based on the maturity of their current practices. 'Its benefit is in narrowing the scope of improvement activities to those key practices that provide the next foundational level for extending the organization's current BD capabilities.'
Advantages:	Non-prescriptive 'open' model. Emerging standard for BD process continuous improvement. Correctly separates Capability for organization and Competencies for its people. Balance of 'soft and hard' goals.
Disadvantages:	*Bias to process.*
Rated Tier:	*Specialist to business development.*

This model (Table 3.11) demonstrates that even salespeople are moving up the risk maturity curve. Developed by the non-profit Business Development Institute International (BDI) in association with the Association of Proposal Management Professionals (APMP), and the Carnegie Mellon Software Engineering Institute (SEI). This directory entry is with the kind permission of the BD Institute and quotes them as follows:

> The Capability Maturity Model® for Business Development (BD-CMM) is designed to guide BD organizations in identifying and implementing high-priority improvement actions in business development (BD). Version 2.0 was released in May 2013 as a major revision to the original model (Version 1.0) released in 2004. This new version restructures content to align with Capability Maturity Model Integration® (CMMI®) and reflects significant, worldwide operational experience, lessons learned and research studies since 2004.
>
> As was true for Version 1.0, BD-CMM V2.0 does not focus primarily on enabling organizations to have their BD operations certified, nor is it intended to provide a 'quick fix' for organizations that may have failing BD projects. Rather, BD-CMM V2.0 helps adopters to create dramatically more robust focus on customer value, dynamic leadership, teamwork, process vibrancy and leading-edge systems. This means having capability to win more opportunities, at greater contract values, while minimizing the cost of winning; however, its greatest goal is to move organizations to a sustainable culture of business winning in an increasingly competitive business environment.

The Capability Maturity Model® for Business Development (BD-CMM) is offered exclusively worldwide by the Business Development Institute International on an 'as-is' basis, with no warranties of any kind. Organizations are encouraged to use the model without restriction internally, subject to required acknowledgements; however, external and commercial uses are restricted, subject to specific permissions and/or licensing. The Capability Maturity Model®, CMM, and CMMI® are registered in the United States Patent and Trademark Office by Carnegie Mellon University.

TABLE 3.12 Benchmarker ™ Antonucci ERM, United States 2015

Features:	Five levels covering n=105 capabilities using a five-point scale evidence-based rating. Rating index scores to 100%. Proprietary online software model v3.3 backed by flexible spreadsheet. Includes practical scoresheets and guide notes against ISO 31000, COSO ERM and expert CRO interpretive commentary. Distributed by STP Specialty Technical Publishers Online and Radar-Risk, United States. Backed by consulting services from the content author Domenic Antonucci, a practising chief risk officer (CRO).

TABLE 3.12 *Continued*

Benefits:	Multipurpose uses as a maturity model, benchmarking tool, a KPI and KRI, an audit tool or a road map for creating a plan of action. Powerful risk management system capability maturity tool to assess risk management effectiveness (as required by IIA mandate). Collects current findings with guide notes. Specifies gap-improvements to targeted maturity levels. Generates a five-year rolling risk management plan, which is objectives-centric and gives effect to a risk maturity strategy (ISO Principle k). Creates inputs to the risk-based Audit Plan.
Advantages:	Appeals to global risk, audit and board professionals. First software to cross-walk benchmarks from both of the leading global codes by a practising CRO. Improved objectivity as it covers 100% of the capabilities within ISO and COSO but also the one-third of capabilities that both ISO and COSO miss and CROs require to be effective. Enhances CEO/board reporting and demonstrates their mandate and commitment.
Disadvantages:	Practitioner-bias.
Rated Tier:	*Benchmark-able.*

This is the first ERM domain risk maturity model (Table 3.12) designed by a practising chief risk officer (CRO) that is benchmark-able to CRO-friendly capabilities that are cross-walked to ISO 31000:2009 and COSO ERM transparent references to generate three sets of assessments. I am the content author of Benchmarker™.

TABLE 3.13 Booz Allen enterprise resilience risk management, United States 2004

Features:	Three levels with eight capability modules. Heralds a post-ERM higher level called 'Enterprise Resilience'. One of a series of proprietary consulting maturity models by Booz that are not confined to ERM but also include cyber security, supply chain etc.
Benefits:	Claims early warning capability linked to strategic planning.
Advantages:	Addresses risks to major earnings. Quantitative approach.
Disadvantages:	*Not well known in the ERM domain?*
Rated Tier:	*Basic.*

Retained at the Basic tier because this is a proprietary consulting model with little known about it except for a reference to a post-ERM higher level called 'Enterprise Resilience' (Table 3.13).

TABLE 3.14 Capgemini Sigma Map™ balance sheet risk maturity, United States 2013

Features:	Maps the assets and liabilities off the balance sheet. Measures them along six components (credit-, market-, operational-, contagion-, liquidity- and reputation risks). Uses radar-map dashboard.
Benefits:	Organization holistic view and management of their financial risk profile.
Advantages:	Addresses risks to major earnings. Quantitative approach.
Disadvantages:	*Not well known in the ERM domain.*
Rated Tier:	*Basic.*

This model (Table 3.14) is targeted to a financial-sector audience.

TABLE 3.15 Causal Capital financial-sector ERM maturity, Singapore 2012

Features:	Six operational and credit risk maturity 'phases' (levels) with various Gantt-charted capabilities across the six phases, being: Framework, Elements, Integration, Capital, Trading Risk and Maturity. Uses ISO 31000 as the foundation for initial phase 1. Proprietary consulting firm high-level map authored by Martin Davies and available online.
Benefits:	A risk maturity and ERM map of the path to enterprise risk maturity from an operational-risk (OpRisk) and credit-risk perspective, with an ISO 31000 starting point.
Advantages:	Unique flow chart hybridizing traditional finance sector OpRisk and credit risk in alignment with ISO 31000. Great source of summary milestone capabilities for tailoring own maturity model for financial-sector organizations.
Disadvantages:	*More OpRisk and credit risk than ERM. If the 31000 'enhanced attributes' are included in the Phase 1 of 6, this seems ambitious.*
Rated Tier:	*Specialized.*

This risk maturity model is a great source of summary milestone capabilities for tailoring your own model for financial-sector organizations or operations risk-dominated organizations (Table 3.15). In the Specialized tier but shares some features of the Intermediate tier.

TABLE 3.16 CEB ERM maturity diagnostic, United States 2013

Features:	Five ascending stages numbered 1 to 5 representing strengths and potential development areas across 16 key attributes of effective ERM. Proprietary consulting firm model by CEB Risk Management Leadership Council of the Corporate Executive Board Company (CEB). Self-assessment by remote web-based questionnaire backed by CEB Executive Advisor™ consulting service.
Benefits:	Evaluate the maturity of your enterprise risk management capabilities using objective, peer-based performance standards. Clarifies how well the organization is doing. Supports short-term and long-term planning, identifying next steps and associated resource. Ensures alignment of strategy and resources with business needs.
Advantages:	Reputed robust content. Testimonials.
Disadvantages:	
Rated Tier:	*Benchmark-able.*

Testimonials from financial service and large US corporates indicate a robust model (Table 3.16) tailored to the US corporate market. Consultants provide supportive analysis and some 'best practices' based on the priority areas identified by the diagnostic.

TABLE 3.17 CERT®-RMM Resiliency Maturity Model, United States 2010

Features:	Five CMMI process maturity levels are applied specifically and in detail to software or systems engineering processes with x26 process areas from asset definition and management to vulnerability analysis and resolution. Part of SEI series authored by Caralli *et al* (Caralli, Allen and White, 2011). Three critical dimensions: people with skills, training and motivation, process and tools/equipment. Three component categories: required elements, expected elements and informative elements. Four key assets: people, information, technology, facilities/assets. Certification. Capability – not a risk maturity – model.
Benefits:	Specialist maturity model with a capability dimension for managing operational resilience from a single process at a time perspective. Disclaimer that it is not a capability maturity model yet to CMMI standards as it does not yet provide an organizational expression of maturity.
Advantages:	Process areas for operations risk. Detailed. Targeted-improvement road maps to comply with FISMA etc regulations or measuring how well using cloud-services or insider-threats.
Disadvantages:	*IT process-focused model. Complex.*
Rated Tier:	*Certification for operation resilience.*

This model (Table 3.17) is from a book of the same name (Caralli, Allen and White, 2011) that claims to represent practitioners dedicated to the belief that security, continuity and IT operations management processes can be improved and operational resilience can be actively directed, controlled and measured. This model is highly technical and specialized to operations process risk. It seems to be heading for certification in the future.

TABLE 3.18 Ciorciari EnteR COSO-based assessment tool, Switzerland 2008

Features:	Five levels with eight COSO principles, 26 topics, 123 elements and 615 criteria. Proprietary-to-bank EnteR automated guidance too. Claims to help organizations assess the maturity level of the ERM, highlighting strengths and weaknesses and a prioritized list of measures whose implementation helps to fill existing ERM gaps. Multi-period overview.
Benefits:	An effective ERMt provides a reasonable assurance on the achievement of the entity's objectives... identifying the current weaknesses and strengths in the ERM: list of measures that enable the maturity-level enhancement; contributing to a more effective corporate governance; integrating the documentation of the ERMt; contributing to the improvement of the quality of the risk management process and risk mitigation throughout the entity.
Advantages:	Banking specialized content aligned to COSO ERM framework. Advanced and multi-period reporting.
Disadvantages:	*Single-code reference framework. Academic. Complex if 615 criteria. Non-actionable? Dated, harking back to 2004 thinking? Not clear what content is and how rated.*
Rated Tier:	*Specialized to banking, possibly benchmark-able.*

This COSO-aligned model called EnteR (Table 3.18) appeals to those interested in banking-specialized content aligned to COSO ERM framework. It has an academic approach and seems complex. It is only known in the public domain as a thesis and Applied Paper presented by Maria Ciorciari of Banca del Gottardo of Switzerland to the 2008 ERM Symposium 14–16 April in Chicago. Banca del Gottardo offers Swiss bank private-banking services. Ciorciari claims the model was applied within that bank and provides sample information. To quote:

> The approach is transferred into an application tool, EnteR, for an automated and guided maturity-level assessment... it is possible to evaluate the elements of the framework's eight components: internal environment, objective setting, event identification, risk assessment, risk response, control activities, information and communication, and monitoring.

TABLE 3.19 CIPS supply chain capability maturity model, Australia 2012

Features:	Seven-level supply chain capability maturity model by Australian arm of a UK-based network for the Chartered Institute of Procurement and Supply. Purchasing and supply chain management. The CIPS Corporate Certification is 'an in-depth assessment process that measures your procurement function against our world-class standards across five dimensions... These... are essential facets of all organizations, no matter who and where you are, and what you do.'
Benefits:	The whole process aims to ensure that you are operating efficiently and effectively, and can drive constant improvement.
Advantages:	*'World class' purchasing and supply chain management standards.*
Disadvantages:	
Rated Tier:	*Specialist purchasing and supply chain management.*

This modeller claims 'world class' standards in the global supply chain domain (Table 3.19).

TABLE 3.20 CIRANO corporate reputation risk maturity, Canada 2012

Features:	Four levels of 'generations' (levels) matrix by 11 indicators (capabilities) to protect corporate reputation. Online article by Marcellis-Warren and Teodoresco from the Centre for Interuniversity Research and Analysis on Organization (CIRANO) Quebec and Preventa consulting firm respectively. Each indicator assigned a four-scale maturity performance value from one (lowest) to four (highest). Intended for structured interviews at different levels of the organization, in-depth consultancy audits and documentation reviews. White paper, part of a Burgundy Report series by CIRANO.
Benefits:	Identifies underlying causes of organization reputation risks and potential organization weaknesses. Continuous road map. Preventa consulting expertise in reputation risk, which is enterprise-wide.
Advantages:	Quality of the reputation capabilities backed by academic and consulting practice.
Disadvantages:	*Impractical rating method (pick-a-box) as an indicator may have one or more elements described in each of the four maturity 'generations' so it is difficult to choose which rating from 1 to 4?*
Rated Tier:	*Conceptual.*

This is a useful conceptual reference source for corporate reputation risk (Table 3.20). The CIRANO methodology seems to lend itself to optimism bias if practised because the impractical rating method (pick-a-box) as an indicator may have one or more elements described in each of the four maturity 'generations' so it is difficult to choose which rating from 1 to 4 is most appropriate to your specific organization.

TABLE 3.21 COBIT IT process maturity model, United States 2002

Features:	Five levels with a 0–5 scale algorithm scoring/charting 34 COBIT IT processes to four functional domains. These four domains cover 318 objectives of control. Designed by the COBIT Management Guidelines Control Objectives for Information and Related Technology (COBIT) and published by the IT Governance Institute (ITGI) and Information Systems Audit and Control Foundation (ISACF). Support by ISACA. An IT governance tool used to measure how well developed the management processes are with respect to internal controls. Fundamental feature: measure as-is maturity levels, and define to-be maturity levels as well as gaps to fill, ie planning improvements (as-is, to-be, gap analysis). Capability – not risk maturity – model.
Benefits:	Balancing IT risk and control in a cost-effective manner. Organization can grade itself from non-existent (0) to optimized (5). Such capability can be exploited by auditors to help management fulfil its IT governance responsibilities, ie, exercise effective responsibility over the use of IT just like any other part of the business.
Advantages:	Specialist CMM for IT audit assurance. Respected originators. Practical improvements to the system of internal controls of IT processes.
Disadvantages:	*IT Compliance-driven. IT-speak. Auditor-speak.*
Rated Tier:	*Conceptual.*

Auditors, compliance and IT people will find this maturity model (Table 3.21) of interest. It is probably better described as an IT compliance maturity model rather than a risk maturity model. Employs a sophisticated weighting function, to quote:

> The questionnaire is intended to capture the compliance of an IT organization under investigation to the diverse scenarios describing each maturity level... an algorithm computes a 'compliance' vector that describes the compliance of the organization to every scenario. Then, it uses the vector to compute the maturity level as a weighted average of the organization's compliance with respect to each scenario. (ISACA, 2003)

TABLE 3.22 COSO ERM, United States 2004

Features:	No levels, scales or mention of risk maturity but positions the eight cube 'components' as capabilities for effective ERM. Firstly, 'determining whether an entity's [ERM] is "effective" is a judgement resulting from an assessment of whether the eight components are present and functioning properly' (p7) and therefore the eight components 'serve as criteria for determining whether [ERM] is effective' (COSO, 2004: 3, 7, 13). Second, 'reducing operational surprises and losses' is mentioned as an 'enhanced capability' (COSO, 2004: 3).
Benefits:	Accepts trade-offs between components and for small to medium enterprises.
Advantages:	Popular with North American, audit and accountant audiences. Adjunct to COSO internal controls approach.
Disadvantages:	*Dated.*
Rated Tier:	*Conceptual guidance (self-declared).*

COSO ERM is certainly not a risk maturity model and is classified here (Table 3.22) as conceptual, like ISO 31000. What it does offer is a rich source of potential ERM capabilities that may be adapted into a tailored risk maturity model.

TABLE 3.23 CRMS EMPIRISK ERM game simulation, Indonesia 2015

Features:	The Centre for Risk Management Studies (CRMS) Indonesia launched in July 2015 a game-simulation with 'five levels of risk management implementation cycle based on ISO 31000, which takes participants through step-by-step understanding about risk management up to a bit complex risk-based decision making (sic)'. Innovative game-approach designed and targeted to Indonesians in Indonesian. Web-based technology.

TABLE 3.23 *Continued*

Benefits:	Participants can 'accelerate their risk management knowledge acquisition in a new fun-based environment... The approach has been rated very satisfying and easy to earn by those who have already attended and participated in that simulation.' 'The flexibility of game-based simulation allows participants from different levels to learn risk management from the level of knowledge and comprehension of the principles, framework and process to the level of complex risk-management problem solving.'
Advantages:	The game 'could be enhanced and/or adjusted to capture the real case of the customers' risk environment, and therefore, help customers to solve their unique risk problem-solving.' ISO 31000 aligned.
Disadvantages:	Not in English.
Rated Tier:	*1 Conceptual.*

A model that has at least one set of risk maturity component (levels) (Table 3.23). Certainly a first in terms of being a game-based simulation and an emerging market innovation (ie designed by Indonesians for the online and emerging market sectors).

TABLE 3.24 Deloitte Risk Intelligent Enterprise™ maturity, United States c.2009

Features:	Five stages with 22 representative attributes (read as *capabilities*) matrix showing increasing stakeholder value. Downloadable reference. Various white papers including nine fundamental principles of a risk-intelligent programme to develop an advanced state of ERM capability. Reference standard or code neutral.
Benefits:	Increasing stakeholder value. Claims benchmarked to n=1,541 firms surveyed 2009?
Advantages:	Simple and robust ERM content in tables, diagrams, white papers. Robust 'pyramid' of oversight, common risk infrastructure, risk process and risk classes.
Disadvantages:	*Six pillars not enough? Dated?*
Rated Tier:	*Intermediate.*

The Deloitte Risk Intelligent Enterprise™ maturity model (Table 3.24) appears to be a popular and robust proprietary consulting model. Well worth referencing when tailoring your set of capabilities and levels – especially in combination with the Deloitte risk function operating model options. Probably one of the better consulting-firm-style of risk maturity models. The ERM profession needs more contributions like this from the consulting firms.

TABLE 3.25 The Economist Intelligence Unit (EIU) ERM maturity, UK 2011

Features:	Four maturity Levels. Research paper author Rob Mitchell. Includes results of global survey of n=? senior executives from finance, risk, compliance and legal functions. Sponsored by SAP. Findings drew on desk research, a global survey and in-depth interviews with executives familiar with risk and compliance within their organizations.
Benefits:	Effective risk and compliance management will assist a company to improve performance and executive enhanced strategies. Respected source.
Advantages:	Global white paper.
Disadvantages:	*Not known in ERM domain. Dated content?*
Rated Tier:	*Conceptual.*

Surveys of this type (Table 3.25) from reputable firms are always welcome although the views reflected by the survey participants in this one seem dated now – probably because ISO 31000:2009 was barely released at the time the survey was undertaken.

TABLE 3.26 Elmaallam Information Systems MM, Morocco 2011

Features:	Five levels with nine elements of control. Academic paper *Towards a Model for IS Risk Maturity* proposed model based on the information systems (IS) life cycle, IS risk management process and control objectives of its activities, IS constituents and its control elements and control map that defines the IS maturity levels. Draws on risk and capability maturity models from Hillson, INCOSE, RISKIT, Cobit, MMGRSeg and OPM3 PMBOK.
Benefits:	Claims risk management an 'indispensable discipline for any organization to achieve its objectives. As the IS are key assets for organizations, managing IS risks becomes more and more important especially within a world in perpetual change.' Claims 'First, we indicate IS definition that will fix the scope (all things concerned by IS risk management). Second, we define the IS risk management process that will fix the way (activities used in IS risk management). Third, we develop the maturity model for IS risk.' Aligned to ISO 31000:2009.
Advantages:	Information systems (IS) risk maturity model concept.
Disadvantages:	Academic.
Rated Tier:	*Conceptual.*

Included as an IS specialized-capability maturity model (Table 3.26) as this subdomain may well be a growing demand for modern organizations. It is interesting how it also draws on a combination of risk and capability maturity models from Hillson, INCOSE, RISKIT, Cobit, MMGRSeg and OPM3 PMBOK.

TABLE 3.27 EY risk management framework review ERM maturity, UK 2009

Features:	Five practice maturity levels – as basic, average and leading, with intermediate levels between these three. Rating 19 capabilities with scales as established practices=1, embedded practices=3 and enhanced practices=5. Themed by six 'areas' (governance, risk strategy, RM processes, technology, RM functions, culture and capability). Each area assessed for progress from current to recommended future state specific to each area (perhaps rated to seven scales within each of the three levels?). MS Office-software based. Proprietary consulting model. NB: The Ernst & Young survey 'Turning Risk into Results' found specific risk practices that were consistently present in the top performers (ie top 20% based on risk maturity) that were not present in the bottom 20%. The 20 risk practices (read *capabilities*) were organized into five domains (read *modules*).
Benefits:	Improving risk management capability by indicative basic to average to leading practices.
Advantages:	Simpler version of the 'pick-a-box' method. Strong on culture.
Disadvantages:	*Dated to pre-ISO 31000. Auditor-bias to functions and technology content. Unclear methodology: how is the status level rating derived from the five-scale rating per 19 capabilities? How do each of the three levels have a seven-point scale?*
Rated Tier:	*Intermediate.*

This 2009 risk maturity model (Table 3.27) has a laudable focus on culture and practices. The methodology it employs is not publicly known as this is a proprietary consulting model.

Also laudable was the 2012 Ernst & Young survey 'Turning Risk into Results'. This found specific risk practices that were consistently present in the top performers (ie, top 20% based on risk maturity) that were not present in the bottom 20%. The 20 risk practices (can be read as *capabilities* by any risk maturity model user) were organized into five domains (read *modules*). The 20 risk practices (read *capabilities*) are reproduced in Chapter 5. The ERM profession needs more contributions like this from the consulting firms.

TABLE 3.28 FERMA risk management maturity, Belgium 2012

Features:	A periodic multi-criteria membership survey approach based on four categories (risk governance, risk practices and tools, risk reporting and communication, risk management functions alignment) and four maturity levels (emerging, moderate, mature and advanced) depending on respondents' answers to 16 relevant questions. Run by the Federation of European Risk Management Associations (FERMA). NB: Also supported the Ernst & Young survey 'Turning Risk into Results', which found specific risk practices that were consistently present in the top performers (ie top 20% based on risk maturity) that were not present in the bottom 20%. The 20 risk practices (read *capabilities*) were organized into five domains (read *modules*).
Benefits:	Improving risk management capability to leading European practices.
Advantages:	Content appeals to FERMA members. External benchmarking survey n=809 responses representing 20 countries to their 'survey and benchmark to identify and share current practices'.
Disadvantages:	*Potential insurer bias.*
Rated Tier:	*Concept.*

This model (Table 3.28) represents the federated European approach to improving risk management capability by periodic survey to members.

TABLE 3.29 Parkins Fraser Health ERM maturity, 2003–09

Features:	Five levels with 21 'elements' (capabilities) under seven themes. Paper-based solution. ERM readiness assessment tool to benchmark current healthcare ERM capability. Tailored by Sandra Parkins at Fraser Health in 2003 by adapting a tool used by the Internal Audit and Advisory Services of the Office of the Comptroller General of BC Canada (developed by Human Resources Development Canada). Applies change and quality management principles.
Benefits:	Meeting the ERM integration challenge. Cultivating an 'ERM mindset: achieving success against the odds'. Leadership buy-in. Informs ERM implementation strategy.
Advantages:	Specialist ERM capabilities to health sector. Emphasizes tailoring to own organization as the solution. Supported by the ISO 31000 movement.
Disadvantages:	*Dated?*
Rated Tier:	*Specialist with some intermediate elements.*

This is one of the early groundbreaking risk maturity models (Table 3.29). It specializes in adapting an ERM approach to the health sector.

TABLE 3.30 G31000 risk maturity model, Fr/UK 2016

Features:	Built on the 11 principles of the ISO 31000 risk management standard. Five levels of maturity defined: safety and security, compliance and control, partial ERM, full ERM and advanced performance. These establish successive foundations for continuous improvement towards advanced performance are directly linked to the degree of alignment with the ISO 31000 principles. Each of the 11 principles is broken down into five sub-components and the scoring for each of these is defined on a scale of 1 to 5 by reference to predefined responses categorizing the level of maturity of the subcomponent. The alignment with each principle is determined by summing scores from the five subcomponents. The total score across the 11 principles maps to the five maturity levels. Both downloadable Excel and web-based assessments are available.

TABLE 3.30 *Continued*

Benefits:	Promotes continuous improvement by providing a road map of sustainable change to enable an organization to mature their risk managment approach by steadily increasing alignment with the principles, framework and process proposed in ISO 31000.
Advantages:	ISO 31000-centric.
Disadvantages:	*ISO 31000-centric.*
Rated Tier:	*Benchmark-able.*

This is an ISO 31000-specialized but benchmark-able risk maturity model (Table 3.30) by G31000, a well-established ISO 31000 certification-for-individuals training and support institute. It is in-design at time of printing with plans to be launched in 2016.

TABLE 3.31 Gartner various maturity models, United States 2006–13

Features:	Five levels with multiple capabilities for various IT-related maturity models including: 1) IAM-PMM identity and access management programme maturity model; 2) BPM business process maturity model of six-phases; 3) EIM enterprise information management maturity model; and 4) CPM business capability maturity model. Capability – not risk maturity – models.
Benefits:	SEI CMM-style key rating indicator of the effectiveness and efficiency of the various IT-related and business processes etc.
Advantages:	
Disadvantages:	*Technology and process bias. Confusing efficiency with effectiveness benefits.*
Rated Tier:	*Conceptual.*

This is another IT-domain capability maturity model (Table 3.31) that seems to overclaim effectiveness benefits over efficiency. Not a risk maturity model but may be a useful reference for one.

TABLE 3.32 Genius Methods risk culture maturity monitor, RSA/UK 2014

Features:	Five levels with 36 questions under six operational areas (policies, reporting, processes, systems and data, management and control, people and organizational design). Pay-per-user online software tool outputs an assessment measuring maturity level with auto-report by e-mail. A 'Risk Culture Maturity Monitor' marketed by ComplySoft trading as Genius Methods, and content authored by Horst Simon.
Benefits:	Identify and understand the next step in the process of implementing an effective ERM culture in any organization.
Advantages:	Innovative. ERM culture based on banking experience of an OpRisk manager.
Disadvantages:	*Bias to financial services, OpRisk and compliance software. Overclaimed marketing; eg 'global ERM failed!'.*
Rated Tier:	*Specialized to culture and OpRisk.*

It is laudable to find an innovative risk maturity model specialized to ERM culture based on the extensive banking experience of an OpRisk practitioner (Table 3.32). The ERM profession needs more work like this on risk culture and from other subdomains.

TABLE 3.33 Hillson risk maturity, UK 1997

Features:	Four maturity levels each linked to four 'attributes' (culture, process, experience, application) with guidelines for current assessment. White paper. Benchmarks defined in terms of maturity usually reflecting increasing levels of sophistication together with other features. Applies principles from the pre-existing SEI capability maturity model and the European EFQM excellence model to risk management.
Benefits:	Benchmark current versus 'best practice', identify realistic targets for improvement, and develop action plans for developing or enhancing their risk capability.
Advantages:	*Classic white paper from 1997. Inspiration for Hopkinson Project RMM and others. Excellent sections on how to move from one level to the next with precautions. Hillson's strengths are in projects and ERM. He may be considered the 'father of the risk maturity model'.*
Disadvantages:	*Dated.*
Rated Tier:	*Conceptual.*

Hillson was the first to write a classic white paper in 1997 effectively evolving the risk maturity model from the existing SEI-style capability maturity family of models (Table 3.33). For this, he deserves the honour of being considered the 'father of the risk maturity model'. His seminal work has been the inspiration behind the INCOSE and Hopkinson Project risk maturity model and many others. The original paper still holds excellent sections, for example on how to move from one level to the next with precautions.

TABLE 3.34 HM Treasury 'Orange Book' self-assessment tool: Risk Management Assessment Framework (RMAF), UK 2004

Features:	Five levels with matrix descriptors. Paper-based template. Free UK Government tool for assessing ERM maturity. Genesis in the original European Foundation for Quality Management (EFQM) excellence model. First model in 2001 became known as the 'Orange Book'. Enables two types of assessment approaches: broad/impressionistic versus detailed.
Benefits:	Improving government's risk handling. 'Especially useful in preparing for the annual "Statement on Internal Control", which is a public statement about the review of the system of internal control' (HM Treasury, 2004).
Advantages:	Generic design inspiration to many other UK risk maturity models; eg ALARM. Good reputation within UK and audit for practical adoption to commerce and ISO 31000. Considers trade-offs hinted by the two approaches.
Disadvantages:	*Dated?*
Rated Tier:	*Conceptual.*

This model (Table 3.34) was developed in the early 2000s on the back of the European quality management movement. It was the basic design inspiration for many other UK risk maturity models such as ALARM. Still enjoys a good reputation within audit and some circles for practical adoption to commerce and ISO 31000. It was important in its day and is still worth referencing today albeit outdated by more modern ISO 31000-inspired thinking.

TABLE 3.35 Hopkinson QinetiQ project risk maturity model, UK 2010

Features:	Four maturity levels each linked to numerous 'attributes' (capabilities) with guidelines for current assessment. Book with CD working copy of the model enables users to undertake own project maturity assessments. Martin Hopkinson, APMP, is a principal consultant with QinetiQ, specializing in project risk management and project governance. Preface by Dr Hillson. Includes UK Department of Defence case studies and 'hard' success metrics for risk maturity.
Benefits:	Robust 'assessment framework and development pathway. Benchmark project risk processes and support the introduction of effective in-house project risk management. Using this model, implementation and improvement of project risk management can be managed effectively to ensure that the expected benefits are achieved in a way that is appropriate to the needs of each organization.'
Advantages:	Success metrics in cost, schedule and scope for project risk mature project over non-risk mature projects. Claims: 'The RMM [risk maturity model] has been proven over a period of 10 years, with at least 250 maturity assessments on projects and programmes with a total value exceeding £60 billion.'
Disadvantages:	
Rated Tier:	*Specialized.*

This is the best book on project-level risk maturity written to date. It 'walks' where others 'talk' (Table 3.35). Hopkinson sets the benchmark in not just explaining the project risk maturity model but he provides the 'hard' measured proofs of the added value it brings by risk professionals. The first book released with a working risk maturity model on CD, attached to the book.

TABLE 3.36 HRDC HR risk culture maturity model, Canada 2003

Features:	Five levels numbered 1 to 5 with 40 capabilities under five themes. Diagnostic tool to benchmark current ERM culture capability developed by Basil Orsini, director of policy, planning and client support, Human Resources Development Canada. Free non-proprietary generic tool in .pdf downloadable from **http://www.fin.gov.bc.ca/ocg/ias/Risk_Assessment_Tools.htm**; or contacting its producer, the Internal Audit and Advisory Services (IAAS) of the Department of Finance BC Canada.
Benefits:	Claims to 'have proven effective in assessing risk throughout [government] organizations' and to be 'particularly useful in assessing risk management culture'. Adapted by Fraser Health for their tailored ERM risk maturity model for the health sector.
Advantages:	ERM culture maturity specialized, especially for government risk culture and HR.
Disadvantages:	
Rated Tier:	*Specialized to ERM culture and government.*

HRDC (Table 3.36) is one of the great early risk maturity models that has inspired others such as the Fraser Health risk maturity model. An example of the thought leadership Canada has stamped on the ERM domain over many years.

TABLE 3.37 IBM risk maturity model, 2012

Features:	Six 'leading practices' to five maturity levels. White paper available by IBM Global Services Institute for Business Value.
Benefits:	Improved analytics to predict, monitor and mitigate risks in real time.
Advantages:	Financial institutions and large corporates with demand for high-end financial analytics with a balance-sheet focus.
Disadvantages:	*Financial modelling-tool bias.*
Rated Tier:	*Specialized.*

This model (Table 3.37) offers high-end financial analytics with a balance-sheet focus.

TABLE 3.38 IIARF-Sobel ERM maturity assessment, United States 2012

Features:	IIA Research Foundation (IIARF) book entitled *Enterprise Risk Management: Achieving and sustaining success* (IIARF, 2012). Appendix tool is called an ERM Maturity Assessment. It includes the current maturity of the ERM system, specifying a targeted maturity level and closing the gap to desired maturity levels (five levels with six steps covering attributes n=42). Includes details as to why you need to assess the ERM system, gathering information to support a comprehensive assessment, when to assess and basic design elements of a risk maturity model.
Benefits:	Geared to internal auditors. Promotes continuous improvement by providing a road map of sustainable change to enable an organization to mature their risk management approach by steadily increasing alignment with the principles, framework and process proposed in ISO 31000.
Advantages:	Aligned to ISO 31000. Senior auditor and IIA reputation backing.
Disadvantages:	
Rated Tier:	*Conceptual.*

The IIA Research Foundation (IIARF) (Table 3.38) published a progressive book for its time geared to internal auditors, written by Paul Sobel and Kurt Reding, entitled *Enterprise Risk Management: Achieving and sustaining success* (IIARF, 2012). These senior IIA board members and auditor thought-leaders provide direction to help internal auditors continually audit their organization's evolving ERM system. They offer two appendices tools representing approaches to assessing an ERM system. The first is against ISO 31000 as an outline approach, with a long list of questions (questions n=118). The second focuses on an ERM maturity assessment aligned to ISO 31000, as in the vignette above.

TABLE 3.39 INCOSE risk maturity model for projects, UK 2002

Features:	Four maturity levels centred on four capability domains: culture, process, experience and application. INCOSE (International Council on Systems Engineering) was a small business working-team in the field of project risk management, which adapted the Hillson Risk maturity model into a RMMM (risk management maturity model) – a simplified maturity model to target weaknesses for all types of organization and projects across all sectors.
Benefits:	Early adopter of Hillson's 1997 'first' risk maturity model for ERM. Risk management process.
Advantages:	For project manager audience.
Disadvantages:	
Rated Tier:	*Specialized for projects.*

Although surpassed in the field of project risk maturity model by Hopkinson's book/model in later years, INCOSE (Table 3.39) also evolved the Hillson model into its own model. It is a more simplified model than that by Hopkinson.

TABLE 3.40 Influence Inc regulatory risk maturity, UK 2014

Features:	Five phases, opt-in of components from a library per phase. Proprietary consulting services.
Benefits:	Regulatory compliance.
Advantages:	Understanding and mapping regulator requirements. *'Tube-map' visual very appealing and descriptive for a difficult area.*
Disadvantages:	*Prescriptive content.*
Rated Tier:	*Specialized to regulatory category of risk.*

This is an interesting model because of the novel 'Tube-map' visual that is very appealing and descriptive (Table 3.40). This model is highly specialized for regulatory risk maturity.

TABLE 3.41 INSEAD – Arguden 'LOGIC' corporate governance model, Turkey 2010

Features:	Five phases with five capability modules called 'LOGIC' (standing for learning, oversight, guidance, information and culture) rated against 'BaSICS'. Not described as any form of risk maturity model but has capability maturity dimensions – 'a self-assessment questionnaire tool to measure and improve the effectiveness of corporate governance or as the basis of an award scheme like the European Foundation for Quality Management (EFQM) to promote the right sort of behaviours in the board' (Arguden, 2010). Paper-based questionnaire includes guide and key area descriptions.
Benefits:	European style of governance. How a board learns and invests in developing its own performance.
Advantages:	Governance and culture domain capabilities CMM-style. Focus on 'soft' capability: 'governance is a management culture rather than a list of codes'. Backed by highly reputed King Committee Chairman South Africa. Evaluation and backbone of model is four main areas: three inputs (right people, right team, right process) and one output (improved business results). *Bias to European quality management approach.*
Disadvantages:	*Claims of 'best in class' not transparent. Bias to European quality management approach.*
Rated Tier:	*Specialized to governance.*

Auditors and followers of either the South African King-style governance or those interested in risk culture will enjoy this capability maturity conceptual piece (Table 3.41). Backed by the highly reputed King III Committee Chairman himself.

TABLE 3.42 IRM risk appetite maturity, UK 2011

Features:	White paper available via IRM Institute of Risk Management UK website; authored by Richard Anderson.
Benefits:	How to approach risk appetite at ERM level.
Advantages:	One potential capability within a tailored ERM risk maturity model. Detailed.
Disadvantages:	
Rated Tier:	*Specialized to risk appetite.*

A useful IRM thought-piece on an often complex and confusing topic (Table 3.42). A useful reference for designing one 'risk appetite' capability within your ERM risk maturity model.

TABLE 3.43 IRM RM Professional Magazine ERM risk software maturity curve, 2013

Features:	Five levels of 28 vendor risk software maturity capabilities. First IRM survey supplement to magazine, autumn 2013. IRM disclaimer not endorsing any particular vendor. Not a risk maturity model.
Benefits:	Claims to show the 'highest point of organizational risk management maturity that each provider caters for'.
Advantages:	Risk information systems capabilities. ISO 31000-inspired functionality matrix.
Disadvantages:	*Includes Risk Management Information System (RMIS) softwares for insurers not ERM. Bias to vendors.*
Rated Tier:	*Specialized to risk management information systems.*

This is not a risk maturity model but it may be useful as a reference if considering maturity capability specialized to risk management information systems and software (Table 3.43).

TABLE 3.44 ISACA Risk IT maturity framework, United States 2009

Features:	Six levels with six themed attributes (capabilities) and three 'domains' (being of risk governance, risk evaluation and risk response) specialized to IT risk management. Each domain has a detailed maturity model. Claims 'not a standard but a framework, including a process model and good practice guidance'. Main characteristics of the Risk IT framework that set it apart from the other standards and frameworks include the following: • Risk IT focuses on IT • Risk IT fits with any of the generics/cross-domain enterprise risk standards • Risk IT seamlessly aligns with CobiT and Val IT (and from there to other standards, such as PMBOK and PRINCE2, as explained in the detailed CobiT mapping documents) • Risk IT provides an umbrella for risk across other more focused IT frameworks, practices and process models (eg 2700x, 25999, DRI International [DRII] GAP, Business Continuity Institute [BCI] Good Practices, Information Security Forum [ISF], Information Technology Infrastructure Library [ITIL).'

TABLE 3.44 *Continued*

Benefits:	Integrates IT-related business risk management into overall ERM. Brings together all aspects of IT risk, including value, change, availability, security, project and recovery. Based on ISACA CobiT® but extends CobiT® and Val IT approaches. ISACA 110,000-strong over 180 countries – a leading global provider of knowledge, certifications, community, advocacy and education on information systems assurance and security, enterprise governance of IT, and IT-related risk and compliance. Huge online knowledge base includes a range of IT maturity subtopics such as cloud maturity and information security CMMs. Risk IT complements and extends COBIT and Val IT to make a more complete IT governance guidance resource. The associated *The Risk IT Practitioner Guide* is probably better and more detailed than most ERM equivalents and includes risk scenarios and flow charts.
Advantages:	Innovator – the only provider to date combining a detailed process model with management guidelines and maturity models. Detailed analytical models suited to ISACA professional members of IT and information systems professionals covering a range of titles and disciplines, many with a focus in IT assurance, control, security, governance and risk. Claims to be based on the principles of ERM codes such as COSO ERM and AS/NZS 4360 (precursor to ISO 31000).
Disadvantages:	*IT- and COSO- bias (as pre-ISO 31000?). Overdetailed? Dated?*
Rated Tier:	Specialized to IT.

ISACA was an innovator in the IT risk and assurance domain as the first to combine a detailed process model with management guidelines and maturity models (Table 3.44). Described above at length in due respect to the strong ISACA reputation and to the robustness of the risk IT model. A very detailed analytical model suited to IIA and ISACA professional members of IT and information systems professionals covering a range of titles and disciplines, many with a focus in IT assurance, control, security, governance and risk.

TABLE 3.45 ISO 31000:2009 Risk Management Standard, Switzerland 2009

Features:	Cites risk maturity strategy but not a risk maturity model. Leading document of reference for ERM initiatives. International standard for principles-based guidance for risk management. Three interlinked pillars of principles, frameworks and processes aimed at improving risk-informed decision making in the pursuit of organization objectives. Not certifiable for organizations. Supported by two additional ISO documents: the ISO Guide 73 for vocabulary and the IEC/ISO 31010 risk assessment techniques. Additional reference such as ISO/TR 31004:2013 and HB436:2013 Guidance for the implementation of ISO 31000 could be useful.
Benefits:	A high-level document presenting principles and concepts, which may be used as a content reference for many risk maturity models. It encourages organizations to have components of risk management to 'carry out a critical review of its existing practices and processes in the light of this ISO 31000 standard'. Important concepts for any risk maturity models such as 'risk maturity strategy' and a three-tiered proto-maturity model, being: three 'foundation components' (eg risk policy, mandate), seven 'organization arrangements' (eg resources) together with five 'enhanced features' (eg continuous improvement).
Advantages:	*The only international standard or major code to cite ERM maturity. Adopted by 61 countries including most of OECD and all BRICS. Succinct but powerful 24 pages. Proven pedigree and international implementation track record. Easy to implement. Easy to cross-map for transparency with numbered sections. Being updated.*
Disadvantages:	*Not a certifiable compliance standard for organizations. Not designed as a risk maturity model intrinsically nor contains a risk maturity model, but as a high-level structure for reference in risk management associated with the ISO Guide 73 – Vocabulary and ISO 31010 – risk assessment techniques.*
Rated Tier:	*1 Basic.*

The ISO 31000:ISO PC 262 technical committees are updating 2009 at the time of writing. Topics rumoured to be reviewed include: risk-based thinking and organization certification.

ISO 31000:2009 (Table 3.45) is certainly not a risk maturity model per se and is classified here as conceptual (as is COSO ERM). What it does offer – if disaggregated correctly – is a sort of proto-maturity model, or at the least, a rich source of potential ERM capabilities to be synthesized into a tailored risk maturity model. It describes three underlying levels of increasing maturity sophistication from the foundation components up to the organization arrangements up to enhanced features. One may also unpack an increasing sophistication sequence in the risk process outputs from risk sources to intrinsic to inherent to residual to reported risk profiles etc. See Chapters 4 and 5 for more detail.

TABLE 3.46 ITI Global IT reliability process maturity model, India c.2012

Features:	Six process maturity levels are applied specifically to IT process reliability and benchmarking activities. Evaluates maturity in IT reliability methods and processes. Benchmarks at all organization levels via gap analysis between the company process and industry 'best practices'. Defines improvement plan up to desired target and related: processes, organizations, methods and tools, training and skill requirements. Industrial Training Institutes (ITIsd) are government-run training organizations in India.
Benefits:	Lower product development costs and time to market IT via more upfront reliability planning and activities. Fewer prototypes necessary to achieve reliability targets. More accurate reliability predictions.
Advantages:	IT reliability process benchmarking.
Disadvantages:	
Rated Tier:	*Specialized to IT process reliability with some intermediary.*

Financial services and other organizations dependent on IT may reference this complex maturity model (Table 3.46) specialized to IT process reliability.

TABLE 3.47 Kaplan-Mikes ERM maturity, United States 2011

Features:	Three to four levels being board and company commitment, business culture, strategic assets then methodologies and tools, book and proprietary consulting services via an affiliated consulting firm.
Benefits:	
Advantages:	Adapted to business strategy and performance management.
Disadvantages:	*Early foray into ERM from business scorecard and strategy academic experts. Prescriptive content.*
Rated Tier:	*Concept.*

This represents an early attempt at alignment between strategy and risk, from the strategy people behind the balanced scorecard concept (Table 3.47).

TABLE 3.48 Kerzner project management maturity model (KPM3™), United States 2001

Features:	Five levels focusing on four critical 'components' (modules): effective communications, effective cooperation, effective teamwork and trust. Five levels: common language, common processes, singular improvement, benchmarking, continuous improvement. Closely aligned with PMI PMBOK® Guide. Online assessment with 183 multiple-choice questions on subject areas including common language, common processes, singular methodology, benchmarking and continuous improvement. 'The focus of KPM3 is that people manage projects; people manage tools; tools manage neither people nor projects.'
Benefits:	Behavioural assessments indicate whether people believe that they are working within their comfort zone. 'If continuous improvements are made correctly (ie, level 5 of the KPM3), and people are happy with their comfort zone, project management maturity can be achieved quickly.'

TABLE 3.48 *Continued*

Advantages:	Significantly more behavioural than quantitative as people manage projects and methodologies function as supporting tools.
Disadvantages:	
Rated Tier:	*Specialized to projects.*

A very interesting perspective specialized to project risk maturity as Kerzner has an innovative focus on people behaviour (the so-called 'soft side' to organization capability) (Table 3.48). Kerzner offers an excellent quote: '[risk maturity is]... significantly more behavioural than quantitative as people manage projects and methodologies function as supporting tools'. Perhaps other ERM risk maturity models can learn from taking more interest in measuring the behavioural attributes to organization capabilities, like Kerzner?

TABLE 3.49 KPMG ERM maturity assessment model, United States 2010

Features:	Website and earlier model in 2010 use three levels (basic, mature and advanced) with five capabilities.
Benefits:	
Advantages:	
Disadvantages:	
Rated Tier:	*Intermediate.*

There is little known in the public domain about the KPMG approach to a risk maturity model (Table 3.49).

TABLE 3.50 Lederman/GARP information governance, United States 2012

Features:	Five levels with eight generally accepted record-keeping practices (GARP) principles for records management or 'information governance'. A paper-based benchmarking and improvement tool by ARMA International **www.arma.org**. Claims the principles 'distilled from information governance best practices and international standards'.
Benefits:	Baseline for judging their initial state of information governance maturity and for measuring progress as they develop policies and procedures.
Advantages:	Electronic records for records-management benchmark capabilities.
Disadvantages:	
Rated Tier:	*Specialized to record keeping.*

It is interesting to note from the perspective of the evolution of the maturity model how it continues to branch out. So, now you can even find a capability maturity model for record keeping backed by a record-keeping institute (Table 3.50).

TABLE 3.51 LogicManager™ ERM maturity model, United States 2006

Features:	Fifty-two underlying indicators with five root-cause categories with 25 factors/attributes with 10 rating scales for effectiveness with 10 for proactivity with 10 for coverage, all combine to arrive at a maturity score between 0–1,000 divided by quintiles into five levels (ad hoc, initial, repeatable, managed, leadership). Reports, dashboards and charts. Cloud-based subscription software with content co-developed and co-marketed with the RIMS Maturity Model™ free online assessment tool on RIMS website. The indicators (read *capabilities*) in both sets are exact replicas.

TABLE 3.51 *Continued*

Benefits:	Attractive to the United States/North American market and RIMS-type members. Set of 'ERM standards for effective collaboration by risk functionaries with others' to 'move... entities to higher levels of competency (sic) and maturity'.
Advantages:	Brand and content associated with RIMS USA. Integrates indicators to business processes and to four high-level frameworks (RIMS ERM, CoSo ERM eight principles, COBIT IT six areas, LogicManager Entity-Wide Controls). Users can create indicators and add documents.
Disadvantages:	*Dated. Complex. Content bias. Taxonomy-driven and prescriptive content library and lexicon. Other framework references are not transparent. See comments below.*
Rated Tier:	*Benchmark-able.*

This is one of the earliest and leading proprietary risk maturity models (Table 3.51) that is benchmark-able. It was innovative in its day and backed by RIMS ERM where it is the software behind the RIMS website 'teaser' gratis assessment. LogicManager positions the survey tool as a teaser on the RIMS website for visitors who may link through to buy their LogicManager™ software. This RIMS/LogicManager combined content and framework was created in 2006 by an initial RIMS ERM committee and a workshop led by the LogicManager CEO who sat on the RIMS Executive. The indicators (read *capabilities*) in both sets are exact replicas and have not changed since 2006. This risk maturity model committee devised their own assessment method of three dimensions of rating by Effectiveness=Impact × Proactivity=Timing/Likelihood × Preparedness=Assurance/Coverage.

The methodology and approach to the model are complex and reflect pre-ISO 31000:2009 and North American risk thinking. The claim that this model is an umbrella framework that incorporates multiple standards (as in RIMS ERM, CoSo and COBIT) is not transparent (as there is no cross-mapping and it seems too high-level as they use roll-up from the same LogicManager library of indicators to either the 'COSO cube' with eight fronts to the cube, or seven for RIMS or a multiple for COBIT). The rating methodology is complex with cumbersome ratings of up to 1,560 considerations per scoring round. The content indicator library and lexicon are prescriptive and taxonomy-driven. The software represents a heavy investment in software and training.

TABLE 3.52 LTRC/EFQM risk management performance ladder, UK 2010

Features:	Five capability and two result areas. Rated to four evidence scales, being 1=nil; 2=some; 3=clear; 4=excellent. Maturity levels are: 1=awareness and understanding; 2=implementation in progress for all key areas; 3=embedding and improving; 4=excellent capability. Capability areas are: leadership strategies and policies; people; partnerships and resources; and process. Result areas are: risk handling and outcomes. Content and structure a direct adaptation of the European Framework for Quality Management (EFQM) excellence model. Proprietary consulting firm Liz Taylor Risk Consulting. MS Office-based.
Benefits:	A framework for helping management manage all aspects of ERM using a balanced model showing inputs and outputs. Multipurpose uses as an audit tool, a maturity model, a benchmarking tool or a model for creating a plan of action.
Advantages:	Bias to EFQM and appeals to their supporters. Implies robustness from the success claims and name of the EFQM movement in the UK, Europe and elsewhere.
Disadvantages:	Bias to EFQM.
Rated Tier:	*Integrated.*

This is an interesting 2010 model (Table 3.52) distinctive in the market for two associated reasons. First, for being a clever and close adaptation of a capability model based on the authoritative quality management model called the European Framework for Quality Management (EFQM) excellence model. This will appeal to quality management supporters. Second, it implies robustness not only from the name of the EFQM movement in the UK, Europe and elsewhere but the business performance success claims that EFQM have published.

The author Liz Taylor has also written an updated chapter on risk maturity in her 2014 book *Practical Enterprise Risk Management: How to optimize business strategies through managed risk taking* (Taylor, 2014). Taylor is a recognized practitioner in ERM industries, with 35 years' experience. She was formerly chief executive of ALARM (the forum for risk management in the public sector), senior vice president for Marsh Europe and winner of Europe-wide Risk Manager of the Year. Currently running her own training and consulting company, Liz Taylor Risk Consulting, she is a Fellow of the Institute of Risk Management as well as the Business Continuity Institute.

TABLE 3.53 Luyckx enterprise business process maturity, United States 2012

Features:	The Enterprise Business Process Maturity framework is a 4×4 matrix. The horizontal axis is four project phases: strategy, design, implementation and control. The vertical axis is four driving forces within an organization, which should work together to make an organization flexible: business management (CEO owner), operational management (COO owner), organizational management (HRM owner) and management control (CFO owner). Book by ex Capgemini SAP specialist. Claims results in 16 BPM process areas are those required to fully utilize BPM and that BP maturity can be determined based on CMMI concepts. May be used for cross-domain maturity analysis, BPM benefit and ROI calculations and the implementation of a BPM platform viz: **1** The relationship between maturity levels, ROI and the BPM stakeholders. **2** The relationship between the BPM process areas, the required BPM projects and the SAP/BPM implementation platform. **3** The relationship between BPM maturity models, BPM governance and the day-to-day BPM maturity control.
Benefits:	Claims to 'help you: 1. to perform a BPM road-map assessment and create a BPM road map; 2. discover the business issues; 3. explain the required BPM tools and projects; 4. create a financial BPM benefits case... the results of the BPM maturity research in more than 1,000 companies and the results of BPM road-map assessments within industry leaders... explain why the operational excellence group and the ERP CC should work together and why the role of the chief processing officer (CPO) is so important.'
Advantages:	Business process maturity with GRC links. Claims 'the first [holistic] framework where the different BPM topics are integrated into one framework to create a BPM road map'.
Disadvantages:	*Bias to processes, GRC, IT vendor and implementer/SAP. Cryptic?*
Rated Tier:	*Specialized to enterprise business process.*

Not a risk maturity model but a capability maturity model that is specialized for business process maturity with GRC links (Table 3.53). Claims to be 'the first [holistic] framework where the different business process management (BPM) topics are integrated into one framework to create a BPM road map'.

TABLE 3.54 Marsh Risk Consulting ERM maturity, UK c.2010

Features:	Six pillars (modules) with underlying capabilities to progress from current to target state to five levels: undeveloped, formalized, established, embedded, fully integrated. Six pillars are: governance and infrastructure; risk identification assessment and prioritization; risk treatment and controls; reporting, monitoring and communications; ERM internal culture; managing partnership risk. Formerly 10 pillars but collapsed into six with minor rewording. MS Office-software based. Proprietary consulting model based on initial questionnaire. Also see Marsh Insurance RM. Past claims to client database of 2,000? Neutral to codes.
Benefits:	Delivering value from building risk-management capability.
Advantages:	Encourages integration of maturity target into long-term strategic and business plans as formal KPIs and integration with RM information systems. Robust ERM content from the largest ERM international consulting firm.
Disadvantages:	*Six pillars not enough? Dated?*
Rated Tier:	*Benchmark-able.*

This model (Table 3.54) deploys a robust methodology developed over some years and backed by the largest ERM consulting group in the world. Like many consulting firms at this level, the risk maturity model deliberately avoids any benchmarking to ISO, COSO other voluntary codes in order to appeal to as wide a client base as possible and to preserve 'independence'. So the 'benchmark-ability' is based on their prescriptive content backed by claims to its 'usage by x number of clients'.

TABLE 3.55 Marsh Insurance and ERM maturity models, UK 2013

Features:	Five levels x six pillars (modules) with underlying insurance function capabilities to progress from current to target state. MS Office software-based. Proprietary consulting model based on initial questionnaire to rate against 'best practice made in key areas such as governance; insurable and non-insurable risk identification, analysis and evaluation; cost of risk approach; risk reporting and monitoring; risk transfer resourcing; and the management of third-party providers'. Sister product to Marsh ERM RMM.
Benefits:	Measure value of insurance resources and the 'effectiveness of their insurance departments, develop a road map to achieve added value, deliver operational efficiency and ultimately ensure the optimum ROI is achieved from the insurance function'.
Advantages:	Insurance function RMM. Claimed as the *'first methodology of its kind'* by one of the largest international insurance brokerage firms with a track record in ERM RMM. 'Best practice' claimed.
Disadvantages:	*Only available in UK?*
Rated Tier:	*Specialized to insurance and may be benchmark-able.*

This model (Table 3.55) is an expected recent evolution from the sister ERM risk maturity specialized to an insurance-function risk maturity model. Claimed as the 'first methodology of its kind' by one of the largest international insurance brokerage firms with a track record in ERM risk maturity. Also a 'teaser' product to broker insurance products.

TABLE 3.56 Marsh Risk Consulting 'Risk Focus' ERM maturity, Australia 2000

Features:	? levels x nine risk categories. Risk Focus proprietary software running on the Marsh STARS TrendTracker platform. Produces a stand-alone ERM benchmarking study against 600+ clients with an auto-generated report to client. Requires inputs from fee-for-service consulting interviews, workshops and client collaboration. Not marketed as a RMM but effectively one that predates more recent Marsh ERM and insurance RMM products.
Benefits:	Delivering value from understanding the risk profile of the organization. Separating insurable risks to buy insurance cover from non-insurable risks for management to focus on (hence the name Risk Focus).
Advantages:	ERM RMM content based on 600+ client experience from the largest ERM international consulting firm. Later claims it is aligned to AS/NZ 4360:1995 (the 2004 update became the precursor to ISO 31000:2009).
Disadvantages:	*Dated. Expensive and complex STARS system. Not easy to implement. Insurance bias as it is used as 'door-opener' marketing tool for 'wrapped' insurance broking. No cross-mapping to 4360 so not transparent. No evidence of wide acceptance outside of Australia. Benchmarking robustness dubious over time as the database is difficult to mine.*
Rated Tier:	*Benchmark-able.*

This was an innovative early risk maturity model from 2000 (Table 3.56) producing a standard template report as a 'teaser' to win insurance work. It represents the first known *working* risk maturity model in the marketplace after the Hillson paper in 1997. It is not known if it is still marketed by Marsh Australasia or if it was ever available outside that region.

TABLE 3.57 Marx management control systems maturity model MCS-MM, Germany 2011

Features:	Doctoral paper outlines three partial maturity models for reporting, planning and consolidation, which are integrated into one holistic maturity model for management control systems with five core domains. The five levels are: financial and corporate centre-centric MCS (level 1) to a basic corporate MCS (level 2), and a comprehensive corporate MCS (level 3). Additionally, the MCS recommends a strong strategic orientation (level 4) and leveraging potentials in modern IT support (level 5). Combines: corporate management; management accounting; management control systems; business intelligence; maturity models; design science. Capability – not risk maturity – model.
Benefits:	'An empirically and algorithmically constructed MCS-MM.'
Advantages:	Specialist management control systems CMM. Holistic. IT as strategic enabler for MCSs. Claims that 'Despite MMs' popularity in IS research, the concept has not gained much popularity in management research.'
Disadvantages:	*Academic. Conceptual. Technology bias, eg the highest level is 'IT-enabled MCS' over 'Strategic MCS'.*
Rated Tier:	*Conceptual.*

This is an academic conceptual paper regarding 'IT-enabled' management control systems (MCSs) and 'strategic MCS' for those interested in such capability maturity (Table 3.57).

TABLE 3.58 McGraw BSIMM-V software security maturity model, United States 2013

Features:	Five levels with a 0–5 scale algorithm scoring/charting 34 COBIT IT processes to four functional domains. These four domains cover 318 objectives of control. Designed by the COBIT Management Guidelines Control Objectives for Information and related Technology (COBIT) and published by the IT Governance Institute (ITGI) and Information Systems Audit and Control Foundation (ISACF). Support by ISACA. An IT governance tool used to measure how well developed the management processes are with respect to internal controls. Fundamental feature: measure as-is maturity levels, and define to-be maturity levels as well as gaps to fill, ie planning improvements (as-is, to-be, gap analysis). Capability – not risk maturity – model.
Benefits:	Balancing IT risk and control in a cost-effective manner. Organization can grade itself from non-existent (0) to optimized (5). Such capability can be exploited by auditors to help management fulfil its IT governance responsibilities, ie exercise effective responsibility over the use of IT just like any other part of the business.
Advantages:	Specialist CMM for IT audit assurance. Respected originators. Practical improvements to the system of internal controls of IT processes.
Disadvantages:	*IT compliance-driven. IT-speak. Auditor-speak.*
Rated Tier:	*Conceptual.*

This model (Table 3.58) is a good example of how sophisticated the SEI-evolved capability risk modellers have become. The result of a multi-year study of real-world software security initiatives from data observed in 67 software security initiatives from global firms such as Fidelity, Fannie May, Marks and Spencer, Nokia, SAP, Sony and SWIFT.

TABLE 3.59 Mayer MMGRSeg information security, United States 2009

Features:	Five levels with three stages (maturity, immaturity and excellence) and 43 objectives of control with n=35 questionnaire (capabilities). Includes: tool for assessing the maturity level of the risk management process activities, map of control, RACI matrix relative to each risk management process activity, and dashboard of the risks. See Elmaallam (Table 3.26) for more on information security.
Benefits:	Information security risk management process maturity capabilities. Concerns a part of IS: the information security.
Advantages:	Information security maturity. Integration and product improvement.
Disadvantages:	
Rated Tier:	*Specialized to IT information security.*

This risk maturity model (Table 3.59) specialized to IT information security is worth a look from a tailoring-your-own-model design point of view, due to its neat set of features and the rise of cyber risk. These include: a map of control, RACI matrix relative to each risk management process activity and dashboard of the risks.

TABLE 3.60 Monda ERM Index (ERMi), Italy 2013

Features:	Conceptual model for organization self-assessment. Questionnaire of 22 parameters as closed-end questions (read as *capabilities*) on ERM practices, analysing company risk culture, the organization and the ERM process of ERM. Rating ERM maturity ranges from 0 to 100 and can be expressed as a percentage. No tool. Academic paper based on input from 16 international practitioner/consultant/ academic ERM subject-matter experts. Claims the model tested on a small sample of five (or 12?) firms.

TABLE 3.60 *Continued*

Benefits:	Claims 'a model to assess the maturity of the ERM implementations in non-financial firms. The ERMi is the first ERM maturity model available in literature that is built in a rigorous and scientific way.' Objective answers to common questions: 'How good is the ERM programme?' and 'Which ERM areas to prioritize and improve on?' (Lau, 2013).
Advantages:	*Most significant RMM international research release of 2013.* Particularly useful when tailoring your own RMM for a start-list or 'core' capabilities or ones that may be up-weighted. Short-form up-to-date self-assessment based on scientific method, design rigour and derivation from an international mix of Delphi-experts. Platform for future quantitative and qualitative research. Questions and weighted scores that form the index were arrived at via ranking-type Delphi method facilitated by the authors from a panel of ERM experts then cross-tested with real data from firms obtained through a survey.
Disadvantages:	No levels. Acknowledged as not a comprehensive evaluation tool as limited to the 'top' 22 parameters originating from literature. *Early reference bias to COSO risk definition.*
Rated Tier:	*Conceptual.*

Monda ERMi is the most significant piece of international research specifically on ERM risk maturity models released since 2013 (Table 3.60). It is particularly useful when tailoring your own risk maturity model for a start-list or 'core' capabilities, or capabilities that may be up-weighted. The academic authors acknowledge that ERMi is not a comprehensive evaluation tool as it is limited to the 'top' 22 parameters (read *capabilities*) but this paper makes the most robust use of published RMM Delphi subject-matter experts. Where better can you find a starting-list of subject-matter expert (SME)-agreed capabilities to design or redesign your tailored risk maturity model?

One of those Delphi SMEs was William Lau. His blog comment on 4 April 2013 is quoted here:

> I feel outputs of an effective maturity assessment need to give objective answers to 'How good is the ERM programme?' and 'Which ERM areas to prioritize and improve on?' to whomever asks – auditor, board, management – knowing

> that most people will never care for ERM as much as practitioners do. Towards those aims I highly recommend the 'ERM Index (ERMi)... The ERMi balances the trade-offs perfectly IMHO [in my humble opinion] for the people that ask the questions. I do hope that it takes root and grows in our industry where consensus on what works is still difficult after so many years'.

Below are extracts from the Monda abstract to the Monda research paper of April 2013. This will give the reader more insight into the robustness of the methodology employed:

> No studies have been conducted yet to propose robust and rigorous models to evaluate the quality, or maturity, of ERM programmes implemented by firms... In order to build a rigorous ERM maturity model, we have run an e-mail Delphi procedure... The output of the Delphi method is a scoring model that can be used to assess the maturity of an ERM programme by administering a questionnaire composed of 22 closed-end questions to firms: answers are collected and scored, and all scores are combined in a single final score, the ERM Index (ERMi)... The difference with other existing maturity models is its solid scientific base, the rigour with which it has been designed and the fact that it is derived from a Delphi procedure involving leading ERM experts who reached consensus on the model detailed design (Monda and Giorgino, 2013).

TABLE 3.61 Murphy 4e model project managing the value system, Ireland 2012

Features:	Five maturity levels, four value levels, four success levers, and eight areas from framework to oversight with 32 'carefully tailored questions designed to test all levels of the value system' representing a 'new framework... measures value across these dimensions: success levers, value levers, capability layers, growth drivers, maturity profile'. The risk maturity model is the fifth dimension of the 4e model. Downloadable academic papers by an author risk manager, Ronan Murphy.
Benefits:	Maturity profile 'route map' to improved corporate performance. 4e model helps the project management profession to address the challenges of strategy and growth across all sectors. Establishes a value-measurement culture for project management initiatives to ensure the long-term interests of all their stakeholders are taken into account. Empirical research support. Compass and comparison charts.

TABLE 3.61 *Continued*

Advantages:	For project managers – organization-level metrics.
Disadvantages:	*Academic. Practical?*
Rated Tier:	*Specialized to projects but may be benchmark-able if ERM relevant?*

The Murphy model (Table 3.61) is specialized to project risk maturity model and quite conceptual. Future public disclosure may clear up if it is of an intermediate or benchmark-able to ERM tier. Murphy claims that the risk maturity model 'is the fifth dimension of the 4e model'.

TABLE 3.62 NSW Government Treasury ERM risk maturity, Australia 2012

Features:	No levels but various 'success indicators' define five maturity attributes (capabilities) with four 'maturity rating scales' (low, inconsistent, consistent and fully addressed). Online gratis spreadsheet-based templates provide a simple ISO 31000-based risk maturity model. Additional templates provide potential RMM input for risk people-competencies as well as analysis matrices for stakeholders, communication needs and communication strategy.
Benefits:	Generic and simple model and risk capability templates. Designed for government agency use and tailoring to meet each agency's specific needs as part of wider risk management toolkit.
Advantages:	Simple. Easy-to-tailor or a 'get-started' risk maturity model for novices. Based on ISO 31000 proven pedigree and international implementation track record. *No reason why for-profits and all sectors cannot use the simple RMM template.*
Disadvantages:	*Simple. No levels. Confuses capability with people competencies.*
Rated Tier:	*Basic.*

This model (Table 3.62) by a government agency is a wonderful place to start to tailor your own ERM risk maturity model. It is ISO-31000:2009 aligned and the website offers a free easy-to-use spreadsheet.

TABLE 3.63 OCEG Redbook GRC Capability Model™ v.2.1, United States 2003–12

Features:	No risk maturity levels or ratings per se. Eight global risk and compliance (GRC) universal outcomes achieved via eight integrated components with 33 elements each embodying high-performing practices discussing related principles, subpractices, success factors, actions and controls. Online 200-page 'open-access' OCEG Red Book guide plus related materials – technology and assessment guides (**www.OCEG.org** store). OCEG 'is a non-profit think tank that helps organizations drive principled performance by reliably achieving objectives while addressing uncertainty and acting with integrity'. Open compliance and ethics group assisted by leadership council voluntary members from over 50 US-based organizations that are claimed as 'cross-industry, cross-disciplinary and trans-global'. Certifiable.
Benefits:	Provide assurance to management and the board that the [GRC] capability is reliable, effective, efficient and 'responsive'. 'Achieving principled performance by integrating the governance, assurance and management of performance, risk and compliance.' Principled Performance® means 'reliably achieving objectives while dealing with uncertainty (both risk and reward) and acting with integrity'. Reported cost savings of 30% or more and a raft of other benefits.
Advantages:	*Ambitious early attempt to provide holistic integration of all-organization activity via root-element of 'information'. Recognition of 'soft' elements, particularly culture. Well-written, cross-referenced and cogent for certification purposes.* Represents a large inventory of potential capabilities for tailoring your own risk maturity. *Appears ISO 31000:2009-consistent – but are most of the risk-related elements a cleverly re-badged ISO 31000 overlay on traditional compliance/audit foundations?*
Disadvantages:	*Still-emerging 'GRC' concept. Technology bias to IT vendors, IT analysts, IT/Big 4 implementers, compliance and insurance. Bias to big-spending corporate sector.*
Rated Tier:	*Certifiable.*

This is a certifiable GRC maturity model (Table 3.63) backed by the commercial and marketing weight of the IT vendor sector. It claims an enormous number of deliverables.

TABLE 3.64 OGC Management of Risk (MoR®) Projects, UK 2010

Features:	Five rating scales with n=? criteria. Based on MoR® principles. Developed by UK reference group of SME consultants for the UK Office of Government (OGC). Paper-based tool. MoR® describes how risk management applies to government or private-sector long-, medium- and short-term objectives by describing four organizational perspectives: strategic (LT) to programme to project (MT) and operational (ST). Certifiable. Also see Axelos P3M3.
Benefits:	Assessing the maturity of project risk management. Self-claimed 'best-practice' guide to measure the current level of RMM and to identify areas for improvement. Also refers to other RMMs and provides a high-level description of the portfolio, programme and project management maturity model (P3M3). Includes tools and techniques.
Advantages:	Projects risk maturity guidelines designed for APMG UK certification for focus on strategic (LT) to programme to project (MT) and operational (ST). Claims strong overlap with HM Treasury model and ISO 31000 (albeit 31000 for the life of the organization).
Disadvantages:	Focus on process improvement.
Rated Tier:	*Specialized to government projects.*

This is a certifiable risk maturity model (Table 3.64) specialized to projects. Also refer to Axelos P3M3.

TABLE 3.65 Pergler-McKinsey & Co risk management maturity, United States 2012

Features:	Claims all business sectors fit within four stages of a maturity spectrum. Value drivers and key tools may represent maturity capabilities. Business models for corporates and financial institutions compared, as well as risk function models. White paper.
Benefits:	Risk management effectiveness across the board.
Advantages:	Good resource for tailoring capabilities. Differentiates corporate from financial sector. Supports combining tailoring (due to differences in business models) with appropriate cross-over learnings of 'emerging good practices' between sectors. Excellent macro-sector capability analysis and comparisons. McKinsey name for strategy.
Disadvantages:	*Finance and big corporate bias?*
Rated Tier:	*Conceptual.*

This is a good conceptual resource for tailoring capabilities that differentiates corporate from financial sectors (Table 3.65). It supports combining tailoring (due to differences in business models) with appropriate crossover learning of 'emerging good practices' between sectors. It offers excellent macro-sector capability analysis and comparisons.

TABLE 3.66 PMI OPM3® v2 organizational project management maturity, United States 1998–2003

Features:	Four levels with three domains (project, programme, portfolio) and analysis of an additional 17 organizational enablers into one maturity model. Project Management Institute (PMI) claims to be 'the global best practice standard for enterprise improvement. Uncover hundreds of best practices. Evaluate your current project management capabilities. Map out the steps needed to achieve your improvement.' Origins in 1998, first edition 2003, second in 2008 recognized as an American National Standard (ANSI/PMI 08-004-2008). Different commercial product and service offerings on-sale. Certifiable. Capability – not risk maturity – model.
Benefits:	Project management maturity capabilities. Projects delivering the value you expect. Targeting project management offices (PMOs), similar centralized project management departments, project and programme practitioners in organizational project management. 'Tie your projects to your business strategy and make sure they support your organizational goal.'
Advantages:	Robust and exemplary development pedigree from a reputable institute with legitimate claims to global coverage. Guidance not prescriptive.
Disadvantages:	*Not directly risk management-related.*
Rated Tier:	*Certifiable.*

This is a certifiable projects risk maturity model (Table 3.66) with a robust and exemplary development pedigree from a reputable institute with legitimate claims to global coverage, being the Project Management Institute (PMI). Albeit overclaimed, the commercial product and service offerings on-sale have evolved from origins in 1998, a first edition in 2003 and a second edition in 2008, which was recognized as an American national standard (ANSI/PMI 08-004-2008).

TABLE 3.67 Protiviti process maturity matrix, United States c.2008

Features:	Five levels with a six-capability matrix intersected with current versus desired line-chart. Downloadable reference. Proprietary consulting model behind this not known.
Benefits:	Simple current versus desired maturity gap analysis.
Advantages:	ERM capabilities with a process and IT maturity focus.
Disadvantages:	*Process and software engineering bias. Dated. No reference set but a COSO ERM supporter.*
Rated Tier:	*Basic.*

This is an early basic risk maturity copy (Table 3.67) in the SEI capability maturity model-style (like the PwC model) dated to the pre-ISO 31000 era.

TABLE 3.68 PwC risk management maturity model, United States 2011

Features:	Five levels to the standard SEI capability maturity model lexicon of ad hoc, managed, standardized, integrated and optimized. Downloadable white paper reference. Proprietary consulting model created for internal consulting use.
Benefits:	Assess risk maturity: 'This approach enables an organization to efficiently build their ERM capabilities and ultimately drive towards higher maturity levels.'
Advantages:	ERM capabilities with a process and IT maturity focus à la SEI CMM style. Appeal to COSO ERM audience.
Disadvantages:	*Bias to: COSO ERM, process, SEI-style methodology, the formal side of risk management and physical evidence that does not guarantee a strong culture of risk management. No reference codes except COSO framework, which PwC authored. Very compliance driven, as is entirely based on COSO, which PwC authored for the COSO committee from 2002–04. Dated.*
Rated Tier:	*Basic.*

This is an early basic risk maturity copy (Table 3.68) in the SEI capability maturity model-style (like the Protiviti model) dated to the pre-ISO 31000 era.

TABLE 3.69 RIMS Maturity Model™ for ERM, United States 2006

Features:	This is a free online initial assessment tool accompanied by a free State of ERM Report. The RIMS ERM Development Committee selected Steven Minsky, CEO of LogicManager software and RIMS Executive member, to develop the tool with initial input from a RIMS RMM committee. Additional RMM features and functionality are available via purchased LogicManager software, refer to LogicManager.
Benefits:	Claims many benefits on behalf of: risk professions, stakeholder organizations, reduced costs, increased efficiencies and top-line revenue (RIMS, 2015b). Quote: 'a road map for your risk management programme that can deliver on today's expectations... to develop sustainable ERM programmes and infrastructure reflecting their organizations' strategies and business objectives'.
Advantages:	Backed officially by RIMS USA. Content and benchmarking suited to RIMS/insurance-style audience. Claims to build 'best practice ERM infrastructure according to RIMS State of ERM Report 2008' with more than 2,400 report users (2015) and over 500 in second benchmarking year. Excellent for benchmarking against others in RIMs member firm database – eg Advisen Ltd/RIMS 2013 RIMS ERM Survey. Can be used alongside other maturity models.
Disadvantages:	*Bias to LogicManager methodology. Dated content.*
Rated Tier:	*Intermediate, but benchmark-able if buy the LogicManager software.*

This model (Table 3.69) was groundbreaking when released in 2006 and powerful in the pre-ISO 31000 era for a North American audience. The free online RIMS website assessment is still accessible to non-RIMS members at time of writing. The free online assessment acts as a lead-generator for the software vendor LogicManager and their full product also called LogicManager™ . Refer to the separate entry for LogicManager for more detail (see Table 3.51 on pp 106–07).

TABLE 3.70 Risk Academy risk maturity model, Russia 2015

Features:	Four key risk maturity components (integration of risk management into decision-making and business processes, risk culture and awareness, disclosure and transparency, continuous risk management improvement) with three capabilities each, totalling 12 capabilities. Rated to a three-scale scoring methodology of low, medium or high maturity level of integrated risk management (ie absence, formal/compliance process, integrated). 'Check-the-box' matrix spreadsheet format in Russian and English languages. Proprietary consultant model authored by Alex Sidorenko. No overall levels of organization maturity as in most models, instead... 'risk management can only be considered effective when high level of maturity is achieved for each of the four components'.
Benefits:	Effective risk management that is systemically integrated into organization processes and decision making. Author was involved in drafting PwC risk maturity model and has researched leading global models before creating a model with a unique focus on risk integration and risk culture with users such as Russian regulators and government.
Advantages:	Succinct methodology and modern content. Provides for risk processes to be aligned to ISO 31000:2009 principles. Succinct guidance for risk functionaries and top management.
Disadvantages:	*Standard 'check-the-box' matrix constraints.*
Rated Tier:	*Intermediate, albeit aspects of Tailored.*

This Russian model (Table 3.70) is one of the newest models on the market in 2015. It will appeal to those wanting a succinct and modern content approach, focused on risk management integration and risk culture. The model's author strongly feels that absolutely every point has to be applied for an organization to be mature otherwise none of the elements or levels are relevant: 'I am basically saying unless you have all elements at integrated [the highest maturity level], you probably shouldn't call your risk management effective.'

TABLE 3.71 Riskonnect ERM technology maturity model, United States 2012

Features:	A cabability maturity model (CMM) – not risk maturity. Specialized to the maturity of risk technology tools. Three levels (low maturity, engaged, advanced) with a % survey rating response from ERM managers concerning six technology tools. The six are: spreadsheets, simulations, database, presentation graphics, dashboards/heat maps, communications. Survey of n=? by Riskconnect software vendor of what US risk functionaries are saying about use of ERM tools. Presentation by Russell McGuire to RIMS Conference 16–18 Apr 2012. Some conclusions as your organization climbs from low maturity to advanced: 'all but spreadsheets become increasingly essential' and 'fewer believe spreadsheets are required'.
Benefits:	Lists 10 benefits of technology for ERM.
Advantages:	Well-suited capabilities if moving up the more sophisticated technology curve is appropriate to your organization context and maturity level, or a key driver to organization success.
Disadvantages:	*Software vendor bias to moving potential clients off spreadsheets. Respondee numbers and the methodological robustness of the survey is not known. The list of benefits are dominated by* efficiency *not* effectiveness *drivers, which is the key measure for assessing ERM maturity.*
Rated Tier:	*Specialized to risk technology.*

This is an odd sort of capability maturity model (Table 3.71) rather than a risk maturity model. It seems to be a marketing promotion specialized on the theme of the maturity of risk technology tools, so it will not surprise that this risk software vendor's survey relegates spreadsheets and promotes software tools.

TABLE 3.72 SCRLC supply chain risk maturity model, United States 2013

Features:	Five categories (leadership, planning, implementation, evaluation and improvement) of 25 capabilities with five rating scales (reactive, aware, proactive, integrated, resilient). SCRLC also use the rating scales as the maturity levels for risks. Free spreadsheet .xls model from the website for Supply Chain Risk Leadership Council (SCRLC), a cross-industry organization including world-class manufacturing, and services supply chain organizations and academic institutions that work together to develop and share best practices in supply chain risk management. Three types of output charts show both the average maturity for each category as well as the range of maturity levels in each category.
Benefits:	Help managers assess their organization's capabilities and metrics with respect to managing supply chain risk. Identify areas for supply chain risk management improvement within the organization.
Advantages:	Specialty SCRM model in ready-to-use format. Backed by US peak body for big-name firms such as Zurich, Boeing, Rand. Claims to be aligned with ISO 31000:2009.
Disadvantages:	
Rated Tier:	*Specialized for supply chain.*

The SCRLC website is one of the first places you may go if you want to start your own tailored risk maturity model (Table 3.72). It is a simple spreadsheet model by the Supply Chain Risk Leadership Council, which is kindly downloadable for gratis.* You may then use your own spreadsheet either retained in its original form as a specialized risk maturity model for supply chain; or, adapt it for enterprise-wide risk management (ERM) purposes. For others with any form of supply chain, this is a reputable submodel you may use in tandem with your ERM risk maturity model and have the score feed up to your supply-chain-related capability at the ERM level.

* We thank the board at the Supply Chain Risk Leadership Council USA (SCRLC) who has kindly granted permission to any reader of this book to download and use their spreadsheet model, available from **http://www.scrlc.com/**.

TABLE 3.73 S&P ERM for corporate governance, United States 2012

Features:	Four levels of management and governance credit rating factors (strong, satisfactory, fair and weak) using a three-point scale of positive, neutral or negative to milestone 'factors'. No mention of risk maturity or a risk maturity model but the four 'subfactors' and 14 sub-subfactors may equate to capabilities for effective ERM, particularly for management and governance.
Benefits:	Standard & Poor's global reputation for credit rating and a key influencer or external stakeholder for ERM.
Advantages:	Corporate entity 14 sub-subfactors represent potential risk maturity capabilities with a focus on management and governance capabilities attractive to creditors and lenders. Refer to S&P ERM for insurers for an additional two sub-subfactors tailored to them.
Disadvantages:	*Bias to management and governance creditworthiness rating factors means not holistic ERM.*
Rated Tier:	*Concept.*

This is a great reference for potential risk maturity model capabilities (regarding risk oversight, corporate governance and rating of senior management), particularly if your organization is concerned about credit rating agency, lenders and market opinion (Table 3.73). Whilst some criticize S&P and other credit agencies for not going far enough with ERM, S&P have to be commended as the first credit-rating agency to support ERM.

TABLE 3.74 S&P ERM for insurers, United States 2012

Features:	Three levels of management and governance rating (strong, satisfactory, fair) using a three-point scale of positive, neutral or negative to milestones. No mention of risk maturity or a RMM but the four 'subfactors' and 16 sub-subfactors may be taken to equate to capabilities for effective ERM, at least in terms of management and governance.
Benefits:	S&P global reputation for credit rating and a key influencer or external stakeholder for ERM. Fourteen of the 16 sub-subfactors overlap with corporate entities.
Advantages:	Insurance entity 16 sub-subfactors represent potential risk maturity capabilities tailored by S&P to insurers with a focus on management and governance capabilities attractive to creditors and lenders.
Disadvantages:	*Bias to management and governance creditworthiness rating factors means not holistic ERM.*
Rated Tier:	*Specialized for insurers.*

This is a model (Table 3.74) specialized for insurers with the addition of a few different capabilities from the one for corporates.

TABLE 3.75 Syntex Management Systems OpRisk and financials maturity, United States c.2011

Features:	Four levels with four categories: strategic (high-level goals aligned with a company's mission), operational (efficient and effective use of the organization's resources), reporting (reliability of company reporting), and compliance (with applicable regulations).
Benefits:	For risk reduction, the organization improves compliance (fines/penalties), reduces the likelihood of a loss, and reduces the total cost of the losses that occur. For operational effectiveness, the framework improves reliability and process integrity, shortens process cycle times, and increases both accountability and visibility across the company.

TABLE 3.75 *Continued*

Advantages:	OpRisk process maturity for compliance and financials.
Disadvantages:	*Bias to quantitative and the financial sector.*
Rated Tier:	*Specialized to OpRisk and financial sector.*

This is one (Table 3.75) that may appeal to those with an interest in quantitative risk and financial-sector risk maturity capabilities.

TABLE 3.76 Tiel business intelligence and corporate planning combined maturity model, Germany 2010

Features:	An algorithm-based capability maturity model combining capabilities for business intelligence and corporate planning. Academic paper. Matrix of seven capabilities with five maturity levels (from informal planning to corporate operational planning to corporate financial planning to corporate strategic planning to corporate strategic management).
Benefits:	Science research approach appeals to strategic planners and finance functionaries.
Advantages:	Applies the Rasch algorithm for design science-research.
Disadvantages:	*Academic.*
Rated Tier:	*Conceptual.*

This is one (Table 3.76) that may appeal to a design science-research audience or corporate strategists.

TABLE 3.77 Treasury Board of Canada risk maturity capability model, 2010

Features:	Three levels with five areas of ERM excellence. Downloadable pdf diagnost'c tool to assess current ERM capability. Part of a suite of guides and tools to accompany the board's *Framework for the Management of Risk* effective August 2010 for Canadian government departments. 'Not intended to be used in a linear fashion.' ISO 31000-aligned.
Benefits:	'To embed [RM] is a critical element in all areas of work, at all levels of the organization... to inform a discussion [by government departments] whether resources need to be allocated or diverted to fill gaps to improve capability in key areas of risk management excellence.'
Advantages:	Government ERM – progressive succinct guidance on RMM implementation. Focus on only key excellence capabilities. Flexible for departments to 'tailor' to own needs.
Disadvantages:	
Rated Tier:	*Basic.*

You cannot be more succinct than this ISO-aligned ERM risk maturity model (Table 3.77). This model was intended to be tailored by government agencies in Canada but will be of interest to novices and anyone starting to tailor their own model or interested in the basics.

TABLE 3.78 Willis Risk Consulting risk maturity model for ERM performance, UK c.2009

Features:	Thirty-eight capabilities rated to five scales from 1 (word-box matching ad hoc level) through to 5 (exemplary level). Progress from current to target state. Five levels: ad hoc, fractured, organized, coherent, exemplary. Eight themes (modules): internal environment, objective setting, event identification, risk assessment, risk response, control activities, information and communication and monitoring. Proprietary consulting based on a software model involving a questionnaire-based approach. Certainly Excel-based but unclear if also software-based.
Benefits:	Road map of improvement activities to support shift from compliance to business performance through effective risk management over a several-year rolling period.
Advantages:	Most detailed of the known 'pick-a-box'-style ERM maturity methodologies by consulting firms. Excellent use of objectives. Encourages integration of maturity target into long-term strategic and business plans. Robust ERM content from the UK consulting arm of a reputable international insurance-broking firm.
Disadvantages:	*Dated? Pre-ISO 31000. Bias to insurance. Marketing claims ISO and COSO compatible but not transparent or cross-walked.*
Rated Tier:	*Integrated.*

This risk maturity model (Table 3.78) has lots of appeal for its robust ERM content from the UK consulting arm of a reputable international insurance-broking firm. It is tiered as intermediate bordering on benchmark-able. The model makes excellent use of objectives and encourages integration of maturity target into long-term strategic and business plans.

TABLE 3.79 Zurich risk maturity model, Switzerland c.2011

Features:	Ten-capability risk management questionnaire. Nil levels. Free online.
Benefits:	May provide ideas for separating insurable from non-insurable capabilities.
Advantages:	Simple.
Disadvantages:	*Insurer bias. Will not stand up to audit or serious scrutiny on its own.*
Rated Tier:	*Basic.*

This is a basic risk maturity model (Table 3.79) that may provide ideas for separating insurable from non-insurable capabilities.

Results and analysis of the directory of risk maturity models

The following are some results from an analysis of the preceding directory entry data.

Directory total by domains

The number of risk maturity models that appear in the directory total 77 (n=77). These are divided by domain in the pie chart in Figure 3.1.

FIGURE 3.1 Directory total maturity models by domain

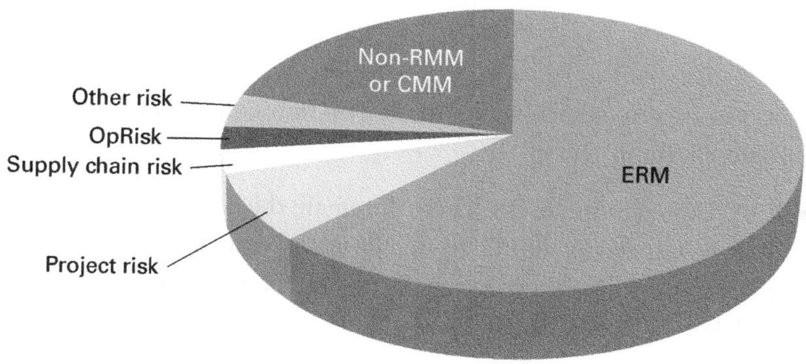

The domains covered are segmented as follows:

- 71% n=54 are ERM and risk-specialty domains.
- 63% n= 48 are dedicated to the ERM domain, which is indicated by the term 'ERM' at the end of their vignette titles.
- 21% n=16 are capability models of one sort or another in IT or other corporate non-risk maturity domains such as reputation, culture, governance, business process and corporate planning.
- 8% n=6 are dedicated to the project risk maturity domain.
- 2% n=2 are dedicated to the supply chain risk maturity domain.
- 2% n=2 are dedicated to the operations risk maturity domain.
- 4% n=3 are dedicated to the other (ie regulatory, insurance, business continuity, business development).

Directory total by geography

US- and UK-originated models dominate the directory with a sprinkle from Europe, Canada, Asia, Australia and Africa. See pie chart in Figure 3.2.

FIGURE 3.2 Directory total maturity models by geography

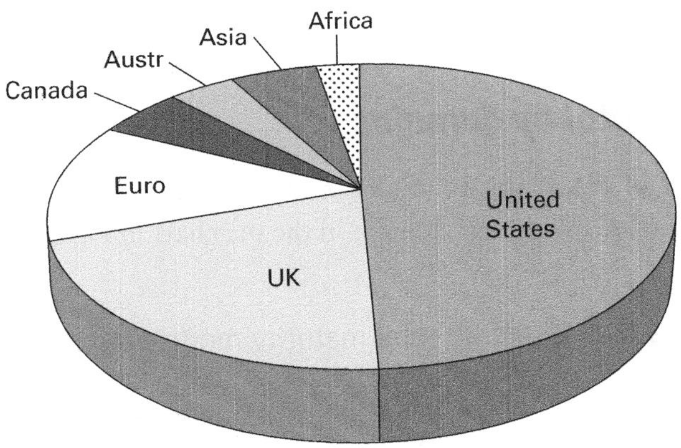

The models are ranked below by origin, with notes on any apparent content over-representation:

- 49% United States n=38. These dominate the certifiable, benchmarkable, risk-specialty and IT-related domains with flagship contributions to the evolution of the risk maturity model from RIMS and Aon-Wharton for ERM.

- 21% UK n=16. These dominate the projects subdomain and have delivered flagship contributions to the evolution of the model from Hillson ERM, Hopkinson projects, Willis ERM and Marsh ERM.
- 13% Europe n=10, is over-represented in conceptual tiered models with flagship research by Monda ERMi 2013.
- 5% Canada n=4, is over-represented in ERM.
- 5% Asia n=4.
- 4% Australia n=3, is over-represented in ERM.
- 3% Africa n=2.

Directory total by capability models

Sixteen (n=16) of the 77 models are not risk management but capability maturity models (21%). These are included in the directory because they may be useful reference sources for those wanting to tailor their own model, and the subject may inspire one or more capabilities that can be designed within a risk maturity model. The six domains covered by the capability maturity models are:

1. corporate performance reputation, culture, governance, business process and corporate planning;
2. business development;
3. resiliency;
4. information technology, information security, IT reliability and record keeping;
5. business processes;
6. project management.

Directory total by tier type

The largest tier membership is the *specialized* models at 43% (n=33), which is not surprising considering the evolution process we described in Chapter 1 ('Background'). The next largest size as a tier is *conceptual* at 21% (n=16). Together these two of the six tiers represent a majority two-thirds (64%) of the number of models.

Next are a bunching of *intermediate* (12%), *benchmark-able* tier (9%), *basic* (8%) and *certifiable* (8%). The increasing need to systemize and measure probably accounts for the 17% of models represented in the benchmark-able

FIGURE 3.3 Directory total maturity models by six-tier matrix

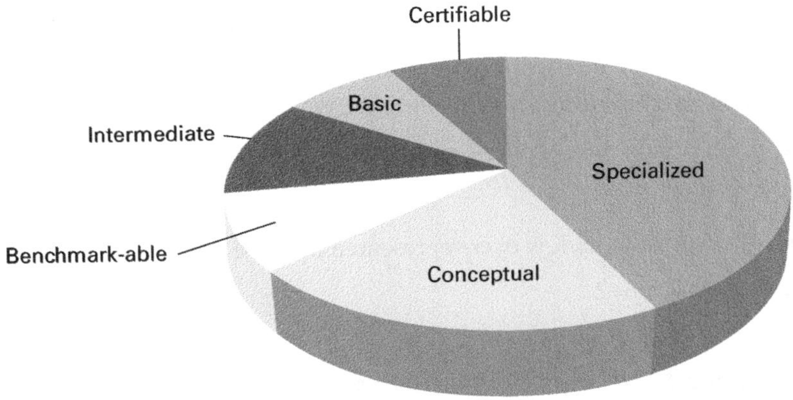

and certifiable tiers. See Figure 3.3 for a pie chart representing these segments.

Directory total ERM models by growth

The evolution of the 48 ERM models in our directory shows an initially slow then steady growth in the number of new models released to a peak in 2012. There was an understandably slow beginning after Professor David Hillson's innovative paper in the UK in 1997. The first-known working risk maturity model appeared in 2000 with Marsh Australia's Risk Focus. There followed a smattering of one to three new models every year or so until the period 2011–13 inclusive, when it rose to four to six a year over a three-year period. Since the peak of 11 in 2012 it has averaged about three per annum.

Summary

Biases are tendencies. They are mostly helpful but can be an issue if they result in a negative consequence by making risk maturity models less fit-to-the-organization. Natural bias in risk maturity models can be managed with the right awareness. Some of the common forms of bias for these models include, in no particular order, biases to: insurable risk, information and technology-related systems, processes, 'door-opener' or 'check-the-box' approaches, and to external benchmarking.

Our practitioners reflect the variety of needs by users in the marketplace related to risk maturity models. Asha goes for the 'best' ERM model,

Chris needs to keep it simple, Alan pursues certification and Megan just wants to explore first.

Our comprehensive alpha-ordered directory represents a treasure trove of 77 different models or key sources as proto-models. These are easily referenced using five standard criteria: features, benefits, advantages, disadvantages and a tier-type. The majority of the directory focuses on *ERM models* (71%). One-fifth of the directory gives a flavour for the rich range of capability models that are available in corporate *non-risk maturity domains* (21%) such as IT, reputation, culture, governance, business process and corporate planning. The remainder of the directory represents a sample of *risk-specialty domains* (18%) such as project risk, supply chain risk maturity, operations risk and others.

The largest directory tier memberships are for *specialized* models at 43% and *conceptual* at 21% that together represent two-thirds of the total models in the directory. Half the models originate in the United States (49%) and together with Canada (5%), represent a 55% dominance to North America, whilst the UK at 21% dominates over Europe at 13% and a smattering contribution from the remainder of the world. The developed world contributes a disproportionate 82% of all models. New ERM model releases seem to have tapered off to a few per annum since rising to a peak of 11 in 2012.

Tailoring and benchmarking a risk maturity model

04

This chapter covers:

- Tailoring and benchmarking:
  - By ERM standards and voluntary codes
  - By corporate governance codes
  - By sectors
  - By organization operating model
  - By risk function operating model
  - By economic value chain
  - By key performance indicators
  - By organization context and model design
- Summary

Introduction

Megan was almost ready to get started on designing her own maturity model but just wanted to prepare herself a little better before moving on to designing. Now that she understood what the range of maturity models looked like, she started to think of where else she could source guidance and information on the right capability set to use in her own model that was best tailored and benchmarked to her NGO. If she missed a good source then either the investment case might be lacking, or the board or her boss may ask her a 'challenge question' that she may not be able to answer.

The 2015 sixth annual study by the American Institute of Certified Practicing Accountants (AICPA) and North Carolina State University asked the 'challenge question' for the board of directors, senior executives and other key stakeholders. The 'challenge question' is: 'How confident are we in our organization's ability to effectively identify and navigate the unfolding uncertainties surrounding our current business model and new strategic initiatives?' (Beasley, Branson and Hancock, 2015).

Whilst comparing risk maturity models in our last chapter helped us understand them better, it does not necessarily address the critical 'challenge question' above. Before we move on to how to design or redesign your model (in Chapter 5), we need to address this challenge question because stakeholders will ask it in different forms for an investment case in risk maturity and in the normal course of business.

In this chapter, we survey the remaining field of potential reference sources that risk maturity modellers can go to for help to respond to whatever form their 'challenge question' may take. These supplementary sources to Chapter 3 also help modellers to understand how the risk management system can be integrated into the existing organization way of working, its business operating model and strategies so as to do what a risk maturity model does best. That is, compare the current risk management state to where it needs to be if the organization wants to optimize benefits and decide on the value and cost of further investment in risk maturity.

Beginner risk modellers would be wise to look to supplementary reference sources to improve how they compare, select and design their tailored risk maturity model. Existing risk modellers would be wise to do the same because it can improve how they redesign and continuously improve their models. Moreover, some of these same sources (eg regulators) can also be the sources of change on their model. It is not necessary for a risk or audit professional to become an expert in operating models or the like. However, any maturity model will improve how it is tailored and benchmarked to assess risk management effectiveness if it takes into account such drivers to organization performance.

Tailoring and benchmarking

Benchmarking and tailoring defined for risk maturity

Our definition of *tailoring* a risk maturity model rests on two assumptions. First, every organization is unique. Second, ERM is best aligned with every unique organization's objectives, external and internal context and risk profile(s). These are the sources of uniqueness.

No single risk maturity model to date represents a standard or automatic 'one-size-fits-all' solution to the challenge of assessing risk management effectiveness. The objective of 'tailoring' a model is to find the optimal fit-for-purpose to that organization (or fit-to-organization). A tailored model need not be unique but its fitness is framed to at least some extent by organization objectives, internal context and external context and risk profile.

Benchmarking is a natural part of a risk maturity model. Every model is essentially and inherently also a *benchmarking* tool or diagnostic. In one way or another, the models we compared in Chapter 3 incorporate a benchmarking format of current/actual/as-is/baseline versus future/targeted/to-be/revision. The Fraser Health model, for example, expresses this as a 'readiness-gap' from the present state of capabilities. The Deloitte model may express this as increasing stakeholder value from the present value state. No matter what the expression, it basically refers to internal benchmarking for organization self-improvement by gap-improvement.

Benchmarking is the search for one or more points of reference or standards against which risk management effectiveness may be compared or assessed. Benchmarking is often thought of as the search for industry-leading practices and metrics, resulting in superior performance. It may be external or internal source-based, or a combination of both. As the quality management discipline has proven over time, benchmarking is a recognized benefit to organizations and is often used to bolster investment cases. Benchmarking may employ external or internal self-improvement reference sources.

External benchmarking challenges and disadvantages

External benchmarking usually demands one set of criteria for risk management capabilities, which can be consistently rated against multiple entities and achieve repeatability over a long period of time measured in years. This set should be an unchanging set and not unique to the single organization; hence it is typically non-tailored by its very nature. Benchmarking research usually involves industry competitors or like-organizations or external standards and codes but can also include models from our Chapter 3 directory. You may not find a risk maturity model specific to manufacturers, for example, but if you are interested in understanding industry capability maturity for business continuity and supply chain risk management – as key drivers for manufacturers – then you may look at the BCCM® Virtual Corp and the SCRLC models.

Practitioner Chris looks for external benchmarking in risk maturity models

Working in construction and a lot with insurance, Chris was keen on metrics and benchmarking. Chris reported to the chief financial officer (CFO). The CFO liked benchmarking and when he noted Chris's growing affinity with ERM he requested his feedback as to: *Which source could externally benchmark their construction company for risk maturity, and where did they rate?* Chris gleaned a shortlist of nine from our Chapter 3 directory. This shortlist included (in alpha order):

1. Aberdeen Group Op Risk Maturity Model UK November 2013 quantified KPIs benchmarking survey n=142.
2. Aon-Wharton Risk Maturity Index RMI United States 2011 ongoing online database.
3. Deloitte Risk Intelligent Enterprise™ maturity United States c.2009 n=1,541 firms surveyed c.2009
4. Economist Intelligence Unit (EIU) ERM Maturity UK 2011survey n=?
5. Federation of European Risk Management Associations (FERMA) periodic multi-criteria membership survey supported the Ernst & Young 'Turning Risk into Results' 2012 survey n=809, 20 countries.
6. Marsh Risk Consulting and 'Risk Focus' c.2010 n=600+ c.2009.
7. QinetiQ Project Risk Maturity Model UK 2010 n=250+ maturity assessments on projects and programmes.
8. RIMS Risk Maturity Model for ERM United States 2006 client users n=2,000+ and co-sponsored Marsh survey n=1,000+ survey called *Excellence in Risk Management 10: Delivering strategic value through risk management*, available online since 24 April 2013.
9. Riskonnect ERM Technology Maturity Model United States 2012 client survey n=?

Chris reported to his CFO that the above research could not *directly* benchmark against other construction firms albeit Chris could glean some very useful *operational risk benchmark data* from Aberdeen Group. Chris and his CFO liked the way the Aberdeen Group backed up what they said with 'hard' success metrics. The exercise gave Chris an idea to try in the future to contact an industry peak body or the larger accounting/consulting firms if they had any industry-specific benchmarking data. In the meantime, the Aon annual benchmarking data was useful for general external benchmarking as it came out every November or December with an accumulating data update. Chris withstood the 'heat' he got from his own insurance broker, Marsh, when they heard Chris was leaning towards Aon's data.

External benchmarking challenges and disadvantages

ISO 31000:2009 is an example of one prominent external benchmarking source. ISO 31000 allows an organization to carry out a critical review of its existing practices and processes in light of the 31000 International Standard (ie as an external benchmark). However, ISO 31000 presents two challenges for those favouring external benchmarking to other organizations, which need careful management. First, ISO 31000 declares it does not intend to promote uniformity of risk management across organizations, which of course, may occur if an organization adopts exactly the same practices as competitors, or other benchmarked organizations. Second, the more tailored a risk maturity model is, the less able to be *externally* benchmarked it becomes as it will erode the same set of benchmarking criteria.

Moreover, external benchmarking has other general disadvantages. It risks confidentiality/intellectual property rights of participating organizations. It looks fine in theory but, in practice, it is heavily constrained by costs in dollars, and time and effort to execute. Then there is the effort to repeat the benchmarking exercises. As time passes, external benchmarks become quickly redundant – whereas time is on the side of internal self-benchmarking wherein quality tends to increase over time.

Internal benchmarking has advantages over external benchmarking. It avoids the investment and delays made systemic by using external references. It will tend to be sustainable, more tailored and benchmark-able.

This does not mean abandoning external benchmarks, rather just balancing them. These can still be used to verify, adapt and adopt the ideas for model components – particularly for new or reweighted capabilities for advanced model users. We will return to prove this point in Chapter 5 when we show how to use multi-models.

At the end of the day, this is just to reinforce that risk maturity modellers need to keep in mind that tailoring your model is imperative and that a risk maturity model naturally acts as an internal 'benchmarker'. Adding external benchmarking by researching the following sources is valuable, whilst allowing for the above precautions.

Tailoring by ERM standards and voluntary codes

Clarifying the issue of 'standards' versus other 'codes'

The IRM UK website is worth quoting for an umbrella statement regarding risk management standards (IRM, 2015). It generalizes that:

> A number of standards have been developed worldwide to help organizations implement risk management systematically and effectively. These standards seek to establish a common view on frameworks, processes and practice, and are generally set by recognized international standards bodies or by industry groups. Risk management is a fast-moving discipline and standards are regularly supplemented and updated. The different standards reflect the different motivations and technical focus of their developers, and are appropriate for different organizations and situations. Standards are normally voluntary, although adherence to a standard may be required by regulators or by contract.

Voluntary reference code is an apt umbrella term that includes all the family of 'standards' and non-standards. They are all 'codes' providing guidance of one sort or another, either regulated or voluntary. It describes a natural hierarchy or 'bush' taxonomy that holds an array of external codes available to help design or improve your risk maturity model. Of course, all voluntary external reference codes are not the same or equal. Two are set apart as primary sets of guidance (as we shall see below). Each code has a unique history and purpose, let alone characteristics biased to their author-originators. In the end, choosing is about what is best tailored to your organization.

For our purposes here, there is only one *official standard* for risk management: ISO 31000:2009. ISO 31000 correctly self-states as an 'international standard' that acts as a 'guideline'. COSO ERM 2004 self-states as a 'conceptual framework' and does *not* cite itself as a 'standard' (see Glossary), but states its usefulness to educators and others, so it can share a guidance/guideline role with ISO 31000. Other professional bodies have in the past used the term 'standard', as we shall see below, but these have not had the international gravitas that ISO 31000 enjoys and should be treated as internal-to-membership or common parlance levels of usage.

It is not our purpose here to provide a *qualitative* comparison between ISO 31000 and COSO ERM approaches to risk management. There is much content freely available that has discussed this topic, and a declining debate about their respective merits. What can be said here is something from a *quantitative* perspective.

Imagine an exercise on a blank spreadsheet where we leaf through every page of each code and we enter these into two stacked cell columns, each cell with just a title describing each capability topic covered. We then compare the two stacked columns of raw capabilities that are covered by each code. Now, look at the results of such an exercise from a numbers-only point of view. Question: are the two codes vastly different by their extent of coverage of capability topics? No. Do they both cover every capability that should be covered? Most practising risk managers would probably answer: definitely not. Do they both cover every capability compared to an example set of capabilities in a modern-day risk maturity model used by a practising CRO (such as the set of 105 capabilities in Benchmarker™)? No.

Compare the two spotted bars in Figure 4.1. It shows that the two codes cross-cover or share between half to two-thirds of the capabilities they expect in an organization. ISO 31000 covers 66% of COSO, and COSO covers 46% of ISO 31000. The small gap is understandable given that ISO 31000 enjoys the benefit of fresher ERM thinking by at least half a decade. What the chart also says is that a modern risk maturity model can cover 100% of all the capabilities described in both codes (see light grey shade bars). However, over one-third (33–37%) of what is required is not covered by both codes (see dark grey bars). The message for every risk professional is: do not solely rely on assessing or 'cross-walking' to either or both of the two current top codes.

Practitioner Alan opts not to rely solely on the two leading codes

Alan shares Asha's feelings that all the talk of a 'jigsaw puzzle' of differing voluntary guidance and corporate governance codes is harmful to all parties if it obstructs risk management practice. Alan strongly believes that for the sake of clarity, the IRM website reference above to multiple risk management 'standards' is misleading. He feels that the term 'standard' should be reserved for a special status to separate it from other non-standard codes. He is cynical of 'standards' being announced by the media and every new commercial entity or a new management/board of an association, certifier or trainer. He feels that no matter how 'common' or 'popular' the term *standards* has become, the risk discipline needs to rally behind *one* standard (whilst respecting a family of augmented voluntary codes, frameworks and guidance) if it was to raise itself into a profession. He therefore prefers to call both COSO ERM and ISO 31000:2009 the two leading risk management voluntary guidance codes, but reserves the title of the true current and international 'standard' for ISO 31000.

Alan interprets the results from Figure 4.1 as offering two clear learnings for his ERM manager. First, do not rely on either, or both, the two leading risk management guidance codes to cover all the capabilities required for a risk maturity model with comprehensive capabilities. Second, that the divide between the two camps (ISO 31000 and COSO ERM) behind the codes is not as great as the emotion attached to the debate.

FIGURE 4.1 Capabilities coverage as a percentage of ISO 31000 versus COSO ERM

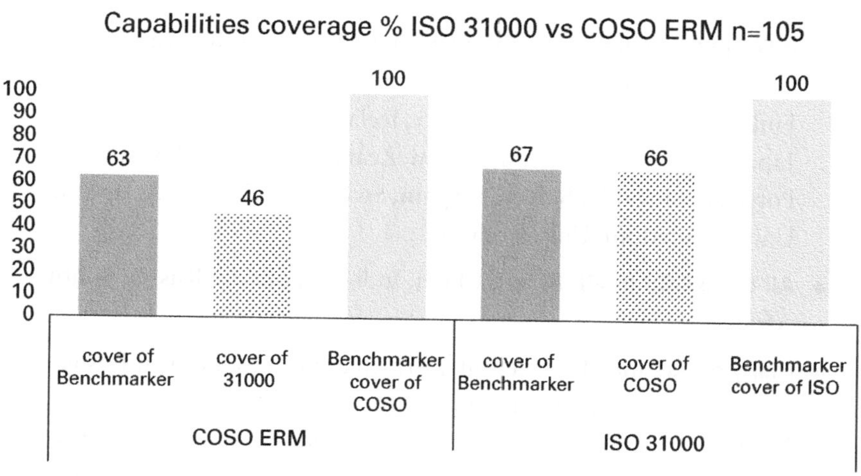

ISO 31000:2009: summary as the only official global standard

ISO 31000: 2009 – Risk Management Principles and Guidelines ('ISO' or '31000') issued in November 2009 by the internationally recognized International Organization for Standardization (ISO), based in Geneva, is the only accredited global standard for risk management. All ISO management standards, including ISO 9001 for quality management, need to introduce the concept of risk and risk management as required by the internal ISO document called Annex SL, a new management system format that provides a base structure and standardized text for ISO management system standards (MSS), making the implementation of multiple ISO standards within one organization easier.

ISO 31000 is founded on the Australian and New Zealand standard, named AS/NZS 4360. This was first published in 1995 then revised in 1999 and 2004. It was popularly adopted in many other OECD as well as developing countries over the years prior to 2009. Hundreds of professionals from different sectors and industries representing over 30 countries such as from the UK, France, Canada, South Africa and elsewhere have contributed new content to AS/NZS 4360 (such as the framework) to create the international ISO 31000 risk management guidance standard.

According to the Global Institute G31000, an international non-for-profit organization with the mandate to raise awareness on ISO 31000, there are, on 28 February 2015, at least 61 countries that have adopted ISO 31000 as their official national risk management standard. These include:

- **ISO 31000 covers most of the OECD (n=31):** Australia, Austria, Belgium, Canada, Chile, Czech Republic, Denmark, Estonia, Finland, France, Greece, Hungary, Iceland, Ireland, Israel, Italy, Japan, Mexico, Netherlands, New Zealand, Norway, Poland, Portugal, Slovakia, Slovenia, Spain, Sweden, Switzerland, Turkey, United Kingdom, United States.
- **All the BRICS (n=6):** Brazil, China, India, Indonesia, Russia, South Africa.
- **Many others (n=24):** Argentina, Armenia, Belarus, Bolivia, Bosnia and Herzegovina, Bulgaria, Colombia, Costa Rica, Croatia, Cuba, Ecuador, Iran, Latvia, Kazakhstan, Macedonia, Malaysia, Morocco, Peru, Romania, Serbia, Singapore, Thailand, Uruguay, Vietnam.

ISO 31000 can trace a long-evolved pedigree since 1995 in accredited risk management technical committees. The international Technical Committee

ISO TC 262 and national mirror committees try to balance long-term inputs from a range of cross-national risk management professionals drawn from all sectors and backed by risk practitioners who have worked the standard at the front line. The root drivers sustaining the ongoing growth of the standard are these risk-specific practitioners and professionals from broad sectors looking to the long term and without a commercial mandate. ISO 31000 is non-mandatory, generally non-prescriptive and non-certifiable for organizations. At the time of writing, an update is being worked on.

ISO 31000 is only 24 pages long. It is streamlined and clearly section-number referenced for ease of reference and implementation. It prefers a 'less is more' and guidelines-based approach to encourage organization tailoring. The key graphic icon for the ISO 31000 three pillars structure – Principles-Framework-Process – is a mnemonic that is easy to recall. See Figure 4.2.

FIGURE 4.2 ISO 31000:2009 official diagram

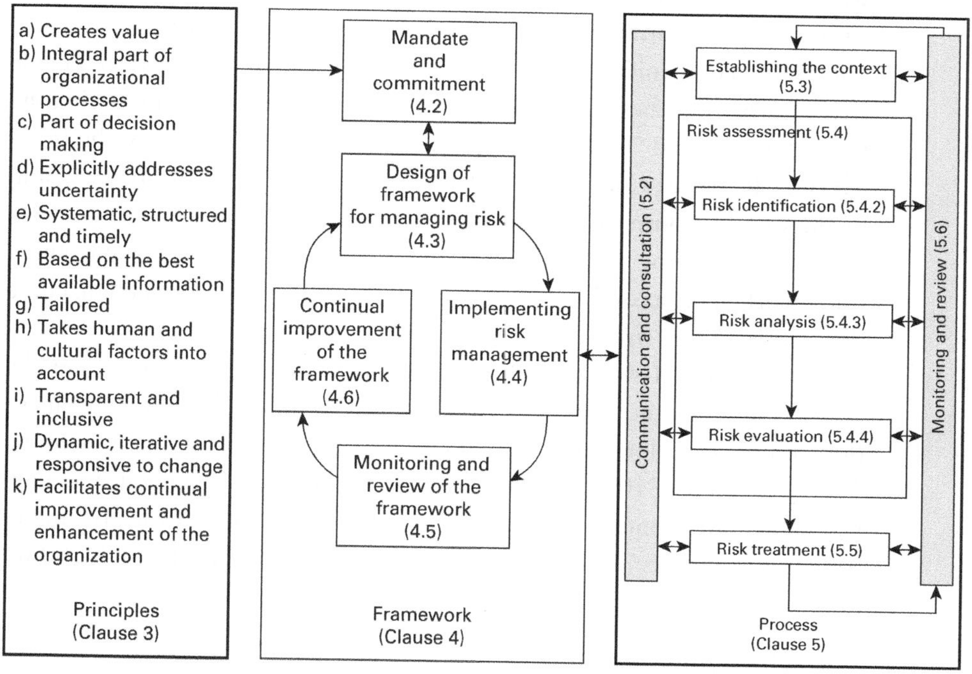

SOURCE: This figure is taken from ISO 31000:2009 Risk management – Principles and guidelines and is reproduced with the permission of the International Organization for Standardization, ISO. This standard can be obtained from any ISO member and from the website of the ISO Central Secretariat at the following address: www.iso.org. Copyright remains with ISO

ISO 31000 provides a supporting body of guidance on enterprise risk management published since 2009, known as the 'ISO 31000 family'. This includes ISO Guide 73: Risk Management – Vocabulary; and ISO/IEC 31010:2009 – Risk Management – Risk Assessment Techniques. Some also add SA/SNZ HBR436-2013 Risk Management Guidelines – Companion to AS/NZS ISO 31000:2009; SA/SNZ HB89:2013 Risk Management – Guidelines on Risk Assessment Techniques; and AS/NZS 5050:2010 Business Continuity – Managing Disruption-Related Risk.

ISO 31000 prefers an 'open-framework' approach. It promotes the additional use of other frameworks rather than hold itself out as a prescriptive checklist or exclusive compliance and audit tool. It espouses that:

- There is no 'one-size-fits-all' solution to effective ERM.
- An ERM standard should match the uniqueness of each organization ('tailoring').
- ISO 31000 outlines capabilities and enhanced capabilities for effective ERM.

The ISO 31000 fraternity support risk maturity albeit in an undeveloped way. The 'Principle k' in ISO 31000 requires strategies to improve risk management maturity alongside all other organization aspects. A so-called 'ISO 3004' companion guideline to ISO 31000 has been mooted to include risk maturity but the published document is not explicit. In an illuminating presentation called 'Transitioning', Kevin W Knight, chairman of the International Technical Committee ISO TC 262, refers to the 'risk journey' and to the two key outputs for risk oversight (Knight, 2009). The first is risk maturity, being the maturity and performance of the risk management framework. The second is the risk profile and how/why it has changed, ie the *managing (of) risks*.

But the ISO 31000 story for risk maturity is more complex than the above. ISO cites the need to assess the effectiveness of risk management (4.1 and 5.6) but does not specify how. However, a reductive analysis of the 24 pages of ISO 31000 (to disaggregate or 'unpack' all content and then reaggregate the content as themed capabilities in a rough order of implementation sequence) might produce a clearer outcome. That is, ISO 31000 implies a three-tier proto-risk maturity model, being:

1. a base-tier of three foundation components;
2. a mid-tier of seven organization arrangements;
3. five attributes of enhanced risk management (Annex A).

Other ERM voluntary codes as useful references

The second of the two most referred and popular voluntary codes and guidelines for risk management apart from ISO 31000 has been COSO ERM 2004. Different surveys from different countries and membership bases may differ regarding the extent of their current uptake but these two reference codes are probably head-and-shoulders clear of other codes. Of the two, ISO 31000 is the fastest growing since its release in 2009. One RIMS ERM survey revealed that it had already overtaken COSO ERM in terms of North American adoption by 2013 by 23% over 22% (RIMS, 2013a).

Below we look at seven other codes that are not technically 'standards' but potentially useful for any risk maturity modeller in order to source capabilities to go into a model and/or to be potentially 'cross-walked' to specific sections of the code.

1. COSO ERM (United States)

COSO Enterprise Risk Management – Integrated Framework 2004 (known as COSO ERM 2004) is a self-described ERM 'conceptual framework' authored by audit and accounting consultants. Its pedigree originates in one report by one audit firm, PricewaterhouseCoopers (PwC). This was commissioned by one private committee called the Sponsoring Organizations of the Treadway Commission (COSO) centred in one city, New York City. COSO is a joint initiative of five private-sector organizations that are audit and accounting professional bodies. The COSO sponsors represent the leading global audit and accounting firms, US accounting bodies and the NYC-headquartered Institute of Internal Audit.

The COSO ERM report was the result of a one-time consulting exercise over the period 2001–04. It balanced short-term inputs drawn primarily from audit consultants and audit/accounting professionals. The root driver of the framework was a desire by post-Enron/Sarbanes-Oxley-era audit and accounting professionals to extend the previously released COSO Internal Controls into the growing discipline of ERM. COSO ERM is non-mandatory, part prescriptive and non-certifiable. COSO has not updated the 2004 framework to date but has declared in 2014 an intention to do so, again through PwC.

COSO ERM is 300+ pages over two volumes and lacks section-number referencing (COSO, 2004). It encourages organizations to build out from and link to COSO's previously issued framework, *Internal Control — Integrated Framework*. It identifies the interrelationships between ERM, internal control and entity management. The key visual icon 'COSO cube' has met with mixed reaction, with critics arguing it is too complex to implement.

COSO have provided a supporting albeit ad hoc body of guidance since 2009 (COSO, 2015). COSO's stated goal is to provide thought leadership dealing with three interrelated subjects: enterprise risk management (ERM), internal control and fraud deterrence. COSO has released various ad hoc white-paper updates by authors drawn from US audit firms on specific subjects of a topical interest (such as risk appetite).

COSO claims to provide a benchmark for organizations to consider when evaluating and improving the effectiveness of ERM processes. The COSO website (COSO, 2015) states that COSO ERM provides:

- the essential eight components of ERM as the key criteria to evaluate whether ERM is effective;
- the context in which they are effectively implemented;
- key ERM principles and concepts that relate to effective application of the components (eg ERM philosophy, risk appetite, risk tolerance, portfolio view of risk);
- a suggested common ERM language;
- direction and guidance promoting an enterprise-wide approach to risk management.

COSO ERM 2004 does not use the term 'risk maturity'. Instead, COSO ERM 2004 devotes attention to ERM components as the eight components driving the 'cube'. However, a COSO-approved report was authored by academics in 2010 called 'Current State of Enterprise Risk Oversight and Market Perceptions of COSO's ERM Framework'. This report included a graphic of the current state of ERM for survey responders where the top level is 'systematic, robust and repeatable process with regular reporting of aggregate top risk exposures to board'. This would typically rank in the low-to-mid levels of more modern risk maturity models such as that by Aon or Benchmarker™.

Practitioner Alan clarifying SEC and SOX mandates

Alan supported ISO 31000 but had to field queries as to whether there was a mandate or support for COSO ERM by US regulators. After some research he found that, despite some common misconceptions, the NYC Stock Exchange Commission (SEC) and the Sarbanes-Oxley Act 2002 (SOX) for US companies do *not* cite nor specify a preference for any particular risk management external code. Nevertheless, he found that a chain of market associations has developed since 2004 that has created a false impression in the market that the regulators prefer COSO ERM over other voluntary codes.

Alan found the answer complicated but it seems to work like this: Sarbanes-Oxley 2002 (SOX) changed the internal audit and compliance landscape. SOX mandated internal controls but not providers or codes to deliver it. The SEC mentioned COSO Internal Control — Integrated Framework 2002 as one of several examples of available codes. The NYC-headquartered COSO sponsors that market the voluntary COSO Internal Control compliance solution to satisfy the SOX regulation also market voluntary COSO ERM as an extension solution to build on COSO's previously issued framework.

2. RIMS ERM (United States)

The Risk and Insurance Management Society, Inc. (RIMS) is the North American equivalent of the IRM for the UK or the Federation of European Risk Management Associations (FERMA) for Europe. RIMS is a professional association for insurance and risk managers founded in 1950 and is headquartered in Manhattan. It publishes the industry-focused magazine *Risk Management*. RIMS represents more than 3,500 industrial, service, non-profit, charitable and governmental entities. It counts more than 10,000 risk management professionals around the world within 81 chapters across the United States, Canada, Mexico and Japan. Like FERMA, it has a strong insurance focus.

RIMS was a pioneer in risk maturity by promoting its own leading model back in 2006. Innovative in its day, the RIMS risk maturity model is well worth the free online RIMS website assessment, which is also accessible to non-RIMS members. This assessment acts as a lead-generator for the content author of the RIMS model, a software vendor LogicManager and their own risk maturity product also called LogicManager™. Refer to the two tables and accompanying author comments in Chapter 3 comparing RIMS (Table 3.69) and LogicManager™ (Table 3.51) for more detail.

Also useful for keeping up to date with what risk and insurance managers believe are leading ERM practices and potential capabilities is the periodic member survey by RIMS and sponsors. The recent survey, called 'Excellence in Risk Management 10: Delivering Strategic Value Through Risk Management', by RIMS and Marsh, has been available online since 24 April 2013.

These surveys usually have over 1,000 responders and represent a US perspective.

3. Standard & Poor's ERM (global)

See Chapter 3, Tables 3.73 and 3.74 for the S&P directory entries.

4. FERMA (European Risk Associations)

The Federation of European Risk Management Associations (FERMA) is the European equivalent of RIMS for North America or IRM for the UK. Established in 1974, FERMA brings together the national risk management associations of 20 countries from its headquarters in Belgium. Like RIMS, it has a strong insurance focus. FERMA has a non-voting, liaison role on the ISO/TC 262 risk management technical committee and a ISO/TC 262 working group towards a revision due in 2016 or 2017. FERMA supports the AIRMIC/ALARM/IRM guide to ERM and the requirements of ISO 31000.

FERMA has been conducting benchmarking surveys of its members since 2000. These offer a potential reference pool of risk maturity capabilities for a tailored model that is also benchmark-able to other FERMA members. FERMA reported that they repeated in 2012 the risk management maturity analysis last performed in 2010 in order to analyse the evolution of maturity within European companies and enable risk managers to compare the maturity of their risk management practices against others (FERMA, 2012):

> In order to illustrate companies' different maturity levels with regard to risk management practices, we defined a multi-criteria approach based on four categories (risk governance, risk practices and tools, risk reporting and communication, risk management functions alignment) and four maturity levels (emerging, moderate, mature and advanced) depending on respondents' answers to 16 relevant questions.

The FERMA website states that FERMA has adopted the Risk Management Standard, published in the UK in 2002 (FERMA, 2015):

> Versions in several languages of this pan-European standard of best practice in risk management are available for risk managers. The Risk Management Standard is the work of three UK risk management bodies in the UK, the private and public-sector risk management associations, AIRMIC and ALARM, and the Institute of Risk Management (IRM), the profession's educational body. The Risk Management Standard sets out a strategic process, starting with an organization's overall objectives and aspirations, through to the identification, evaluation and mitigation of risk, and finally the transfer of some of that risk to an insurer.

The FERMA 2012 Risk Management Benchmarking Survey claimed a positive correlation between the level of risk management maturity of a company and its performance, in terms of EBITDA and growth over a long-term basis (FERMA, 2012). FERMA went on in the same report to quote the 2012 Ernst & Young survey, Turning Risk into Results, which found that while most organizations perform the basic elements of risk management, the top performers do more in terms of the leading practices (we can see this by scanning forward to Chapter 5, Figure 5.2 Ernst & Young leading practices as potential maturity capabilities). The FERMA Risk Management Benchmarking Survey 2014 7th edition does not, however, refer to risk maturity.

5. IRM-AIRMIC-ALARM:2002 risk management standard (UK)

Now outdated by ISO 31000:2009, this self-described 'Risk Management Standard' was published in 2002 by a collaborative team. This team was drawn from the major risk management organizations in the UK – the Institute of Risk Management (IRM), the Association of Insurance and Risk Managers (AIRMIC) and ALARM, the national forum for risk management in the public sector. The IRM was founded in 1986 in the UK as a professional association for risk managers. AIRMIC is a UK association for insurance (and risk) managers with 1,100 members representing nearly 500 companies.

6. OCEG Red Book 2.1: 2012 Governance, Risk and Compliance Capability Model (United States)

Refer to Chapter 3, Table 3.63 for the OCEG capability model.

7. Various government Treasury Board frameworks

Government Treasury agencies in Australia, the UK and Canada have led the way in the public sector by issuing risk management and maturity guides designed to educate their respective agencies in promoting the risk maturity model.

From Canada, the Canadian Government Treasury Board of Canada (TBS) Secretariat (TBS, 2015) has published their risk management capability model online since August 2010. This model claims to assist organizations in analysing their risk management 'capacity' as it compares to key attributes of an integrated risk management approach and encourages a discussion on 'current capacity versus optimal capacity in these areas' (taken to mean risk maturity capabilities).

Refer to Chapter 3, Table 3.34 for the UK, HM Treasury 'Orange Book' Self-Assessment Tool: Risk Management Assessment Framework (RMAF), published in 2004 (HM Treasury, 2004).

From Australia, the NSW Government Treasury ERM Risk Maturity Model of 2012 (Table 3.62) is a modern model based on ISO 31000:2009 (NSW Treasury, 2012). It is designed as part of a wider risk management toolkit for government agency use. It encourages their risk management model to be tailored by each agency to meet each agency's specific needs as part of a wider risk management toolkit. The model comes as a free tool available online in spreadsheet format, so it is excellent for novice RMM modellers.

Aligning codes to maturity models

Some risk modellers will be interested in a ready reckoner of which codes may be aligned with which model because they prefer one code over another or they want to avoid bias to a code.

Practitioner Chris considers bias and how to combine the two leading codes

Chris wants to understand which maturity models claim they are *aligned* with which voluntary guidance codes and if they are perhaps biased in some way. He is not concerned if they are biased one way or another, he just wants to take any bias into account. He pays attention to Table 4.1 quite carefully and looks at the models grouped against the code they claim an alignment with. He saw that most were neutral, but some were ISO-aligned, a few older models were COSO ERM-aligned and a couple claimed alignments to both. Chris found the latter couple interesting as he had thought ISO 31000 and COSO ERM were opposed but realized now that maybe this was not the case.

When Chris finishes considering Table 4.1 he finds it whets his appetite and he has a new higher need. He has a CFO and chief of audit who seem keen on COSO ERM but do not know much about ISO 31000 so they may query Chris in detail on ISO 31000. The CEO and Chris are neutral on either ISO 31000 or COSO ERM. Chris wants to find if any maturity models go further than a claimed 'alignment' because Chris wants such claims to be clearly evidence-based and transparent. Chris wants clear references in his maturity model that take him to the specific relevant section in that

TABLE 4.1 Models claiming alignment to a guidance code

Code	Risk Maturity Model and Related	Capability Maturity Model and Related
ISO 31000	Aberdeen Group. Causal Capital. CRMS. Fraser Health. G31000. IIARF-Sobel. ISO 31000. Managenable®. NSW Treasury. OGC-M_o_R®. ReviewIT. Risk Academy. Treasury Board Canada. SCLRC. SecureIT.	
Both ISO and COSO	Benchmarker™.	ISACA.
COSO ERM	Ciorciari. COSO ERM. LogicManager. Protivity. RIMS.	COBIT IT. COSO Internal Controls.
Neither or Neutral	Accenture. Active Risk. ALARM. Aon-Wharton. BCCM®-VirtualCorp. Booz. Deloitte. EIU. Elmaallam. EY. Genius Methods. Hillson. HM Treasury. Hopkinson. HRDC. INCOSE. IRM-RMP. Marsh ERM. Marsh Insurance. Marsh Risk Focus. Mayer. Monda. Murphy 4e. OCEG. Pergler-McKinsey & Co. Riskonnect. S&P ERM Corpcrates. S&P ERM Insurers. Syntex. Willis. Zurich.	Aho. BD-CMM®. CERT®-CIPS. RMM. Gartner. INSEAD–Arguden. ITI. Lederman/GARP®. Luyckx. Marx. PMI OPM3®.

NOTE: Listing based on public claim of some alignment or another to a code, not tested.

code. This way, he can not only judge how accurate the claimed 'alignment' is but he can find extra evidence in that code for each capability that is cross-referred to that code so that his assessment is more accurate and robust.

After a bit of research, Chris finds that this advanced technique is called 'cross-walking'. He discovers it is only available in certain maturity models. He reduces by elimination from the list in Table 4.1 and leaves only those that are cross-walked. The result is represented in Table 4.2.

TABLE 4.2 Maturity models cross-walked with specifics to guidance codes

Code Need	Risk Maturity Model	Non-Risk Maturity Model, ie CMM
ISO 31000	BCCM®. Benchmarker™. G31000.	
COSO ERM	Benchmarker™	COSO Internal Controls
Both ISO and COSO	Benchmarker™	
Other		ISACA

NOTE: Alpha-order listing based on publicly available information or claim to specific cross-mapping to a key code, so proprietary sources may be missing above.

Tailoring by corporate governance codes and guidance

Risk modellers under various jurisdictions may be asked (by internal audit or others) if their model is in accord with, or at least not at odds with, their relevant corporate governance-related legislation. Often the regulatory corporate governance reports and surveys contain ideas for risk management capabilities that can be tailored into your model, especially those belonging to a risk oversight module/theme.

The leading code for universal application in terms of quantity and quality of risk management guidance is King III Code. The next tier of authoritative guidance includes corporate codes from Australia's ASX, Singapore, Malaysia and the UK. Less authoritative guidance than those preceding is provided by the remainder of those listed here, including those from the United States (barring perhaps the NACD Blue Ribbon Committee). These 12 codes are summarized below.

Practitioner Asha finds a guidance code mini-directory useful

Asha finds quite bewildering all the talk of a 'jigsaw puzzle' of differing voluntary guidance and corporate governance codes that the risk profession should draw on. On the one hand, she feels that people in the risk discipline should stop using either one term too broadly (eg a 'standard' versus a 'framework') and, on the other hand, should stop confusing each other by mixing up a large array of differing terms, including but not limited to: standards, frameworks, conceptual frameworks, models, principles, guidelines, codes, rules, regulations, road maps and so forth. In the end, Asha is clear in her mind that it is up to the unique organization as to which combination of codes are relevant. So Asha took comfort that she just has to be aware of the core codes out there and 'deep-dive' if the need arose in the future. Given below are the summaries she finds useful as a mini-directory for this purpose.

KING III Review (South Africa) is the leading code for risk management guidance

King III (2009) or King III – the King Code of Governance Principles and the King Report on Governance – came into effect on 1 March 2010 by the Institute of Directors in South Africa. It is highly regarded in international audit and governance circles. It has a long pedigree with three reports issued in 1994 (King I), 2002 (King II) and 2009 (King III). The report includes many emerging governance trends such as risk-based audit plans, alternative dispute resolution, and evaluation of board and directors' performance and shareholder approval of non-executive directors' remuneration. It also added a number of new principles such as: business rescue, IT governance, and fundamental and affected transactions in terms of directors' responsibilities during mergers, acquisitions and amalgamations.

King III 2009 does not specifically cite *risk maturity* but the crispness and quantity of its detailed guidance offers many risk management system capabilities that should be tailored into risk maturity models. Our Western Cape Government South Africa case study in Chapter 5 gives an example of a practical implementation (Western Cape Government, 2014). King III 2009 specifies in clear detailed terms 26 requirements on boards. No other governance code places more risk management responsibilities on boards than King III and these are paraphrased here at length, because risk modellers will find they summarize a 'core' of risk management system capabilities that should appear in any risk maturity model. We have taken the liberty *in italics* of further adding risk maturity-specific details. These include:

- 2.7 and 4 Governance of risk
  Including a board-approved and documented risk management policy and plan and process, integrated report on the effectiveness of the risk system and process of risk management, risk tolerance and risk appetite level, at-least annual review of the implementation of the risk management plan, risk tolerance and risk appetite level, risk committee of at least three meetings at least twice per year, risk strategy executed by management by means of risk management systems and processes, qualified CRO, risk assessments and register, continual risk monitoring responsibilities defined in the risk management plan, board disclosure yearly of its views on internal audit's assessment of the effectiveness of the system of internal controls and risk management to the board.
- 2.2 Inseparability
  Appreciating the inseparability of strategy, risk, performance and sustainability, *including the risk maturity strategy*.
- 2.10 Effective risk-based internal audit
  This takes into account *risk maturity* and risk managers to assist auditors with combined assurance.
- 2.20 Director development
  Training and development of directors *to include training in risk maturity models for effective risk governance. Risk managers to cooperate or assist with the above.*
- 2.23.6 Risk committee
  To promote and oversee risk maturity.
- 3.2.5 Audit committee to keep up to date with required skill set
  And risk managers to cooperate with auditors who need to *improve their ability to use the risk maturity model to assess independently, to suggest improvements to the model and to include risk maturity model inputs and outputs* to assess the effectiveness of risk management in their integrated report to the board.

- 3.5.1 Audit committee to ensure combined assurance received is appropriate to address all significant risk
  As outputs from the risk maturity model-driven improvements on the risk (and risk maturity) strategy executed by management by means of risk management systems and processes; and which should include combined assurance as a risk maturity capability. Risk managers to cooperate with the above.

The progressive philosophy behind King III and the clarity and quantity of its risk-related requirements will influence global long-term adoption and implementation. These are, in summary:

- *Effective leadership:* essentially equates to good governance and leaders should rise to the demands of modern governance.
- *Sustainability:* as the primary moral and economic imperative of the 21st century.
- *Corporate citizenship:* extension from concept to practice. That is, every company is a person and should act sustainably.

ASX Principles of Corporate Governance (Australia)

The ASX website provides an excellent description of their approach to corporate governance (ASX, 2015) and access to the current annual version of the Council's Corporate Governance Principles and Recommendations, which are highly regarded internationally for inclusion in risk oversight capabilities for any listed organization.

Singapore Corporate Governance Council (2012)

The Risk Governance Guidance for Listed Boards includes risk management process in daily routines, strategy setting and other progressive requirements.

Securities Commission of Malaysia (2012)

This Code on Corporate Governance update for listed companies is on a par with that for Singapore.

FRC Combined Code (UK)

The UK had a long line of corporate governance reports released prior to 2014. The key reports included Cadbury Report (1992), Greenbury Report

(1995), Hampel Report (1998), Turnbull Guidance (1999), Higgs Report (2003), Cadbury Report (2002) , Turner Review (2009) and Walker Review (2009). These variously led up to the one code that modern risk modellers may take note of, the Financial Reporting Council (FRC), 2014 Review of the Combined Code: Final Report requires board review on the effectiveness of the risk management and internal control systems.

OECD Guidelines (global)

The Organisation for Economic Co-operation and Development (OECD) Guidelines for Multinational Enterprises are an annex to the OECD Declaration on International Investment and Multinational Enterprises. It was first published by the OECD in 1976 and revised in 1979, 1982, 1984, 1991, 2000 and 2011. The guidelines focus on business ethics, codes of conduct and corporate governance matters and are useful content for a maturity model.

NACD 2009 Blue Ribbon Report (United States)

This is one of the better governance codes from the United States. The National Association of Corporate Directors (NACD), an independent non-profit organization, is composed of board members across the world and is dedicated to improving corporate board performance. NACD created a Blue Ribbon Commission to consider the board's role in risk oversight. The 2009 Blue Ribbon Commission Report aimed to inform the corporate world of best practices related to risk oversight in the boardroom. The report includes guidance for aligning strategy and risk, a description of the board's role regarding risk oversight, and finishes with 'Ten Principles of Effective Risk Oversight'. These are all potential capabilities that may be tailored into your risk maturity model.

SEC (New York)

The SEC release 12/16/2009 only touches on the extent of board role for risk oversight and if compensation policies and practices create risks. There is no reference to board or management comment on whether there exists a risk management system that meets the needs of the organization. There is not even a requirement to disclose whether they have a formal risk management policy or a chief risk officer.

Sarbanes-Oxley S404 'SOX' (United States)

The Sarbanes-Oxley Act (July 2002), commonly known as 'SOX', is a US federal law. It followed the Enron scandal in 2001 that eventually led to the bankruptcy of the Enron Corporation, and the dissolution of Arthur Andersen, one of the five largest audit and accountancy firms in the world. Enron represented both the largest bankruptcy in US history at that time as well as the biggest audit failure. SOX was enacted to expand the reliability of financial reporting for public companies and to increase the accountability of auditing firms to remain objective and independent of their clients.

BASEL II Sound risk management practices and Basel III and SOLVENCY II (Europe)

Basel III (or the Third Basel Accord) is a global, voluntary regulatory framework on bank capital adequacy, stress testing and market liquidity risk released by the Basel Committee on Banking Supervision in 2010–11. Implementation has been serially extended until 31 March 2019. The third instalment was developed in response to the deficiencies in financial regulation revealed by the financial crisis of 2007–08 and aims to strengthen bank capital requirements by increasing bank liquidity and decreasing bank leverage.

The Solvency II Directive (2009/138/EC) is an EU Directive that codifies and harmonizes the EU insurance regulation, particularly the amount of capital held to reduce the risk of insolvency.

COBIT IT Guidelines (global)

The COBIT Management Guidelines Control Objectives for Information and related Technology (COBIT) are published by the IT Governance Institute (ITGI) and Information Systems Audit and Control Foundation (ISACF). These guidelines are supported by ISACA, which is the IT arm of the Institute for Internal Audit (IIA). COBIT IT is an IT governance and risk assurance tool used to measure how well developed the management processes are with respect to IT internal controls.

CIPS Gold Certification (global)

The Chartered Institute of Procurement and Supply (CIPS) is a UK-based network with branches in Australasia, China and Hong Kong, MENA, Africa and Singapore. It 'exists to promote and develop high standards of professional skill, ability and integrity among all those engaged in purchasing and supply chain management'. The CIPS Corporate Certification is:

> An in-depth assessment process that measures your procurement function against our world-class standards across five dimensions... These five dimensions are essential facets of all organizations, no matter who and where you are, and what you do. The whole process aims to ensure that you are operating efficiently and effectively, and can drive constant improvement.

CIPS Australia also released a supply chain capability maturity model (Table 3.19) with seven levels in 2012 (CIPSA, 2012).

Tailoring by sectors

There are many industry sectors and many different ways to classify them, from government official sources to recruitment job-site classification. What makes industry sectors different may influence your choice of organization capabilities required for effective ERM and therefore tailoring of your risk maturity model. These are unique to each organization.

Practitioner Megan adds sector guidance to standards and codes guidance

Megan is the quality manager at an NGO that works within three diverse sectors – education, mental health and welfare. Being new to ERM and risk maturity models, and unfamiliar with the for-profit sector, she was interested in what the key drivers were that characterize her not-for-profit workplace. Megan already had a liking for EFQM but took a new liking to the King III Corporate Governance Code because it had more specific, clear and numerous guidance for capabilities in a risk management system than any other global corporate governance code. Megan quickly scanned the following Chapter 4 sections for a high-level understanding and found Table 4.4 (see below) for the sector origins of risk maturity models the most useful. Here, she found the names of ALARM, Fraser Health, HM Treasury, Hopkinson, HRD, NSW Treasury and the Treasury Board Canada as a shortlist she could narrow down to. She wanted to do a bit of research on those from her not-for-profit sector to identify any capabilities that she could design into her own risk maturity model (in Chapter 5).

Not-for-profit, public sector and NGO

Not-for-profits (NFPs) such as non-government organizations (NGOs) require no capabilities specific to generating profit objectives. Risk maturity models that are littered with these will not be relevant to NFPs. Government and public sectors look to more specialized capabilities than for-profits. They may prefer capabilities for aligning product and service outputs to outcomes largely framed by three stakeholders: policy-makers and politicians, the communities they serve and the specialized government governance and regulation they abide by, enforce and administer. Sub-capabilities in quality management may come to the fore.

For example, the Western Cape Government in South Africa adopted a risk maturity model benchmarked and cross-walked to ISO 31000:2009 called *Benchmarker*™. It then deleted its profit-related capabilities then added their own cross-walk to the King III corporate governance guidelines. That is tailoring and benchmarking combined. For more detail, see our case study: Western Cape Government of South Africa risk maturity (Chapter 5).

NGOs look to more specialized capabilities than NFPs. They often have to answer to stakeholder-specific vision and mission statements. For example, these may be focused on war victims or the poor or the human-trafficked. Capabilities related to programme management and marketing, including grants to generate income, may come to the fore.

Non-financial private sector

It could be argued that the financial sector dominates the literature and content of conference, media and public discussion over the non-financial sector. Regardless, the point here is that the latter-sector risk modellers should be aware of this bias when trawling risk content for potential capabilities to tailor their own risk maturity model and guard against such bias. For example, one risk maturity model for culture-building positioned for the general ERM market is littered with reference to sanctions and other artifacts mainly suited to the culture of the finance sector. These may or may not be best-fit for a non-financial organization.

Financial and non-financial private sectors

The for-profit sector broadly divides between the financial services and the non-financial sector for ERM. We started to discuss this split in Chapter 1 ('Background'). McKinsey highlights the differences between the two sectors, as summarized in Table 4.3. These differences include how they approach

TABLE 4.3 Business model differences – corporate versus financial services, by Pergler/McKinsey, United States 2012

Capabilities	Corporates	Financial Institutions
Risk taxonomy	Non-standardized/ customized work better. More complex and situation-specific. Less leveraged and less compliance.	Standardized into market, credit, liquidity, ops as central to model, ie allocating risk capital effectively, defining risk limits and complying with regulations.
Nature of risk exposures	Chunky' key risks – 'which are my key risks?', 'what risks am I willing to take on?'	Leveraged but can 'dial up or down' level of exposure and appetite – settled at Stage 2 with 'measure my exposure to standard set of risks and choose where to set my dial'.
Non-linearity	Linear and discrete, eg oil price-tipping points.	Linear.
Data	Data-poor risks are key or dominate, eg strategic, reputation, ops, supply chain.	Data-rich to feed quantitative analysis.
Analysis	More qualitative, quantification highly variable and targeted.	More quantitative.
Risk insight and transparency	Identifying, assessing and prioritizing wide range of risks so key outputs are unravelling relationships across the company and understanding company risk responses within different areas of organization.	Quantifying core risks (credit etc) so key output is understanding degree of risk being taken and scarce risk capital needed within different areas of organization.
Risk appetite and strategy	More qualitative policies. Broader overall appetites, stakeholders and expectations. So effective risk-appetite allocator is a strategic financial thinker who brokers dialogue between board and management.	Highly leveraged. Strong internal competition for scarce capital. Low flexibility on appetite so effective risk-appetite allocator is a technical and regulatory specialist.

TABLE 4.3 *Continued*

Capabilities	Corporates	Financial Institutions
Risk decision-making and processes	Front-line managers less comfortable & confident as risk-takers. Their decisions not purely risk-decisions and influence others more so role of RM is to frame risk-trade-offs and provide insight to support informed management and board dialogue.	Act as intermediary (disaggregate and consolidator) of risk. Part of all decisions so role of RM is to answer question 'what else is necessary?'.
Risk organization and governance	Less C-suite CROs and risk committees. Four different central risk function models fit-to-organization, not even to sector.	More C-suite CROs and risk committees. Central risk function typically only one model, ie actively manage risks.
Lines of Defence	Each of the four risk function models vary in which line of defence to prioritize over the other, or not at all.	Three lines of defence originate here and still are the common framework.
CRO	Less defined or requires it fit-to-organization. Report to top management team, typically CFO or strategy or corporate audit.	Steward of the bank's risk capital. Specific well-defined function. Part of top management team.
Risk elements focus	Risk-related decisions and processes, plus risk appetite and strategy.	IT and other infrastructure fundamentals.
Biggest concerns	Risk in crucial business decisions and processes. Risk-appetite and culture is sector and organization-specific.	Appetite, culture, IT, evolving regulation. Risk-appetite and culture is sector – and organization – commonly shared.
Solutions and future	Tailored expertise and approaches, with 'insider' expertise-orientation.	In past 'external industry professionals' deploying next generation standardized approach. But in future will add tailored expertise and approaches as for corporates.

risk-related taxonomy, exposures, data, quantitative versus qualitative analysis, insight and capital, appetite and strategy, decision making, organization, lines of defence, CRO, key concerns and solutions and failures.

Sector origins

Users with a need to understand the provenance of their preferred maturity model reference may refer to Table 4.4. The provenance or sector origin matters in at least some cases, particularly if positive or negative bias needs to be taken into consideration. Table 4.4 takes our sample of over 70 maturity models and reclassifies them by where they originated from.

TABLE 4.4 Sector origin of maturity models

Origins in...	Risk Maturity Model and Related	Non-Risk and Capability Maturity Model, eg CMM
Financial Services	Causal Capital. Ciorciari. Syntex. Genius Methods. Marsh ERM. Marsh Insurance. Marsh Risk Focus. S&P ERM for Corporates. S&P ERM for Insurers. Willis. Zurich.	
Non Fin.Serv. – Private Sector	Aberdeen. Accenture. Active Risk™. BCCM®. Booz. COSO ERM. Deloitte. Economist Intelligence Unit. EY. Hillson. Influence. ISO 31000. Kerzner. KPMG. LogicManager™. LTRC/EFQM. OGC-M_o_R®. Optimit SecureIT. ReviewIT Optimit. Pergler-McKinsey & Co. Protivity. PwC. Riskonnect. SecureIT.	CERT® Resiliency. Gartner. INSEAD–Arguden. ITI. Lederman/GARP®. Luyckx. OCEG 2.1®.
Private Sector Risk Functionary	Benchmarker™.	

TABLE 4.4 *Continued*

Origins in...	Risk Maturity Model and Related	Non-Risk and Capability Maturity Model, eg CMM
Professional Bodies, Institutes	CIPS. INCOSE. ISACA. IRM. RIMS. SCRLC.	BD-CMM®. COBIT IT. COSO Internal Controls. ISACA. ITI. Lederman-GARP®. OPM3®.
Government Joint Ventures	Axelos P3M3.	
Government	ALARM. Fraser Health. HM Treasury. Hopkinson. HRDC. NSW Treasury. Treasury Board Canada.	
Academic, Not for Profits	Aon-Wharton. CIRANO. Kaplan-Mikes. Monda ERMi.	Aho. Elmaallam. INSEAD-Arguden. Luyckx. Marx. MMGRSeg. Murphy 4e.

NOTE: Examples only based on publicly available information or claim to an alignment or overlap to a Sector, so proprietary information is missing.

The majority of the models in the sample shown in Table 4.4 originate from the private sector. One-quarter of the models come from insurance, credit agency and other financial sector representatives. Three-quarters come from the non-financial sector. Here, big and smaller accounting and consulting firms dominate, followed by software firms then followed by a small group made up of business service firms or committees representing the interests of the auditing/accounting firms or of risk professionals. Only one model originates from a practising risk functionary CRO (rather than academic or technical papers).

Tailoring by organization operating model

The organization operating model, also known as the business operating model ('OpMod'), is probably the single most important internal context driver (apart from leadership). The more the risk management system can be integrated and aligned to or sit alongside the existing organization management systems, the more tailored the former. The most common overlapping or fulcrum point rests on the organization *capabilities* that they both share as the same component.

If culture is the way people behave and work together, then the operating model or OpMod is the highest-level design of how your organization expects its people to work within an organizational structure to pursue its objectives. An OpMod has a functional/people accountability focus and is not to be confused with a 'business model' that has a financial/quantitative and budgeting focus. That structure may be informal, because most organizations evolve over time without reviewing their operating model until a step-change or restructure is required or demanded of them. Some boards and organization leaders, however, invest in formally designing or redesigning some, or all, of their operating model. The objectives typically are to run the organization better and faster on a reduced cost-base. This can mean balancing cost and investment through risk management and return on investment with service and product reliability for customer satisfaction. The drivers behind such OpMod initiatives may be many but are typically categorized as either the need to improve the existing OpMod (evolution) or to move to a new paradigm, step change or transformation.

Practitioner Asha uses organization operating model to focus her maturity model

Asha has a need to better understand how her recruitment company's overall internal management system works *before* she can design her risk maturity model, in order that the risk management system maturity it improves is as integrated as possible. Being influenced by the human resource (HR) industry, Asha has HR and culture-related needs that bring her to the specific subject of fit-to-organization operating models (OpMod).

So Asha follows this chapter to understand the structure for an effective OpMod. She begins to understand what an OpMod means in terms of how the structure maps out and defines *objectives* that cascade in an aligned way down to key *process maps*, to *functional accountability maps* and eventually down to *job descriptions*. She interprets the *functional accountabilities* as her key focal point of interest because these represent capabilities that are needed to be covered by the content in her risk maturity model, especially in her risk culture and risk treatment capability modules. She likes the tips from subject matter experts like Bain but she likes even more the way that the PatelMiller example focused on *process, people* and *technology*-themed capabilities. Asha decides to make these three her core capability sets when she applies the steps in Chapter 5 to design her own maturity model. Contrary to Alan, Asha does not need the more advanced technical discussions and a template offered at the end of this section and skips them.

Understanding how the operating model structure unlocks capabilities

Operating models (OpMods) start to explain how an organization management system works by clarification of *decision-mission-objectives*, the business plan drivers and the operating principles defining culture, values and information usage and the strategic assumptions underlying the above. These may be subject to change or carry false assumptions and therefore represent risk. The above are aligned to key *process maps* and supporting process maps. These cascade to an aligned set of *functional accountability* maps (here read organization capabilities). These in turn cascade down to the functional structure comprised of units, teams, projects and individual jobs and finally to *job descriptions* for individuals (here read individual competencies).

Let us stop to absorb the potential of an OpMod for a risk maturity modeller. A risk maturity modeller can ensure that their model is tailored to their organization OpMod, particularly through aligning the capability set in the risk maturity model with that set defined by the OpMod – particularly by the functional accountability maps. Process maps, functional accountability maps and new job descriptions map out in combination the organization to-be/target/future-state capabilities. Plus, they can clearly separate out individual competencies (from organization capabilities) as these are found in the final cascaded subset of *job descriptions* for individuals who are organized into teams and units to deliver the desired OpMod.

Where to focus on OpMods to help your risk maturity model design

There are a number of areas to focus on OpMods to help your risk maturity model design. The first focus for OpMod designers and process re-engineer experts is usually on how the organization key process *interfaces* can be optimized. Interfaces are critical because 'gaps' there are a proven risk. This means combining unit-to-unit, process-to-process, project-to-project and people-to-people interfaces and including the key combinations between these. Dysfunctional interfaces are a key 'make or break' for an operating model. This is akin to any chain where the weakest link is a 'make or break' risk. Some OpMod designers call these the 'pain points' or 'profit leak points'.

The second focus by OpMod designers is on execution and implementation – how well the OpMod is put into effect and monitored and reviewed, ie for *effectiveness*. This represents the second shared characteristic to the risk management system that reinforces our recurring point that risk maturity models represent a powerful tool to assess management effectiveness. Are boards and managers putting their OpMod to *full effect* and keeping it there? Change managers will argue, for example, that hiring great managers within a bad OpMod is a waste of time and investment in good people, and a root cause of a dysfunctional culture. It will lead to bad decision making and therefore bad risk management systems and bad risk-informed decision making.

Bain & Co have a view on what characterizes a winning operating model that every maturity model should consider. They consult with clients to ensure that they 'get fit-for-purpose' (read *tailored*) and that these following six elements work together (Bain & Co, 2012):

1. superstructure of the primary business units and how the profit and loss statement (P&L) maps to them;
2. accountability principles for where and how decisions are made and executed;
3. management mechanisms to prioritize cross-group processes and interfaces to support strategic and operational decisions;
4. talent requirements to make the operating model work;
5. key strategic metrics that align the top team and the broader organization around clear strategic objectives and priorities;
6. behavioural expectations, unique cultural heritage and teamwork.

Another way to think of OpMods is in terms of the key internal capabilities. Sometimes, these are labelled by a number of popular names coined for various OpMods such as lean–mean, small-business mindset, digital or entrepreneurial models. Regardless of popular name tags, how key internal capabilities are described and understood in order to execute strategy and objectives is vital to performance and success.

Look at the retail OpMod in Figure 4.3. Asha spotted several capabilities that she adapted when designing her own risk maturity model. The OpMod consultants who designed it, PatelMiller, like to think of:

> How each capability is linked and further designed in terms of three components (process, technology, people) to drive efficiency and effectiveness. Distinctive capabilities are the things that a retailer does better than anyone else in the market; creating compelling reasons for customers to choose to shop with it. For example, Amazon's free one-day delivery is not something that can be easily copied. The *process* component includes the overall process flows, inputs, outputs, who does what, where, how, what metrics and what levels of consistency. The *technology* component includes architecture, applications, data, infrastructure and levels of standardization required to deliver them. The *people* component includes structure, organization, skills, culture, governance, rewards, sourcing and locations. (PatelMiller, 2015)

More technical OpMod approaches to validate your risk maturity model

There are more technical OpMod approaches that may be used to validate your risk maturity model that in the end may provide better ways to define tailored capabilities in your model.

For example, look at the template Table 4.5 that depicts a sample of OpMod approaches. The examples are summarized by either how they cascade down capability sets by levels (from high to low and left to right on our table template rows) or, for the Porter example, how they flow across in value-causation (from low to high and left to right on our table template rows). Note these levels are *not* maturity levels but hierarchy or flow levels. These approaches include my own preferred approach that I have been using since my previous business management consulting days, the Michael Porter Economic Value Chain approach (more later). These range from OCEG v2.0 to how business process optimizers may approach OpMods from different perspectives.

How does your organization compare? Or, how does your leading competitor or an industry model for your organization compare? You can get help internally from HR, Finance, Operations and from quality and standards managers. For example, you may not find detailed process maps from the Corporate or Strategy team but you may find many for operations

FIGURE 4.3 Example of a high-level retail operating model

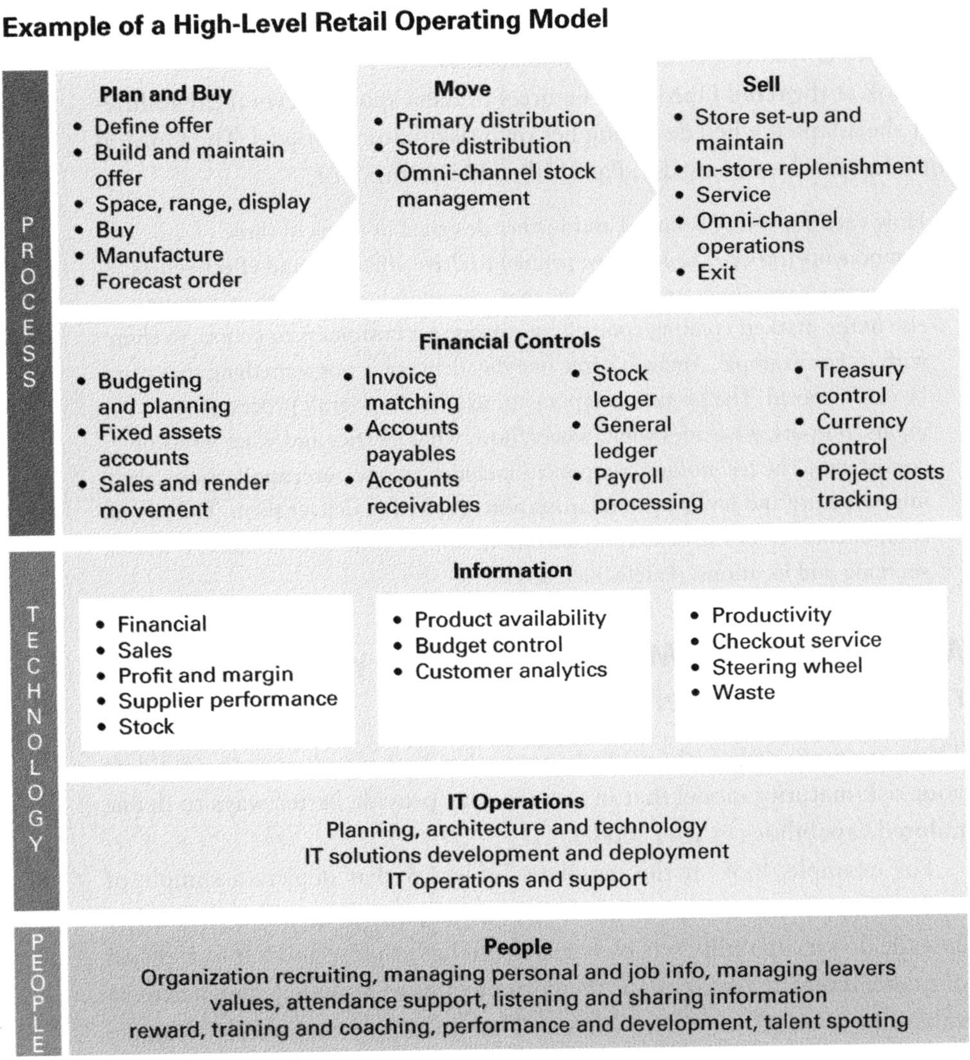

SOURCE: Reprinted with kind permission from PatelMiller http://patelmiller.com/what-we-do/operating-model/operating-model-design/

in the ISO 90001 manuals. Enter the notes that are relevant to your organization as to where to source more information, or the results, into the empty row for your organization. These should relate to either how they may validate and act as a 'gap-checker' to your existing risk maturity model, or serve to suggest the core capability themes when designing the capability content of your first risk maturity model (see Chapter 5).

TABLE 4.5 Template for organization operating model comparing a sample of approaches

Approaches	Level 1	Level 2	Level 3	Level 4	Level 5	Level 6	Level 7
Antonucci OpMod general	Objectives defined	Strategies aligned	Imperatives aligned	Processes aligned	Accountabilities aligned	Job Descriptions aligned	Performance aligned
OCEG v2.0 IT	Objectives	Strategies	Processes	Information	IT systems		
OGC P3M3 projects	Strategic (LT)	Portfolio (MT)	Programme (MT)	Project (MT)	Operational (ST)		
Porter Economic Value Chain flows across	Enablers support Drivers	Driver Input as Logistics	Driver Operations	Driver Output as Logistics	Sales and Marketing	After-Sales Services	Customer Contacts and Revenue in
Processes general	Macro	Key	Support	Subprocess	Tailored to ISO etc		
HR general	Organization	Function or Department	Unit	Team	Individual		
Your Organizaton's OpMod?:							

KEY: ST = short term, MT = medium term, LT = long term

Different consulting firms have different approaches to OpMods. The Wrigley-Rumelt-Andrews model is a sophisticated approach to macro-capabilities that divides organization OpMods into four general types: *integrated*, *allied-related*, *allied-unrelated* and *holding* OpMods. Each can then be compared against each other by a range of capability criteria such as business strategy, customer types, corporate role and human capital. The descriptors for each criteria flag potential maturity model capabilities you may tailor in to your risk maturity model, as no organization has the same mix – even those competing directly in the same sector. Look at the template provided in Table 4.6. Circle the capabilities most relevant to your organization. Are the circles all under one type of OpMod? If not, why not? Can you add more that typify your organization or the leading competitor or role model for your organization?

TABLE 4.6 Template for listing macro-capabilities compared to Wrigley-Rumelt model

Capability	Integrated	Allied-Related	Allied-Unrelated	Holding
Business strategies	One	Many	Many	Many
Customers	Same	Shared	Some shared	Many
Corporate role	Resource allocations	Define protocols	Define protocols	Financial roll-ups and analysis
Human capital	Common	Some shared	Some shared	Independent
IT systems	Common	Common	Few, interconnected	Different
Enabling processes	Centralized	Centralized	Some centralized	Decentralized
Capability X				
Capability Y				
Capability Z				

SOURCE: Four types adapted from Leonard Wrigley and Richard Rumelt (Andrews, 1986)

Practitioner Alan uses OpMod to improve both audit plan and shared maturity model

Alan did not think much of our Figure 4.3 and Table 4.5 because his internal audit team had experience already with cross-matching the 'processes general' row with the 'HR general' row. He wanted a more macro-level understanding of their utility company. He looked at Table 4.6 to classify his own utility and quickly eliminated it as a holding company or integrated type. He chose the allied-related over allied-unrelated type because his utility was using common IT systems (not several or interconnected ones) combined with centralized business processes (as only the minor processes were decentralized).

This then gave Alan the idea to adjust his upcoming risk-based audit plan. He would ask his audit team not only to focus on the IT-capabilities per se, but to come up with audit consulting observations and recommendations for the two specific areas that effectively were the key drivers for their utility (ie common IT systems and core centralized business processes). These observations and recommendations were taken up by the ERM manager who, as steward of the risk maturity model, used them to gap-fill what was missing in the model. The result one year later: it helped the ERM manager to upgrade the design of the risk maturity model. First, by adding one new IT system-related capability. Second, by improving an existing capability in the model by redefining the description, rating the as-is completion level lower and adding more specific to-be actions. The to-be actions were then added to the ERM manager coordinated risk management plan for resourcing and scheduling purposes. The latter plan, in turn, helped revise the overall risk maturity strategy and vice versa.

Tailoring by risk function operating model

One or more of the capabilities designed in to your risk maturity model typically describes how the risk function and risk officers/managers need to work as part of the risk management system, which is in turn a part of the organization OpMod we discussed in the preceding section.

The risk management function's operating model ('risk function') is a subset within the structure representing the organization OpMod. Every risk function has some form of OpMod even if it is informal or not understood fully or formally designed, or its reporting line is to the board or CEO or both. Failure to understand its fit and interface with the organization OpMod may determine the success or failure of the risk management system and having the risk maturity model sponsored from the top, resourced, communicated and implemented.

For now, let us leave aside one argument within a part of the developed world that risk functions should either not exist at all or that they should speed their own termination by absorption into the organization's regular management systems. Some argue that this position is implied by ISO 31000 because it omits any explicit references to risk functionaries (notwithstanding the fact that ISO 31000 does imply they exist by saying they should not be involved in joint decision making with management). On the other hand, the leading corporate governance codes (King III), COSO ERM and the vast majority of other reference sources from Chapter 3 and elsewhere endorse a CRO and/or dedicated risk function role.

Several factors go into how the risk function may operate. At the macro level, the objectives, context and risk profiles of an organization and its organization OpMod shape the parameters. Attitudes to governance, internal departmental politics and the size of the organization often determine the size and shape of the risk function. The latter may range from a single risk champion as a part-time duty of line managers, to a part-time risk officer/managers with split duties, to full-time risk officers/managers, to a full-scale risk management department headed by a CRO and right up to a risk director on the board.

COSO ERM 2004 provides a chapter detailing the role of the risk function (COSO, 2004) that is still informative to the design of any risk function capability within a risk maturity design. It includes at least seven responsibilities for a CRO or risk manager. COSO ERM envisages that the function may be approached in at least three different ways, as either one centralized function reporting to the CEO; or, part of the senior functions, such as the chief financial officer, general counsel, chief audit executive or chief compliance officer; or, separate assignment and resources within line management.

Audit and advisory firms provide a range of guidance for possible combinations of risk function OpMods. The Deloitte Creating a Risk Intelligent Enterprise™ approach is worth a mention (Deloitte, 2013b). Its structure depicts a cascade of typical roles and responsibilities for the risk function sitting within a risk oversight coalition with the Board and CEO at the top accountable for all but delegating responsibilities down to CRO and risk committee for risk management oversight, then Business areas who 'manage risks' alongside a risk management organization that supports the CRO/Risk Committee/management and board. These business lines work alongside Internal audit that provide independent assurance.

Deloitte go on to describe three potential OpMods for the risk function each with advantages and disadvantages (Deloitte, 2013b). A *control/compliance* model is hierarchical and stresses standardization and bureaucracy with the risk function controlling certain risks and the risk managing architecture. A *centre of excellence* model supports the business lines as a centralized resource centre and business partner. A *reporter/central analysis* model is common amongst holding companies wherein the risk managing occurs within the business units and the risk function gathers trends and reports up. A US Deloitte 2013 poll (n=1,211) suggested that 43% of organizations were control/compliance-oriented, 32% unsure, 13% reporter/central analysis and 13% centre of excellence (Deloitte, 2013a).

Deloitte has a popular way of depicting a risk function's common operating environment as a three-tiered pyramid called the Risk Intelligent Enterprise™ model, as in Figure 4.4. It portrays a layered matrix of the typical groups involved with the risk function. Figure 4.5 complements this 'pyramid' with more detail on how the risk function interrelates with these typical groups around it.

FIGURE 4.4 The Risk Intelligent Enterprise™ model

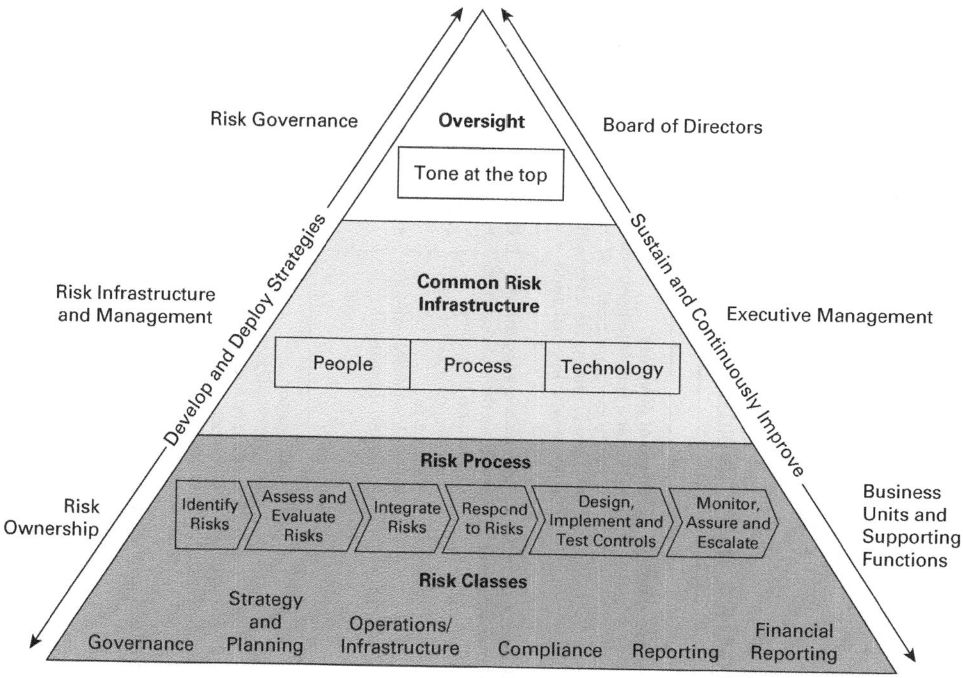

SOURCE: Reprinted with kind permission and Copyright © 2015 Deloitte International LLC

FIGURE 4.5 Typical groups involved in risk intelligent enterprise management

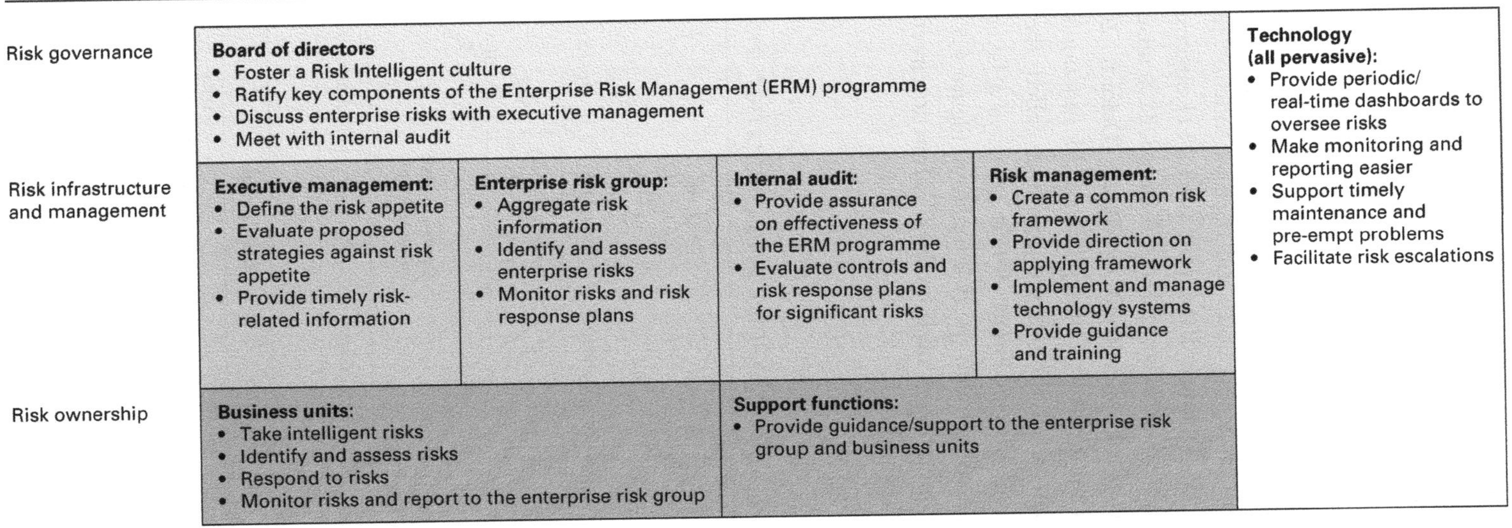

SOURCE: Reprinted with kind permission and Copyright © 2015 Deloitte International LLC

In some respects, the role of the three risk, compliance and audit functions are unique within the organization. Deloitte calls these functions 'the comforters'. Deloitte argues that they are the 'comforters' because they carry a unique mandate and one major responsibility to provide 'reassurance that the internal control and risk structure operates effectively (thereby helping the executive team and board members to sleep at night)' (Deloitte, 2010).

Deloitte argues that these comfort groups are not operational in nature, as they have no responsibility for setting and directing the operations of the business. Rather, they exist to monitor and enhance the effectiveness of the organization's risk management activities. Potential roles that expand the job description include the following eight roles:

- *Visionary*: assessing not only the current state of risk management, but peering ahead to help management divine future risks and opportunities.
- *Dietician*: determining whether the organization's risk diet matches its appetite.
- *Aggregator*: ascertaining whether the organization is appropriately considering how risks interact and cascade.
- *Efficiency expert*: investigating means to eliminate inefficiencies in risk management.
- *Champion:* advocating for resources related to risk taking for reward: addressing those risks associated with increasing profitability and increasing shareholder value.
- *Advocate*: drawing attention to and advocating for resources to address risk areas deemed insufficiently covered.
- *Subject matter resource*: providing deep knowledge and expertise in key risk areas, such as fraud.
- *Troubleshooter*: getting involved in control remediation and design; helping to conduct and interpret risk assessments.

Practitioner Asha aligns organization OpMod with risk function model

Asha finds that, ironically, her recruitment firm has never formalized her own job description or the way her risk function should work (its operating model). Asha took her key learning from the last section to focus on *process*, *people* and *technology*. She uses the simple template from

Table 4.7 to help sort her basic risk function operating model by adapting Table 4.7 to her organization OpMod. First, she lists the key capabilities that she thinks represents the *process* and lists 'Definition and methodology' down the left-hand-side column of the matrix. Second, she lists *technology* as 'RM Info Systems'; and third, *people* as the remainder. She then separates out what should remain decentralized for risk management purposes in the second column, then its opposite in the fourth column, and finally, she puts in the middle (third) column anything that did not fit either side.

Asha drafts her preferred to-be OpMod as indicated in black italics text on the matrix in Table 4.7. By using the matrix to communicate internally, she secures a common understanding and agreement to it by her boss and the CEO that this will become the sort of risk function best aligned to the management systems of the firm. Now, she can look ahead to designing-in the appropriate capabilities to her maturity model (this is covered in Chapter 5).

TABLE 4.7 Template for designing a risk-function operating model

	Decentralized	Hybrid	Centralized
RM Oversight	By business units.	Business unit risk committees manage their level of risks. Remainder with centralized unit reporting to senior management.	***Risk committees associated with centralized function reporting to senior management.***
RM Plans and Policies	Set by BUs with no umbrella.	Corporate risk policy set by the central unit with supporting policies and procedures set by BUs.	***Strictly set at corporate level and cascaded down. Includes RM plan and tracked capability maturity improvements.***

TABLE 4.7 *Continued*

	Decentralized	Hybrid	Centralized
Definition and Methodology	Risk language, processes and methods vary by BU.	***BUs adopt risk language, processes and methods in accordance with central risk policy and risk management plan.***	Central function sets risk language, processes and methods. Mandates across BUs. Monitors compliance.
RM Accountabilities	Primarily rests with BUs.	***Shared with agreed control ranges and demarcation.***	Primarily rests with a centralized risk function headed by a CRO.
Responsibilities	***Primarily rests with BUs.***	Shared. Defined control parameters.	Primary with centralized and/or CRO.
Risk Limits and Compliance	BU managers set risk limits and monitor compliance independently.	***Group-level committee sets risk limits that the business units operate. BUs may define tolerances etc but within group limits.***	Central function sets risk policy, appetite, tolerances. Monitors compliance.
RM Info Systems	No portfolio reporting capability. Systems differ across BUs.	***Group-level system in place. Systems differ across BUs.***	Centralized and deployed across all Bus.

NOTE: Examples only appear above. Tailor to your organization. Italics represent Asha's preference. RM = risk management. BU = business unit.

Tailoring by economic value chain

We already touched on the economic value chain ('value chain') model that the guru Michael Porter made famous in the 1980s. The value chain still has currency today, even for risk maturity modellers and especially the modellers in the developing world. For the sake of simplicity and rephrasing to risk parlance, the value chain represents the capabilities of an organization to realize and sustain end-customer value objectives via two mechanisms – either *drivers* or *enablers*. *Drivers* are the organization capabilities that directly contribute to what the customer directly pays for, or indirectly pays for (such as in general taxes via a government agency service provision). These form a horizontal sequence or chain of component links with generic titles – starting with *Inbound* > to *Production* > to *Outbound* > to *Sales and Marketing* > ending with *After-Sale Service* to *Customer Segments*. *Enablers* are the shared service capabilities that vertically support the drivers that are not seen or do not have direct concern to the end customer (such as Finance, HR, IT and the risk function). In the absence of formal process mapping, this can be a valuable tool to detect performance linkages from end-to-end and to take a customer-centric view on objective-centric capabilities. These can identify new or modify capabilities that are in a risk maturity model.

Not-for-profit organizations may still make use of the value chain. They may prefer to focus on cost-of-service-and-product along the value chain in both financial and non-financial terms (eg time-to-delivery).

A simplified template to use if analysing economic value chain

By definition, then, the effects of any uncertainty as to key capabilities affecting customer objectives are of interest in tailoring a risk maturity model. Whilst few organizations appear to formally map a Porter-style economic value chain matrix, a CRO who cannot find one for their organization need not despair as it is not a huge or expensive hurdle. For a template with a simplified version of the economic value chain to adapt for your organization, see Figure 4.6.

FIGURE 4.6 Template for designing a value chain

Template for designing a value chain for:				owner:		
DRIVERS that create value and margin to the organization.	**INBOUND LOGISTICS** • Receiving inwards product constituents or services • Moving these into operations	**OPERATIONS** • Production of products and services	**OUTBOUND LOGISTICS** Order fulfilment • Warehousing of finished goods • Distribution • Often outsourced	**SALES AND MARKETING** • Pricing • Packaging • Advertising • Market research	**AFTER SALES SERVICE**	**CUSTOMER & MARGIN**
ENABLERS Processes that assist drivers to create value or margin.	**TECHNOLOGY** Technology development to support new products, services to support the above drivers.				**AFTER SALES SERVICE**	**CUSTOMER & MARGIN**
	PROCUREMENT Procurement process for purchases to support the above drivers.				**AFTER SALES SERVICE**	**CUSTOMER & MARGIN**
	PEOPLE People management processes for recruitment, retention, training, labour relations and salaries to support the above drivers.				**AFTER SALES SERVICE**	**CUSTOMER & MARGIN**
	CORPORATE SUPPORT Accounting, Facilities Management, Planning, General Administration, Project Management Office PMO, Risk Management and other corporate support services to support the above drivers.				**AFTER SALES SERVICE**	**CUSTOMER & MARGIN**

Note: High-level only. All activities indicate macro or subprocesses. Potential process flows indicative only by > X > Y >

Practitioner Alan adapts the Porter matrix to update the maturity model

We have seen how Alan leveraged what he learnt from Table 4.6 via his upcoming risk-based audit plan to improve the shared risk maturity model with the ERM manager. However, when Alan saw the value chain template simply laid out, as in Figure 4.6, he put it to good use immediately with a team workshop. Alan's team replicated the Porter matrix on a simple spreadsheet matrix as a simple flow chart, as in Figure 4.6, and tailored the generic chain titles to their utility from the existing process information held by internal audit. With the help of the project management officer (PMO) and Corporate Planning and Strategy functions they adapted the IA macro-processes and subprocess maps to Figure 4.6 and resorted them into the various boxes on the matrix. They analysed where there were any uncertainties in the drivers or enablers, ie any weak links in a chain; then, had the ERM function validate this with relevant stakeholders. When validated, IA and the ERM manager ensured that the risk maturity model and risk management plan were updated.

Tailoring by key performance indicators

If your organization has KPIs to manage corporate performance then this may present an advantage to a risk maturity modeller. You can 'unpack' the KPIs to get to the key management capabilities your organization is measuring and analyse how your risk maturity model is aligned in terms of the corresponding risk management capabilities. For example, if a balanced scorecard (BSC) approach is being used and there are a disproportionate amount of 'learning perspective' KPIs and your risk maturity model does not refer to one capability about quality management and learning, then perhaps there is a need to either revise your model or change your performance management system.

If your organization does *not* have clear and agreed KPIs – as many do not, especially in the developing world – then a risk maturity modeller can resort to a shortcut or proxy. Surprisingly, there are literally thousands of KPIs collated for easy reference and ready to hand via Amazon books. We will talk more of this in Chapter 7 but my personal favourite is Dr Rachad Baroudi's *KPI Mega Library: 17,000 key performance indicators*

(Baroudi, 2010). Do not be daunted by the huge figure of 17,000 as you will find it surprisingly well sectioned for easy navigation of KPI descriptions by:

- Sections: organization, government, international.
- Chapters: industry, sector, topic.
- Group: functions and sources.

Tailoring by context and design-related methods

We have often referred in this book to the need to tailor so that the risk maturity model has fit-to-organization objectives, context and risk profile(s). ISO 31000:2009 proposes that the external and internal context shapes your ERM framework but it is also an open invitation to tailor it this way. A full list of context references appears in the standard and should be cross-referenced by posing this question to your risk maturity model: does the model miss a capability for our organization suggested by the list of context factors? For example, factors such as the external PESTLE factors mnemonic for: political, economic, social, technological, legal and environmental.

We will say more on this and how to use many model design approaches and techniques that integrate some form of tailoring or benchmarking in Chapter 5 on designing.

Summary

Before you start designing, or as you continuously redesign in order to improve your risk maturity model, you should refer to a range of sources that can assist in tailoring and benchmarking apart from comparing the existing maturity models (as we did in Chapter 3).

The first and easiest place to start should be external ERM-related standards and voluntary codes. ISO 31000 is the premier international standard and COSO ERM leads a number of other voluntary guidance codes that may also benefit your model.

Regardless of which governance code is relevant by jurisdiction, the next logical places to research are corporate governance codes. Here, the premier voluntary code for global reference is King III followed by a small number of lesser codes. You may also need to tailor to your sector risk disciplines of interest, whilst factoring for your cost constraints.

You certainly need to consider 'How does my organization work?' if you wish to integrate risk management effectively into management systems and processes. We learnt that the best three ways to do this is to understand how the sector influences the organization, how the all-important organization operating model (OpMod) works and then how the risk function operating model works within the OpMod. Understanding how the organization OpMod operates within an economic value chain, and the KPIs by which the organization chooses to measure performance, may assist. We finished more broadly with how internal and external context, and maturity model design factors may also provide pointers to designing or improving your risk maturity model.

Designing a tailored risk maturity model

05

This chapter covers:

- Components
- Domains
- Capabilities
- Scales
- Levels
- Alternative design formats
- Enhancements to the design
- Optimizing objectivity, tailoring and reporting
- Summary

Introduction

Megan felt confident and equipped from the prior chapters to now move on to the design of her first risk maturity model. She had downloaded the SCRLC gratis spreadsheet. From her Chapter 3 research, she had listed 43 underlying maturity capabilities based on adapting and building on the 22 capabilities from the Monda ERMi model, with other capabilities she chose by researching the quality management-originated and not-for-profit maturity models (such as Hillson, LTRC/EFQM, ALARM, Fraser Health and HM Treasury). She had used Chapter 4 to survey the large field of guidance standards and codes. She preferred the European Foundation for Quality Movement (EFQM) and the leading King III code because, for her, King III had more specific, clear and numerous guidance for capabilities in a risk management system than any other global corporate governance code. She was ready now to start designing.

There can be many purposes for a tailored risk maturity model but the highest purpose is to assess risk management effectiveness to your unique organization. That means designing one that is a best fit for your organization. It does *not* mean you have to create something absolutely new, perfect or become a creative genius. It does mean understanding some basics then synthesizing what models and reference sources are out there (from Chapters 3 and 4) to arrive at what you need to get started.

Designing means a plan to show the construction, function and workings of the risk maturity model. *Tailoring* means its fit-to-organization objectives, internal and external context and risk profiles. We will use a simple spreadsheet matrix format to build up basic content components that will suffice to get started. An organization's size, resources or budget should not stop it from tailor-designing its own risk maturity model.

There are some design basics to be understood. There is a sequence to the basic components. This chapter will follow a simple three-step design process for modellers, ending with tips for enhancements and alternative design options (such as formats, report types, targeting future improvements, score weighting and marketing slogans). We will look at some samples and hear how Megan and all our practitioners approach tailoring their own model.

Components of a maturity model

A new risk maturity model may be built up using components as building blocks. These interlinked units or components are called domains, capabilities, levels and scales. Alternatively, an existing model can be broken down (disaggregated) into some or all of these components and redesigned accordingly.

Components are also called *elements* or *building blocks* by some models. Components should work together to create something more powerful than the sum of their parts, but for now let us understand how to design them one by one. We can summarize them in this sort of hierarchy or sequence as: Components = Domains + Capabilities + Scales + Levels.

Domains as a component of a maturity model

The highest-level component is the *domain* or area of content focus. This represents the subject-matter scope or footprint that the risk maturity model should cover and therefore which capabilities to focus on. For our purposes in this book, our chosen domain is *enterprise-wide risk management* (ERM) and is interchangeable with other common expressions such as *risk management* and *strategic risk management*.

You will recall from Chapter 1 the examples of domains and subdomains in Figure 1.1 ('Value contributed by evolving risk management') and Figure 1.2 ('Maturity model evolution'). For our purposes, we categorize ERM as the umbrella domain over a large number of subdomains being the more specialized risk management disciplines such as project risk, legal, treasury risk, health and safety, security and so on. However, we will also refer to non-risk-related domains and *capability* maturity models as they also may provide inputs to tailoring a better risk maturity model. For example, a process-driven organization may synthesize business process management capabilities.

Let us now turn to design considerations for *capability* meanings, purpose, naming, quantity, module structure and examples.

Capabilities as a component of a maturity model

An ERM domain is made up of a number of underlying *capabilities*. These are the things – the what – that your model is going to assess. ERM represents a 'glue' that holds a holistic umbrella over specialty risk subdomains we have mentioned. A set of capabilities distinguishes one domain from other domains. Our discussions in Chapters 1, 3 and 4 give you a background (Chapter 1) and many capability examples – such as a risk management plan – from the directory of working models (Chapter 3) and references in standards and other sources (Chapter 4).

Here, we define capabilities, consider the aspects of tailoring, quality, theming into modules then undertake design step one by starting your new model with a matrix of capabilities. We add how to get more help to get started and choose your preferred set of capabilities.

Capabilities defined with examples

Capabilities are also known by a potentially confusing array of alternative terms. You should be aware of these if cross-referencing other works but take comfort that they largely mean capabilities. These other terms include: outcomes and attributes (by ISO), elements, milestones, deliverables, drivers, indicators, aspects, characteristics, components, practices, key practice modules, themes, perspectives, areas of excellence, activity areas, work-streams, critical or key success factors (CSF or KSF), key readiness factors, dimensions, and leverage domains. Occasionally, they are also misleadingly termed as competencies or underlying competency drivers. Misleading references to 'competency' should be avoided (refer to Chapter 1 'Definitions' for more detail).

Capabilities describe a set of risk capability performance drivers of ERM. These should be based on *quality* 'evidence-based' detailed output and/or outcomes to meet the standards of 'evidence-based assessment' expected by the quality management discipline.

For example, the simplest wording '*A risk management policy statement is in place*' may represent one ERM capability. If your organization has always had a policy then this sentence may be enough for it to be rated by a few knowledgeable long-time employees, but it cannot be assumed that this level of corporate and specific knowledge will be shared by all assessors and audiences (such as new-to-your organization employees, external assessors or board members). So each capability needs to be described in as much detail as can be evidenced in multiple attributes and in output/outcome terms. For example: '*A risk management policy statement is in place*' may be replaced by: '*A robust risk management policy statement agreed by board and signed off by* CEO. *Addresses the high-level purpose, principles, framework, process, treatment, roles and appetite for enterprise risk management. Communicated to all risk decision-makers and their understanding checked. Regularly updated to reflect organization changes*.'

The latter description grants certain advantages. It gives a far clearer description of 'what good looks like' or a milestone in project parlance. It introduces a number of elements that can all be verified with some form of sliding scale of evidence of quality or completion (that we can later rate to ensure the assessment is robust). Whilst such capability descriptions are not in a question format, they can serve as a cut-down 'silent' questionnaire because they effectively serve to pose as questions, as in: '[Does your organization provide evidence that ...] a robust risk management policy statement agreed by, etc...'

It is not important whether you call capabilities by another name, as long as the meaning is clear within your organization. The differences between the terms are largely academic as they all do the same job of assigning certain characteristics to differentiate one capability from another. In a projects-culture, for example, calling them 'milestones' carries more meaning and may be preferred. In a heavy balanced scorecard (BSC)/ objectives, goals, strategies and measures (OGSM) or other performance management KPI-driven culture, calling them 'indicators' may be better. The idea is to tailor to your existing management systems and processes.

Tailoring capabilities to the organization

The wording for each capability should be *tailored* to your organization and not slavishly copied from outside. If your organization has a 'lean–mean' culture then you may prefer to call a risk management *policy* (taking 12 pages in length) a risk management *statement* (and keep it to a 'crunchy' two pages). If your work culture is tired of overusing the term 'strategy', then the 'risk maturity strategy' ISO refers to may be better dubbed as the risk maturity road map, or similar.

Quantity of capabilities considered

The *number* of underlying capabilities should be 'just right'. Too few and the assessment may become shallow and lack substance. Too many and it may become unmanageable and overly difficult to assess and to obtain buy-in from line managers. Between 30 and 90 is common but some risk maturity models number 120 or more capabilities and some as little as 12. The Aon-Wharton risk maturity model reduced their capability set from 126 to 40. The LogicManager risk maturity model makes assessment rather complicated by requiring 68 underlying capabilities to be rated against a 10-point scale across three dimensions. That means 68 × 10 × 3 = 2,040 considerations – rather too many.

Modules theme the capabilities

Capabilities are often themed together to form capability *modules*. These collect different capabilities under a common theme banner for ease of communication (say a presentation slide to the board), work streaming and use. Capability modules may also be known by an array of terms, such as: capability themes, groups, core-term attributes, key factors, characteristics or, misleadingly, 'core competencies'. Taxonomy-biased models such as LogicManager may also collect them in a hierarchy (ie where *category* ascends over *factors* that in turn ascend over *indicators*).

One benefit of theming into modules is that it lends itself to high-level dashboard and to simplified reporting. Boards and CxOs are time-poor and prefer not to see assessment results and details for each of the 20 to 120 or so capabilities in a model. The Aon-Wharton Risk Maturity Index or 'RMI' (Aon-Wharton, 2013), for example, uses 40 questions (read *capabilities*) themed under 10 'characteristics' (meaning 'themed modules'). These 10 modules are:

1. board understanding and commitment to risk management;
2. executive-level risk management driver;
3. risk communication transparency;
4. risk culture: engagement and accountability;
5. identification of existing and emerging risks;
6. participation of key stakeholders in risk management strategy development and policy setting;
7. formal incorporation of operational and financial risk information into decision making;
8. integration into human capital processes to drive sustainable business performance;
9. sophisticated quantification methods;
10. move from focusing on risk avoidance and mitigation to leveraging risk and risk management options that extract value.

Now we understand that our ERM domain needs modules to theme a set of capabilities, we can go to our first design step of putting these into a matrix.

Design step one: matrix your preferred capabilities

Open up your own new spreadsheet matrix and title it. Enter your choice of ERM *capabilities* and their *modules* on your spreadsheet as rows. These are best located along the y-axis (vertical left-hand side) in a matrix format (boxed cells). A matrix format is a simple format for a spreadsheet. It also acts as database where you can later use rank, sort, calculate and other basic database functions.

You can get started on your own model in two ways. As capabilities are mandatory but modules are optional, it may be easier to start 'bottom-up'.

Start by creating a long list of unsorted capabilities of interest to your organization down your first spreadsheet column. Sort them into a sequence if one follows another by their nature, and/or sort into groups by any shared themes (such as people, technology and process).

Alternatively, the reverse may also apply by starting 'top-down' with themed modules then breaking these down into underlying capabilities. Refresh your memory by looking at the Aon-Wharton modules from our previous section. Alternatively, the ISO 31000 standard has a core process called risk assessment. This can be broken down into three subprocesses of risk identification, risk analysis and risk evaluation. If we take these ISO three capabilities as a sample starting point, then our tailored sample matrix can be seen in Table 5.1.

Other ways to get started

The above methodology is simply based on generic project-planner methodology that project managers are familiar with. For those with the later versions of Microsoft MS Excel they do not even need to create their own spreadsheet but can simply open up the standard template available from MS Excel called GANTT Project Planner. The standard template is shown in Figure 5.1. The rationale here is that ERM as a programme involves a group of exactly the same components as the project planner, that is, a series of activities (read *capabilities*), plan start, plan duration, actual start, actual duration, % complete and period. For risk maturity purposes, the % complete function (or your tailored equivalent) may be used as rating *scales*. This can be a powerful way to measure and track your risk maturity model and to evidence your levels.

Another easy alternative to getting started is to adapt an existing spreadsheet model that is already built, web-accessible and easily tailored to your own organization (SCRLC, 2014). The Supply Chain Risk Leadership Council (SCRLC) website (**http://www.scrlc.com/**) offers one of the first places you may go if you want to start your own tailored risk maturity model. You can download their supply chain risk maturity model in soft spreadsheet format for free (with the kind permission of the board at SCRLC). You can then use your own spreadsheet by adapting the content to your preferred ERM capabilities. Alternatively, you can retain it as a specialized risk maturity model for supply chain and use in tandem with your preferred ERM-level risk maturity model by having the SCRM score feed up to your supply-chain-related capability within your ERM model.

TABLE 5.1 Design step one: illustrative example setting up a set of capabilities

XYZ Risk Maturity Index – Confidential

Module Title and Descriptor

1. Risk Assessment: Risks are identified, analysed and evaluated against objectives and within an established context before treatment.				
1.1 Identification. *Description sentences. Multiple description sentences. Multiple description sentences. Multiple description sentences. Multiple description sentences. Multiple description sentences.*				
1.2 Analysis. *Description ...*				
1.3 Evaluation. *Description ...*				
2. *Module Title: Description*				
2.1 *Capability title.* *Capability description ...*				
2.2 *Capability title*.*Capability description ...*				
3. *Module Title: Description*				
3.1 *Capability title.* *Capability description ...*				
3.2 *Capability title* *Capability description ...*				
3.3 *Capability title.* *Capability description ...*				
3.4 *Capability title*. *Capability description ...*				

Capabilities themed to Module

FIGURE 5.1 Gantt project planner sample

ACTIVITY	PLAN START	PLAN DURATION	ACTUAL START	ACTUAL DURATION	PERCENT COMPLETE
Activity 01	1	5	1	4	25%
Activity 02	1	6	1	6	100%
Activity 03	2	4	2	5	35%
Activity 04	4	8	4	6	10%
Activity 05	4	2	4	8	85%
Activity 06	4	3	4	6	85%

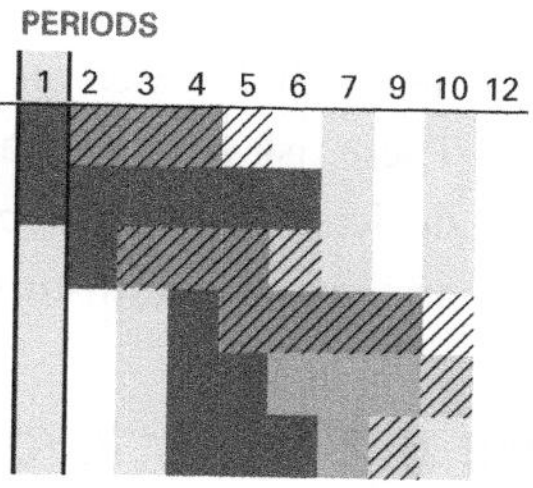

Period Highlight: 1

Plan
% Complete
Actual
% Complete (beyond plan)
Actual (beyond plan)

Getting more help to get started and to choose capabilities

Need help? Do not worry if you are stuck for ideas when choosing capabilities. You have many wonderful sources for capabilities and modules and they are easy to find. Just go back to Chapter 3 (for a large directory of models that you can refer to) or Chapter 4 (for standards, codes and other sources). If you need more details from a particular entry in the directory or other chapters, follow them up in the detailed resources section at the end of this book.

Alternatively, you can go straight to international standards such as ISO 31000:2009, which has only 24 pages and a good place to start, with its five 'Enhanced Attributes' (ISO, 2009a). Or, reference the Monda 22 capabilities researched from subject-matter experts on risk maturity models (Monda, 2013). Or, reference the MECO case study by Alexander Larsen (Fraser, Simkins and Narvaev, 2015). Or, the many capabilities referred to in the book *World-class Risk Management* (Marks, 2015). Or use the many online access points to surveys or product samples with RIMS, Aon-Wharton or Benchmarker™. Or, you may choose to just scan the index to some of the books and publications in the References and Further reading rear sections, as they provide many potential capability titles.

Accounting firm Ernst and Young published an illuminating chart based on evidence-based ERM-leading practices called Turning Risk into Results (Ernst & Young, 2012). It reinforces the point above regarding choosing your capabilities and describing them with a cogent set of sub-capabilities as elements or practices. Figure 5.2 provides more detail (with kind permission from EY). We quote EY as follows:

> We found specific risk practices that were consistently present in the top performers (ie top 20% based on risk maturity) that were not present in the bottom 20%. These risk practices can be organized into the following challenge areas, as depicted in the chart below... Our study findings suggest that these components are critical to transforming risk and driving better business performance.

FIGURE 5.2 Ernst & Young leading practices as potential maturity capabilities

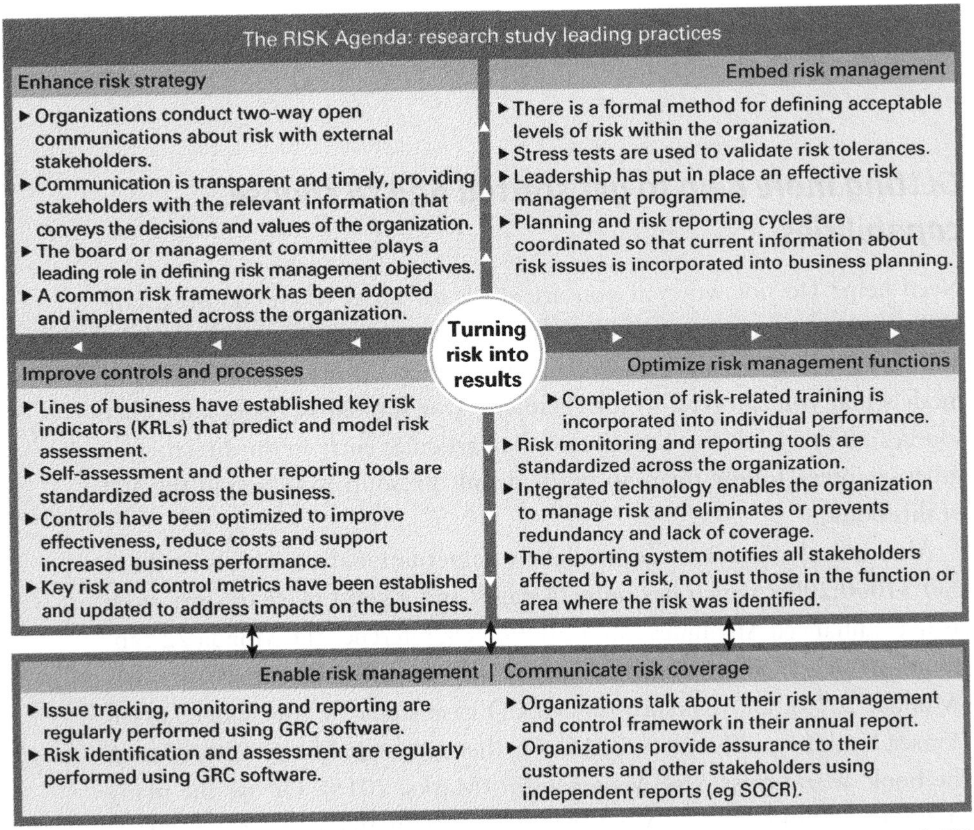

SOURCE: Reprinted with permission of EYGM Limited. Copyright 2012 EYGM Limited. All rights reserved. EYG no. AU1082.

Recap on starting to design your own risk maturity model

To recap, the success of your risk maturity model starts with:

- a tailored set of capabilities fit-to-organization;
- the quality of clear multiple evidences per sub-capability (element);
- tailored descriptions, which are preferred over copied ones.

Now that you know the *what* (the *capabilities* you want to assess), we can move on to the *how* (to assess each capability by *scale* rating). This involves the design considerations for rating scales and their meanings, purpose, naming, qualities and various options.

Scales as a component of a maturity model

The assessing (or evaluating) part in the phrase 'assessing risk management effectiveness' means implementing formal periodic assessments to rate your organization's performance specific to implementing the risk management system. One method to assess is to apply rating *scales* against each of your capabilities. Scales represent the *how* to assess each capability (and their modules) by a stepped qualitative rating protocol.

Here, we define scales then take design step two and add your rating scales to your matrix of capabilities. We also consider how our practitioners deal with the issue of perceived rating bias in three-, four- or five-point scales, and a preference for five-point over other scales.

Scales defined

A *rating*-scale-matrix-approach may use a *numeric scoring description* against each capability row on your spreadsheet. These may combine representative numbers with their text-based explanations. These indicate how far the organization is progressed on each capability on the y-axis based on the evidence represented by the capability description.

The better, clearer and more fulsome the information in the capability cell on the x-axis, the more robust and accurate the rating. In this way, the rating score makes sense and may be thought of as a milestone in project management parlance. This method also leaves lots of column space to the right-hand side to add future advanced features (such as target ratings over future years, or cross-walk references to other codes or sources of desired capabilities).

Design step two: rating your scales

Table 5.2 shows one simple rating approach. Enter a date for the latest rating. Rate each capability with a current score between 0 and 4. The numbers 0–4 represent five-point scales that are typical in the market (also called Likert scales). These can be subtotalled (sub-index) and given a percentage completion score for each module, then an overall maturity score (total index).

TABLE 5.2 Design step two: illustrative example adding scales

XYZ Risk Maturity Index – Confidential

1. Risk assessment: risks are identified, analysed and evaluated against objectives and within an established context before treatment.	**Current Rating mm/dd/yyyy**		
1.1 **Identification**. *Description ...*	0		
1.2 **Analysis**. *Description ...*	1		
1.3 **Evaluation**. *Description ...*	1		
module-index	17%		
2. Module Title: Description			
2.1 ***Capability title.*** *Capability description ...*	0		
2.2 ***Capability title.*** *Capability description ...*	1		
module-index	13%		
3. Module Title: Description			
3.1 ***Capability title.*** *Capability description ...*	0		
3.2 ***Capability title.*** *Capability description ...*	0		
3.3 ***Capability title.*** *Capability description ...*	3		
3.4 ***Capability title.*** *Capability description ...*	1		
module-index	25%		
Overall Risk Maturity Index	19%		

How To Score Rationale for each Scale:
0 = Nil. Nil or not started, no evidence of described capability.
1 = Starting. Started, on capability or evidence of capability intent.
2 = Partly. Partly in place, some evidence of capability.
3 = Largely. Largely in place, substantial evidence of capability.
4 = Fully. Fully in place, all evidence of capability.

Enter rating title and date

Enter score on scale from 0 to 4

Rate each Capability from 0 to 4 then score by module and overall

Enter scoring scales and their meaning

The trick here is to ensure that the five-point scales are given clear text descriptions so that the assessor can stay true to a common scoring system. Experienced practitioners know that it is very easy for assessors to mentally 'shortcut' the rating system and allow their own personal 'optimism bias' or other bias or 'gut-feel' to creep in. This tends to happen either because of natural time-delays breaking up the assessment over an elapsed period, or just human error, frailty and subjective judgement. This is one of the key causes of inaccurate assessments. This is why the text descriptions describing each scale are so important to your tailoring.

Practitioner Chris considers rating bias in three-, four- or five-point scales and goes with four-point

Chris's building company and staff like to keep things simple. Chris was not up with all the technical risk literature but was interested in using rating scales that suited his type of staff as well as to ensure his assessments were simple but as accurate as possible. He heard from ERM-experienced risk managers at a local risk institute event that whilst a five-point scale is very popular, a good practitioner needed to be on guard for a possible bias in scoring to the middle score of '3' if the scorers were risk-naive or risk-immature. Chris weighed up that a five-point scale was probably too 'technical' and complicated for his staff and culture. He heard that a three-point scale could be worse still for scorer bias to 'scoring in the middle'. So Chris decided to start off with a four-point scale for perhaps less-biased assessment, as it seemed the easiest for his staff to use.

The next step is to amplify your scoring index further to improve how robust it is. The 'How To Score...' bottom section in Table 5.2 represents a short summary approach to rating scales; however, it begs fuller guidance descriptions that lend themselves to more accurate assessment. One useful and readily available guidance for the five-scale rating is HB158:2010. This is a joint publication of the IIA Research Foundation, IIA-Australia and Standards Australia that aims to deliver assurance based on *ISO 31000:2009 Risk Management – Principles and Guidelines*. It is an internationally accepted and respected five-point rating scale. Refer to HB158 for a more extensive discussion of these and other issues. Here is a summary of their recommended scales:

1 None: very little or no compliance with the requirement in any way.
2 Very little: only limited compliance with the requirement. Management supports the intent, but compliance in practice is poor.
3 Some: limited compliance with element statement. Certainly agree with the intent, but limited compliance in practice.
4 Good: management completely subscribes to the intent, but there is partially complete compliance in practice.
5 Complete: absolute compliance with the element statement – in intent and in practice – at all times and in all places.

HB158 and others like it are examples of a style of one type of scale that may be termed a *multi-point numeric scale*. These are popular because they lend themselves to more robust qualitative capability content, clearly justifying its scale rating by 'bottom-up' credibility. It also encourages measurement by supporting excellent tracking from a quantitative baseline to %-progress against current status and targeted improvements.

Practitioner Asha changes from four to five tailored rating scales

Asha had aligned her organization operating model to that for her risk function and had now designed her set of capabilities around process, people and technology modules. When it came to rating scales to rate these capabilities on her model she pondered her prior experience. A past boss preferred to use a four-point scale for the maturity model but this produced overall scores that seemed overoptimistic to Asha. She felt that most responders had a bias to scoring '1' over '0' on the four-point scales, as few wanted to admit that the organization was doing absolutely nothing.

Asha now finds that her risk owners in her current recruiting-firm culture are mainly 'touchy-feely-types' who will debate endlessly about nuances and differences (such as that between '0=Nil' or '1=Partly' in place). She knows that the root cause of this is that they have so little guidance.

Asha wants to change to five-scale to give her assessors more guidance. She wants more confidence in the new robust scores they will generate. She wants to reduce any optimism bias and give her overall score more granularity. She wants to tailor her own 'How to Score Rationale' a little more to her own firm. She knows she needs to give her risk owners lots of guidance so they will use one set of consistent scales.

So Asha chooses to adapt and amplify the HB158 five scales. Prior to this, she had checked out a number of alternative scales sources such as ISO-IEC 15504, Marsh, HR-sector Capability-to-Competencies, Projects, COBIT4.1 and the Protiviti Six ERM Infrastructure Elements. But she prefers HB158 and eventually tailors her own ratings-scale descriptions from a bare one-liner to a half-page description for each of the five scales. Each had a common format of: short descriptor, percentage, description, then an example – this being a policy.

Asha is satisfied that her detailed five-scale ratings are more tailored to her organization. They appear in Table 5.3. The alternative scales she researched before deciding on HB158 can be seen later in this chapter in Table 5.5.

TABLE 5.3 Asha's detailed and tailored five-point scales

XYZ Risk Maturity Model

How to Score Rationale for each Scale:	Description	Example
0 = Nil.	Non-existent, nothing in-place, achieved, in-effect (0%) or known. No capability. Unaware or no recognition of need. Not part of culture or mission.	Policy X not in current management mindset.
1 = Starting.	Starting to put in-place, achieve or in-effect (say 0–<30%). Insignificant, limited or starting capability as intent not action. Management mandate or some recognition of intent and need may exist but still lacks engagement or execution. Approach is ad hoc, disorganized, without communication or monitoring. People unaware of responsibilities.	Policy X still being planned or written before approval.

TABLE 5.3 *Continued*

How to Score Rationale for each Scale:	Description	Example
2 = Partly.	Partially in-place, achieved or in-effect (say 30–<60%). Capability exercised to some extent so as to create/protect value. Practices/controls are in place but are not documented. Mandate backed by commitment evidenced by reinforcement practices by management. Operation dependent on knowledge and motivation of individuals. Effectiveness not adequately evaluated. Many practice/control weaknesses exist and are not adequately addressed; the impact can be severe. Management actions to resolve practice/control issues are not prioritized or consistent. People aware in-part of their responsibilities.	Policy X approved in writing or informally communicated by management. Now in early stages of being introduced as a business process with awareness/training etc so people have the knowledge and experience to perform the process.
3 = Largely.	Largely in-place, achieved or in-effect (say >60–<90%). Capability effectively practised or with proficiency, which creates/protects value. There is a largely effective enterprise-wide risk management practice and internal control environment. People aware and largely discharge their responsibilities.	Now in latter stages of being integrated by aware/trained/capable people with evidence of implementation by management for informed decision making (eg reports providing management with the right information at the right time and/or methodologies that adequately analyse data and information).

TABLE 5.3 *Continued*

How to Score Rationale for each Scale:	Description	Example
4 = Fully.	Fully in-place, achieved or in-effect (say > 90%) at all times in all places. Capability practised towards the optimum or serves as model for others so as to create/protect value. People fully aware, trained where appropriate and discharge their responsibilities as an integrated part of the way they work and make decisions. Some use of technology applied appropriately to automate practices/controls to gain efficiencies or reduce cost or duplication. Management checks and balances in place so as to continuously improve.	Policy X fully integrated and continuously improved (where appropriate) with systems and information to meet tomorrow's needs such that practices (and internal controls) are monitored, measured, reported and fed-back so management is confident that they are effective and efficient.

Levels as a component of a maturity model

Now that we have domain, capabilities and scales under way, let us turn to design considerations for risk maturity *levels* – their meaning/naming, purpose, tailoring, qualities, structure and examples. Here, we define maturity levels, consider how to tailor them, then undertake the final design step – step three – by rating your levels. We add how to consider inevitable maturity change in terms of progression and regression and stasis.

Levels defined

Rated capabilities that are ready to denote your risk maturity levels need to carry appropriate names. Levels are also known as grades, generations, phases or labels. Levels indicate the evolution of development stages in the progression (or stasis or regression) of overall organization-wide capability maturity. Invariably, this progression is from some form of 'lower to higher' maturity.

Levels typically have a *name label*. Labels act as a convenient short-descriptor or title that managers and decision-makers will regularly use when they say 'My organization is at an <*Early or X*> maturity level.' It acts as a positioning reflecting on the organization brand and reputation, so labelling or naming your levels should not be underestimated. Inappropriate naming may offend stakeholders.

Giving a level a label or title helps communicate the concept in the everyday, but a longer description of each level is required when assessing. This gives meaning to that level that otherwise may be misinterpreted during rating or may not be obvious to a reporting audience (especially a board or auditor). One technique to arrive at this is to scan your list of detailed capabilities, summarize key words from the list and then expound on each. For example, refer to Figure 5.2 (EY's leading practices): if you had a list of capabilities like the ones in the box titled 'Optimize risk management functions' it would be easy to come to a level called optimize, which can be expounded into a fuller level description.

Tailoring levels to the organization

The name labels and rationales chosen for your levels should be *tailored* to your organization as much as possible. They need to make sense to your staff and stakeholders. The name chosen may be very important for how it positions and communicates your ERM programme. They should fit your business drivers and culture so they are easy to communicate and recall for your people. This improves buy-in.

If you scan ahead to Table 5.9 on page 221 you will find a sample number of maturity level names from our directory models that reinforce the importance of level naming. Here are three examples. The *2012 Lederman/GARP* model six ascending levels being: [Record-keeping > Substandard > In development > Essential > Proactive > Transformational] not only describe the content inside their model for the record-keeping within an organization but the change strategy message they wanted to flag to their industry. The *Elliott Jacques* organization consciousness maturity model has seven quite creative-sounding levels from [Quality] up to [Corporate prescience] which may suit an advertising agency but not a construction company. The *2003 BCCM* maturity levels use an athlete analogy: [Self-governed > Able to walk > Able to run > Fit runner > Integrated (sic) > Olympic runner]. This may suit a fitness business but not a pharmaceutical multinational.

Design step three: rating your levels

Table 5.4 'How to rate Levels...' row shows how you may now define your own set of tailored levels to our working sample model. Divide the 100% overall score into five blocks (percentiles) and assign an ascending maturity level to each block. If your score falls into that block that is the overall level you may label your organization. In other words, each of the five levels represents unweighted quintiles of the 100%-index for the overall score.

Be prepared to argue for or against alternative levels. Sometimes some board directors, top management, business unit heads or audit heads may not accept simple quintiles and want to apportion different-size score blocks to the levels (see ISO-IEC15504, for example). If so, more complex rationales need to be argued to support whatever these blocks represent. Our sample model deliberately avoids becoming complicated by assigning a level rating down to each capability or its module average or total score. Can you argue you are at a level five just because you reach that level on a partial basis via one capability, or even one out of several module scores?

Handling maturity change: progression and regression and stasis

You must anticipate future change now that you rate capabilities and have levels to aspire to. At one level, you will expect that the initial status assessments from an as-is current state to a to-be future state will change on reassessment after a time for each single capability.

At another level, changes in the model come in three broad forms: progression, stasis and regression. Recall here our earlier discussion in Chapter 1 about 'Misunderstanding 3: progression without regression or stasis'. Progression we have covered, but watch out for regression. Regression may occur and may be unavoidable in the case of external factors or internal factors such as restrategizing, reorganization, merger, acquisition or business exit/disposal. Stasis occurs regularly for certain capabilities or modules and may be a friend in terms of sustainably allowing time to re-gear, re-plan, resource and so forth. Working on cultural capabilities is most likely to be an arduous long-term incremental reiterative process with long periods of stasis and some regression à la 'one step backwards, two forward'.

In terms of progression, it is safer to aim small and slow. Avoid moving up across all capabilities in one go as this is typically unrealistic. Stagger your progress, taking into account the risk strategy and risk management plan resource availability, alongside organization objectives, context and

TABLE 5.4 Design step three: illustrative example adding maturity levels and recommendations to improve

XYZ Risk Maturity Index – Confidential

1. Risk Assessment: Risks are identified, analysed and evaluated against objectives and within an established context before treatment.	**Current Rating mm/dd/yyyy**	**Evidence**	**Target Rating Yr+1**	**Target Rating Yr+2**	**Target Rating Yr+3**	**Target Rating Yr+4**	**Recomm-endations for Yr+1**
1.1 Identification. *Description ...*	0	bullet pts	3	3	4	4	bullet pts
1.2 Evaluation. *Description ...*	1	bullet pts	2	3	4	4	bullet pts
1.3 Evaluation. *Description ...*	1	bullet pts	1	3	3	3	bullet pts
module-index	17%						
2. Module Title: Description							
2.1 *Capability title. Capability description ...*	0	bullet pts	1	2	3	3	bullet pts
2.2 *Capability title. Capability description ...*	1	bullet pts	1	1	2	2	bullet pts
module-index	8%						
3. Module Title: Description							
3.1 *Capability title. Capability description ...*	0	bullet pts	0	1	1	1	bullet pts
3.2 *Capability title. Capability description ...*	0	bullet pts	0	0	0	0	bullet pts
3.3 *Capability title. Capability description ...*	3	bullet pts	2	2	3	3	bullet pts
3.4 *Capability title. Capability description ...*	1	bullet pts	2	1	1	1	bullet pts
module-index	33%						
overall maturity index	19%		36%	55%	67%	67%	
target maturity level	Level 1		Level 2	Level 3	Level 4	Level 4	

Regression

How to rate Levels by Overall Risk Maturity Index:

Levels rationale

80–100%	Level 5
60–79%	Level 4
40–59%	Level 3
20–39%	Level 2
0–19%	Level 1

How To Score Rationale for each Scale:
0 = Nil. Nil or not started, no evidence of described capability.
1 = Starting. Started on capability or evidence of capability intent.
2 = Partly. Partly in place, some evidence of capability.
3 = Largely. Largely in place, substantial evidence of capability.

risk profiles. Aim to move up only some capabilities over stages by improving their ratings from as-is to a to-be target over a specified budgeted period. Start modestly and only move in 'digestible-to-organization' chunks that can be integrated into existing management systems and processes.

Be realistic and add some stretch targets when ready. As you gain experience or maturity, you can aim to improve for one module and/or level over another, or by a changing mix of capabilities and the ratings you may need to justify the to-be level. Sustainable steady improvements are normally better than big wins or a big-bang approach. If a big bang fails, it may erode sponsorship and morale.

Summary

Congratulations, you have now finished your three-step process to design your own risk maturity model. You can now move on to enhancing your model by considering several alternative design formats and other ways to tailor your model for an even better fit-to-organization.

Alternative design formats

Now that you have enough to get started there are some handy tips and some interesting optional design alternative formats to the simple working model we have been building so far. Are there many alternatives? Yes. Are they all useful? Depends how you approach tailoring fit to your organization.

Here, we look at some differing design formats for the rating scales and levels for your risk maturity model that move beyond the simple spreadsheet format we have used to arrive at Table 5.4. We look at some advantages and disadvantages of these formats, including: capability completion, process-centric capability, process-centric, scale formats as four-point and percentiles, text-in-box, text page-book format, questionnaire – posed statement, questionnaire. We also consider approaches to both scales and levels using historical and modern examples and choosing the right amount of levels.

We blend in some real company examples to our tips and discussions. We reproduce extracts from the SCRLC 'text-in-box' and the HM Treasury text page-book formatted models. We also blend in differing perspectives from our practitioners. Alan and Chris prefer four-point weighted scales. Asha, on the other hand, prefers five-point scales to rate a capability completion-style format.

Capability completion format

The format you have designed until now to arrive at Table 5.4 is called a *capability completion* format because the assessors can rate the evidence of how complete the capability is in place that they collect during their assessment, so that they can give an overall determination of the organization's capabilities for delivering effective risk management. It draws its strength and starts its assessments from a milestone-style full statement of the capabilities required. This starts the assessor in one correct mental space as to a detailed 'what good looks like'. Each capability typically involves a unique number and a title followed by a detailed multi-sentence capability description explaining the title. In conjunction with robust scale descriptions (akin to the HB158 example), the *capability completion* format aims to assist the assessor with the richest and most fulsome content needed. In this way, the assessor may enter the most robust evidence and then make the effective recommendations in terms of the gap-improvements in capability required over time.

Process-centric capability format

For some, a simple start-strategy may be to be process-centric. That is, agree a small set of the core risk management-related processes and just focus on process maturity. Often your internal audit team may help here.

Two related templates for adopting this method are found in Figure 5.3 and Figure 5.4. See Figure 5.3 for one method of identifying which risk management capabilities are required to make the related processes effective.

Figure 5.4 indicates one set of criteria for assigning process maturity-level effectiveness that may then be averaged up to rate the overall process or macro-process.

Scale formats as four-point and percentiles

Our Table 5.3 uses a five-point scale and Asha may be keen on this scale but a *four-point numeric* rating scale is certainly a useful and popular alternative, as chosen previously by Chris. The largest ERM consulting practice globally by number of dedicated ERM consultants and number of projects (Marsh Risk Consulting) uses four-point scales.

FIGURE 5.3 Sample high-level process map and owner

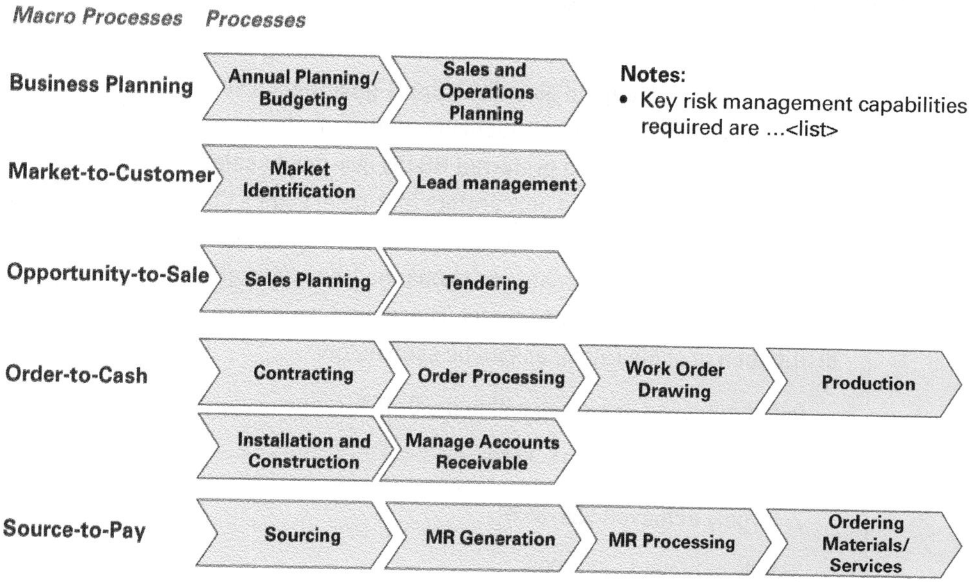

FIGURE 5.4 Process maturity-level-effectiveness-factors sample

Process characteristics	Observation
Clearly defined roles and responsibilities (intra-department)	◑
Clearly understood roles and responsibilities (cross-functional/ inter-department)	◑
Technology-supported	◕
Efficient process flow (eg no waste, duplication or re-work)	◕
Defined/monitored process KPIs	◔
Minimal person-dependency (ie processes/ documented business knowledge/decision rules	◔

○ **Does not exist or lowest maturity process** ◔ ◑ ◕ ● **Exists everywhere or high maturity process**

Practitioner Alan prefers four-point weighted scales

Alan, as internal auditor at a government-owned utility, liked the fact that ISO-IEC 15504 is accepted globally in the IT governance sector. We saw earlier how Chris and other proponents preferred a four-point scale for cultural reasons and Asha preferred HB158 five-point scales for their perceived quality. Alan not only prefers four-point scales ('the assessors cannot sit on any fence as there is no middle ratings scale') but he recommends to the ERM manager to change from unweighted to weighted quartiles for the risk maturity model. These produce a more bell-curved distribution of scale rating, as can be seen below:

0=not achieved, progress within the 0–15% range;

1=partially achieved >15–50%;

2=largely achieved >50–85%;

3=fully achieved >85–100%.

Scales – reference examples from history

Those interested in considering and comparing a range of existing scale alternatives may refer to Table 5.5. This table shows a selection of approaches to the use of scales since about the year 2000. Which are better suited to your organization? Choose between a large range that employs differing techniques or styles. These range from the simpler binary (two scales such as 'yes' versus 'no') or tertiary (three scales), to more developed scales such as those referenced in Table 5.5, being in an audit-style (general audit); scale of ERM progression (such as 2010 Marsh ERM); scale of resilience (2014 SCRLC); or scale of evidence-based completion (see 2008 ISO-IEC 15504).

For example, the HM Treasury 'Orange Book' scales drawing on origins in the popular EQFM excellence model targeted government agencies and is thus useful also for not-for-profits in general (HM Treasury, 2009). It combines a numeric scale of 1–5 tied to a one-word scale title from 'No evidence' to 'Excellent'. This, in turn, is tied to a more detailed but succinct text description. See Table 5.6.

TABLE 5.5 Sample history of risk maturity nominal scales used for rating

Model	Technique	Point 1	Point 2	Point 3	Point 4	Point 5
19?? General	Binary	Yes	No			
19?? General	Tertiary+	Yes	No	Maybe	Not Applicable	etc
19?? General projects	Completion	0=Nil	1=Partly	2=Largely	3=Fully	
19?? General audit	Compliance %	0=Poor	1=Inadequate	2=Satisfactory	3=Exemplary compliance	
? General	Practice quality	Existent	Basic	Reasonably well developed	Well developed	Best Practice
? HR competency	Competency HR	Limited	Basic	Proficient	Advanced	
? HR general	Capability mastery	Limited, no capability	Intent but not yet exercised or evidenced	Capability exercised with some success	Capability effectively practised	Mastery or proficiency, model for others
20?? COBIT IT 4.1	Process optimized %	Non-existent	Repeatable but intuitive	Defined process	Managed and measurable	Optimized enterprise-wide
200? Marsh ERM	Formality	Not present	Conceptually present	Formally under development	Formally implemented	
2004 HM Treasury	Outcome evidence %	Not clear	Limited	Significant	Very significant	Marked

TABLE 5.5 *Continued*

Model	Technique	Point 1	Point 2	Point 3	Point 4	Point 5
2008 ISO-IEC 15504	Achievement weighted %	0=Not achieved, say progress at 0 – 15%	1=Partially achieved >15%–50%	2=Largely achieved >50–85%	3=Fully achieved >85–100%	
2009 EY	Practice degree	1=Established practices		3=Embedded practices		5=Enhanced practices
2011 Hopkinson	Project completion	Not in use, no confidence or involvement	Little in-use, confidence, involvement or informed. Suppressed or withheld	Partly in-use, informed or confident etc	Policy, procedures, reports or agreements written, visible or largely confident etc	Approved, aligned, in-practice or formalized, full confidence and engagement etc
2012 Benchmarker™	Capability evidence %	0 Nil	1 Starting	2 Partial	3 Largely	4 Fully
2012 S&P	ERM positivity	Negative	Neutral	Positive		
2014 NSW Treasury	ERM 'maturity'	Low	Inconsistent	Consistent	Fully addressed	
2014 SCRLC	Resilience level	Reactive	Aware	Proactive	Integrated	Resilient

TABLE 5.6 HM Treasury scales

Summary of Progress				
Level 1 ☐	Level 2 ☐	Level 3 ☐	Level 4 ☐	Level 5 ☐
No evidence	Satisfactory	Good	Very good	Excellent
No clear evidence of improved outcomes.	Limited evidence of improved outcome performance consistent with improved risk management.	Clear evidence of significant improvements in outcome performance demonstrated by measures including, where relevant, stakeholders' perceptions.	Clear evidence of very significantly improved delivery of outcomes and showing positive and sustained improvement.	Excellent evidence of improved delivery of outcomes which compares favourably with other organizations employing best practices.

SOURCE: HM Treasury (2009). Permission kindly granted

Text page-book format

The HM Treasury 'Orange Book' maturity model is not in a spreadsheet format but is an example of an older-style *text page-book* format. The scales above appear at the top of each of the seven capabilities described in the model. A fill-in evidence section follows this with about two text pages of evidence-based questions to assist the evidence section. These pages aggregate to a booklet. This format obviously lends itself to those who prefer to avoid software or spreadsheet models but hampers the use of metrics for tracking.

The advantage of this format is that the assessor responses are usually of a higher quality. The scales at the top of each capability are underpinned by robust and full capability content immediately below it, for quick reference. These scales result in a higher likelihood of consistent evaluation and evidence gathering across the whole model, compared with some of the formats we shall see following. An extract for the last of the seven capabilities described in the above model follows in full (HM Treasury, 2009):

- Successful delivery?
  - Better public services (delivery to meet commitments; eg to quality, coverage, timeliness, with few errors etc; potential disruptions to delivery anticipated and avoided/addressed/mitigated etc)?
  - Sustained improvements in services (continuing improvement over time taking account of stakeholder and public views, lessons learned, government priorities and changing circumstances to ensure meet (and continue to meet) public expectations)?
  - Fewer negative, more positive press reports on delivery?
  - Achievement of business objectives (including intermediate targets, milestones, review criteria etc)?
  - Project success?
  - Programmes and projects deliver as intended (eg good, effective IT systems; intermediate measures, eg traffic lights at 'Gateway' review – may include managing 'red' to 'green'; meeting intermediate targets for delivery of project elements or stages etc)?
  - Risk management assessment framework: a tool for departments?
  - Programmes and projects delivered to time and budget (eg effective IT systems by due date and cost; meeting intermediate milestones for cost and time on profile for project progress; etc)?
  - Few significant failures consistent with risk appetite/tolerance?
  - PSA target achievement (including interim measures, eg traffic light status, milestones, trend analysis)?
  - Few NAO reports citing failures of risk management?
  - Few press reports commenting on failures that relate to failures of risk management?
- Meeting planned financial outcomes?
  - Improved value for money?
  - Delivery within budget (eg fewer calls on reserves arising from inadequate risk management)?
  - Effective control of fraud (eg evidence of less fraud or trend towards less fraud – both fewer instances and reduced size of loss; may involve more fraud identified as an initial phase of better control)?
  - Effective cash management?

- Effective management of risks to the public?
  - Improved public understanding of risks and risk management (eg as assessed by survey results; fewer demands for 'zero' risk; understanding of need for considered and proportionate action in response to risk issues; fewer demands for 'instant' action to increase controls in response to accidents/incidents etc)?
  - Increased public confidence that risks are well managed?
  - Increased trust in government/department risk-based decisions?
  - Better achievement of targets for risks to the public?
  - Improved responsibility by the public in risk matters (eg more willingness to act proactively in response to risk issues; fewer demands for risk-averse action by government; more willingness to accept responsibility where public can control the risk)?
  - Greater satisfaction from the public with the way risks are handled (eg results of surveys; few complaints, protests etc, more positive comments, support for actions etc)?
- Maintenance of high reputation for the organization?
  - Attract positive third-party comments (eg press)?
  - Attract positive public comments (eg surveys, communications on departmental issues, comments to the press etc)?
  - Attract positive comment from staff, partners, stakeholders, professional and other bodies of repute (eg stakeholder surveys, staff surveys, project/programmed reviews, publications in magazines etc).

Text-in-box format

One popular variation on the preceding formats is the *text-in-box* format, or *check-the-text-box* format. Capabilities on the y-axis rows are given short titles and then rated by selecting the best short text-description occupying specific cells against each row. Super-imposed line-graphs or dot-points can be added to indicate current versus target/future status 'rating'. This format lends itself to being transposed from spreadsheets into PowerPoint slides.

Table 5.7 is a sample extract in spreadsheet matrix format for the supply-chain domain called the SCRLC Supply Chain Risk Maturity Model

TABLE 5.7 SCRLC supply chain risk maturity model extract as template

Cate-gory	Sub-category	Your Rating	Rating Notes	Stage 1 Reactive	Stage 2 Aware	Stage 3 Proactive	Stage 4 Integrated	Stage 5 Resilient
1. Leadership	**1A. Executive Leadership**	1	Insert comments about your rating in this space	No supply chain risk management leadership defined.	Functional managers have responsibility for leading risk management within their domain.	SCRM has senior management support, but leadership is found at functional levels.	SCRM has senior management leadership functionally defined and is coordinated across functions.	SCRM has a senior management defined leadership role and active engagement of management is enterprise-wide.
	1B. Line/ Functional Leadership	2		Individuals assume responsibility when an event is triggered.	SCRM activities are led by affected pre-designated functional managers.	SCRM activities are coordinated through supply chain manager(s) with focus on management within the functions.	SCRM activities are led by a collaborative team of functional managers with focus on internal management including critical supply chain partners.	SCRM is coordinated across the enterprise including multi-tier critical supply chain partners with defined roles and responsibilities.
	1C. Governance	3		No supply chain risk management framework.	Functional managers use risk management frameworks appropriate for their function with no cross-function coordination.	SCRM is coordinated across functional units with defined roles of key internal supply chain stakeholders.	SCRM is governed by a cross-functional well-defined framework including critical supply chain partners.	Supply chain risk management framework is well defined across the enterprise including multi-tier critical supply chain partners.

1. Leadership	**1D. Resources & Commitment**	**4**		No designated supply chain risk management resources.	SCRM resources are identified within functional units and risk management is considered a collateral duty.	SCRM resources designated for functional units. Accountability and resource allocation within functional level.	SCRM has committed resources with well-defined roles and responsibilities on a cross-functional level and considering critical supply chain partners.	SCRM is embedded within the organization's culture and seen as a value-added activity with appropriate resources committed. Enterprise-wide accountability and resource allocation considered as part of regular fiscal allocations.
	1E. Programme Communication	**5**		No defined internal or external SCRM communication.	Informal SCRM communication occur within the functional units.	Formal SCRM communications occur within functional units. Supply chain partner communications occur as they relate to individual functions.	Integrated SCRM communications and consultation across functional units and includes critical supply chain partners.	Enterprise-wide communication and consultation includes multi-tier critical supply chain partners.

(SCRLC, 2014) shown here with the kind permission of the Board of the Supply Chain Risk Leadership Council of the United States. Also refer to our directory of models entry in Chapter 3, Table 3.72.

The advantages of this format are that it has a certain logic as it progresses up a curve of capability and it lends itself to PowerPoint presentations to management and PowerPoint-based workshops. The disadvantages with this format are it can be time-consuming and that assessors are always forced to 'agree' with the wording of one cell or another. This in practice makes for 'fuzzy' or 'gut-feel' guessed ratings and overcompensation with text insertions in the current 'Evidence' column cell.

Practitioner Megan prefers capability completion over text-in-box format

Megan from the NGO found that many of the risk maturity models she researched and found from our directory in Chapter 3 were in text-in-box formats. She had a frustrating experience with many of these. Some ran up to an attention-sapping n=100 capabilities or more, multiplied by five cells each, thereby totalling over 500 selections. This was too exhausting; by the time she got to the end of them she felt that the overall score was artificial and not truly reflective of her organization. She found too many of the descriptions-in-a-box 'forced', inappropriate or she intuitively had a 'better' cell description in her mind that was not on offer, or, something in-between two of the forced cells. For example, when she looked at the 'Governance' row of boxes in Table 5.7 she was torn as she felt her NGO was parts of all three middle-box choices, as shown in Table 5.8:

TABLE 5.8 SCRLC three cells

Functional managers use risk management frameworks appropriate for their function with no cross-function coordination.	SCRM is coordinated across functional units with defined roles of key internal supply chain stakeholders.	SCRM is governed by a cross-functional well-defined framework including critical supply chain partners.

She therefore preferred the models using a *capability completion* format. These gave her ample space and unforced freedom to particularize her assessment notes in the spaces allowed in these formats on current versus targeted capability description. In fact, she found that the format lent itself to easier tailoring by inviting the use of the model capability descriptions as wording prompts to 'cut-and-paste-and-tailor' across to the current and future status cells.

Questionnaire – posed statement format

A *posed statement* format is effectively a questionnaire that poses statements requiring an assessor to agree along a pole of scales. The scales represent the strength of your agreement with the statement. These are delivered in either .doc or .xls spreadsheet formats. For example, '*Your organization always acknowledges the potential upside in ERM assessment approaches and tools. Do you: Strongly Disagree, Disagree, Neither Disagree nor Agree, Agree, Strongly Agree, Don't Know*'.

The disadvantage with this format is that it trades-off ease of use for robustness as assessors often give 'fuzzy' or gut-feel' guesses in response. This is because, first, the capability is not detailed enough to warrant one clear 'right' answer for each assessor. Second, their brevity means they do not offer enough clear multiple attributes of the capability to note evidences and gaps for future improvement. In the above example, one may 'Strongly Disagree' with the 'always' attribute and 'Strongly Agree' for the 'approaches' attribute but not for the 'tools' attribute, so does one rate either of the two, or in-between at 'Agree', perhaps? Such uncertainty undermines user confidence in the tool.

Questionnaire formats

A common alternative to the matrix format is the *questionnaire/multiple-choice answer* format. A list of text questions is rated by choosing the most appropriate of a number of options or multiple-choices.

This format leverages a widespread workplace familiarity with questionnaires. The advantages of this format can be prose flow, readability and lighter content. The disadvantages can be light content and too-prescriptive content in that you can only reply within the confines of the answer options framed for you. These may result in the assessor refusing to buy in to the given answers, or confusion where more than one correct answer is perceived to a question. Moreover, there is often poor transparency as to how this model then aggregates the numerous answers and ascribes your organization to one or other maturity level.

Levels – considering historical examples for quantity and usage

Table 5.9 is a sample guide to a history of multi-domain levels as labels since 1988. You may reference these to inspire your own level labels tailored to your risk maturity model.

Historically, levels range from two to seven in number. By far the most popular number is five, followed by six, with a few above or below that range. The level labels represent many copies or spin-offs from the original SEI CMM five, but some have been quite tailored to their domain.

It is wise to avoid indiscriminately using level labels, titles and/or descriptions drawn from the software engineering origins for capability models. These are typically akin to: 'ad hoc, defined, implemented, standardized and optimized'. These sort of level labels have been overcopied in the risk maturity domains. These probably suit IT vendors and their implementer-consultant firms more than your organization. ERM is far more than a software or series of process capabilities. Rote copying for your organization is anathema to good tailoring.

More importantly, you may decide that SEI CMM-type levels have little in common with how your organization communicates. Some or most of your capabilities may have little to do with process 'repeatability', 'standardization' or will need to be 'managed' earlier than a level four and so forth.

Levels – taking a look at some modern examples

Thought-leader Norman Marks prefers five ERM maturity levels (Marks, 2011; 2015). Whilst the labels are partly SEI CMM-style, the descriptions reveal how you can tailor your descriptions away from the predecessors. Marks synthesized these from multiple sources, including the Chelan County Public Utility District, Washington. It is summarized below in ascending order:

1. *Ad hoc*: as in undocumented; in a state of dynamic change; depends on individual heroics.
2. *Preliminary*: as in risk-defined in different ways and managed in silos; and process discipline is unlikely to be rigorous.

TABLE 5.9 Sample history of risk maturity levels as labels

Model	Level 1	Level 2	Level 3	Level 4	Level 5	Level 6	Level 7
1988 Humphrey W.S. (2)	Initial	Repeatable	Defined	Managed	Optimizing		
198? Capability Maturity Model	Ad hoc	Defined	Implemented	Standardized	Optimized		
1994 Capability Maturity M.	Initial	Repeatable	Defined	Managed	Optimizing		
1997 Hillson ERM	Naive	Novice	Normalized	Natural			
1998-08 PMI OPM3®	1	2	3	4			
1998 SPICE>ISO-IEC15504	Incomplete	Performed	Managed	Established	Predictable	Optimizing	
2002 CMM SEI	Ad hoc	Repeatable	Defined	Managed	Optimizing		
2003 BCCM®	Self-governed	Able to walk	Able to run	Fit runner	Integrated	Olympic runner	
20?? Elliot Jacques	Quality	Service	Development	Strategic intent	Corporate citizenship	Corporate prescience	
20?? ISO-IEC 15504	Incomplete	Performed	Managed	Established	Predictable	Optimizing	
20?? IIA UK (1)	Risk naive	Aware	Defined	Managed	Enabled		
20?? ISACA RISK IT	Non-existent	Initial	Repeatable	Defined	Managed	Optimized	

TABLE 5.9 *Continued*

Model	Level 1	Level 2	Level 3	Level 4	Level 5	Level 6	Level 7
20?? ITI-Global.com RPMM	Ad hoc	Conventional	Managed	Initial	Mature	Life-cycle management	Simulation driven
2005? PMI OPM3®	Standardize	Measure	Control	Continually improve			
2006 Chapman	Initial	Basic	Standard	Advanced			
2006 Hopkinson	Naive	Novice	Normalized	Natural			
2006 RIMS	Non-existent	1 ad hoc	2 Initial	3 Repeatable	4 Managed	5 Leadership	
2006 OGC P3M3	Awareness	Repeatable	Defined	Managed	Optimized		
2007 TDWI BI	Pre-natal	Infant	Child	Teenager	Adult	Sage	
2008 Marsh	Undeveloped	Formalized	Established	Embedded	Optimized		
2008 ISO-IEC 15504 ex-SPICE	Immature	Performed	Managed	Established	Predictable	Optimizing	
2010 ALARM	Engaging	Happening	Working	Embedded	Driving		
2010 INSEAD Arguden	Based on definition	Scope	Implementation	Continuous improvement	Sustainability		

2011 Aon	Initial	Basic	Defined	Operational	Advanced
2011 EIU Economist	Reacting	Anticipating	Collaborating	Orchestrating	
2012 Marsh	Undeveloped	Formalized	Established	Embedded	Fully integrated
2012 Halliday, Steven	ERM unaware	ERM under investigation	ERM partial framework	ERM in place	ERM fully mature
2012 Pergler/McKinsey	Systemic risk reduction	Risk-return management	Risk as competitive advantage		
2012 Lederman/GARP	Sub-standard	In development	Essential	Proactive	Transformational
2012 Benchmarker™	Naive	Immature	Maturing	Mature	RiskSmart
2013 Monda ERMi	Ad hoc	Fractured	Organized	Coherent	Exemplary
2013 Aberdeen Group	Laggard bottom 30%	Average 50%	Best-in-class 20%		
2014 SCRLC	Reactionary	Awareness	Proactive	Integrated	Resilient

3 *Defined*: as in common risk assessment/response framework is in place; an organization-wide view of risk is provided to executive leadership; action plans are implemented in response to high-priority risks.

4 *Integrated*: as in risk management activities coordinated across business areas. Common risk management tools and processes used where appropriate, with enterprise-wide risk monitoring, measurement and reporting. Alternative responses analysed with scenario planning. Process metrics in place.

5 *Optimized*: as in risk discussion is embedded in strategic planning, capital allocation and other processes, and in daily decision-making. Early warning system to notify board and management to risks above established thresholds.

The Deloitte Risk Intelligent Maturity Model descriptions offer an alternative (Deloitte, 2010). Like the Marks example above, Deloitte moved away from SEI-style predecessors. These can be seen in Figure 5.5.

FIGURE 5.5 Deloitte stages of risk intelligence maturity

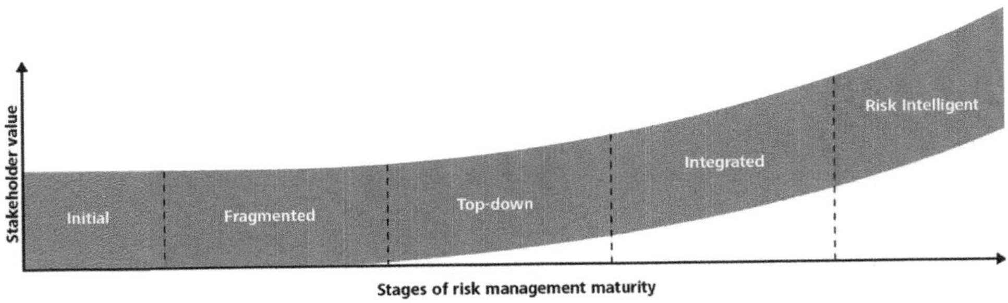

Representative attributes				
• Ad hoc/chaotic • Depends primarily on individual heroics, capabilities and verbal wisdom	• Risk is defined differently at different levels and in different parts of the organization • Risk is managed in silos • Limited focus on linkages between risks • Limited alignment of risk to strategies • Disparate monitoring and reporting functions	• Identified risk universe • Common risk assessment/response approach developed and adopted • Organization-wide risk assessment performed • Action plans implemented in response to high-priority risks • Communication of top strategic risks to the senior management team	• Risk management activities coordinated across business areas • Risk analysis tools developed and communicated • Enterprise risk monitoring, measuring and reporting • Scenario planning • Opportunity risks identified and exploited • Ongoing risk assessment processes	• Risk discussion embedded in strategic planning, capital allocation, product development, etc. • Early warning system to notify board and management to risks above established thresholds • Linkage to performance measures and incentives • Risk modelling

SOURCE: Reprinted with kind permission and Copyright © 2015 Deloitte International LLC

Levels – tip to avoid absolutes

It is wise to avoid loading your highest levels with *absolute* descriptions such as 'best global practice'. Comparative-based descriptions work better. Absolutes are difficult to define and sustain, are open to question by stakeholders and can become outdated. The reasons are many and include:

- the organization external environment will change, especially that for governance, risk and assurance;
- the organization internal environment may change, especially with board, CEO and management turnover increasing;
- disagreement by subject-matter experts (SMEs) as to what constitutes an absolute or best practice even within one country let alone a region or the globe;
- difficulty securing buy-in to absolutes by cynical board, CEO and management; à la, 'Oh no, not another "best practice" management mantra.'

We now turn to a real EGA company case study, which represents an example of one organization that treats their highest level 'Five Maturity Level' more as an aspirational goal than a finite or absolute achievement. Moreover, it doubles as an example of how internal and environment changes required schedule and target adjustment to their long-term risk maturity programme and the related risk management system.

CASE STUDY EGA risk maturity 2011–15 progression and regression

Emirates Global Aluminium PJSC ('EGA') sees the value in using a risk maturity model as a road map but not pushing it into absolutes or idealistic risk maturity terms. EGA was formed when the aluminium smelting assets of Dubai Aluminium PJSC (DUBAL), which was established in 1979, and Emirates Aluminium Company Ltd PJSC (EMAL), which was established in 2007, were brought together under a common umbrella. EGA, located in the United Arab Emirates, is one of the five largest primary aluminum producers in the world. Toby Shore, senior director of Group Treasury, Risk and Insurance, introduced a five-level risk maturity model in 2011 to the DUBAL enterprise risk management programme. It was adapted from his experience in Australia and in working with DUBAL's global risk advisor,

Willis. Toby preferred to move slowly in his targeted roll-out of an enterprise risk management framework and realistically set a target of moving 'from about a two-of-five level in 2011 to a three in 2013'. He prefers to self-improve EGA's capabilities that are tailored to their own internal business objectives rather than a fixed external benchmark or code. Toby believes that the highest level, five, may never be achievable nor desired by EGA and sees it as a more aspirational goal than a finite or absolute achievement.

Interestingly, the DUBAL merger with EMAL in 2014 has led to an overall regressed maturity level for EGA as a merged entity because of the increased size, complexity and operations of the combined group, which now included not only the two aluminium smelters but also a greenfield alumina refinery project in the UAE, a mining project in West Africa and a number of minority equity interests outside the UAE. Figure 5.6 shows the original maturity level targeting for a two-year period from 2011 for DUBAL (now extended). Figure 5.7 shows the structured extent of the ERM roll-out designed by Shore.

FIGURE 5.6 EGA maturity level

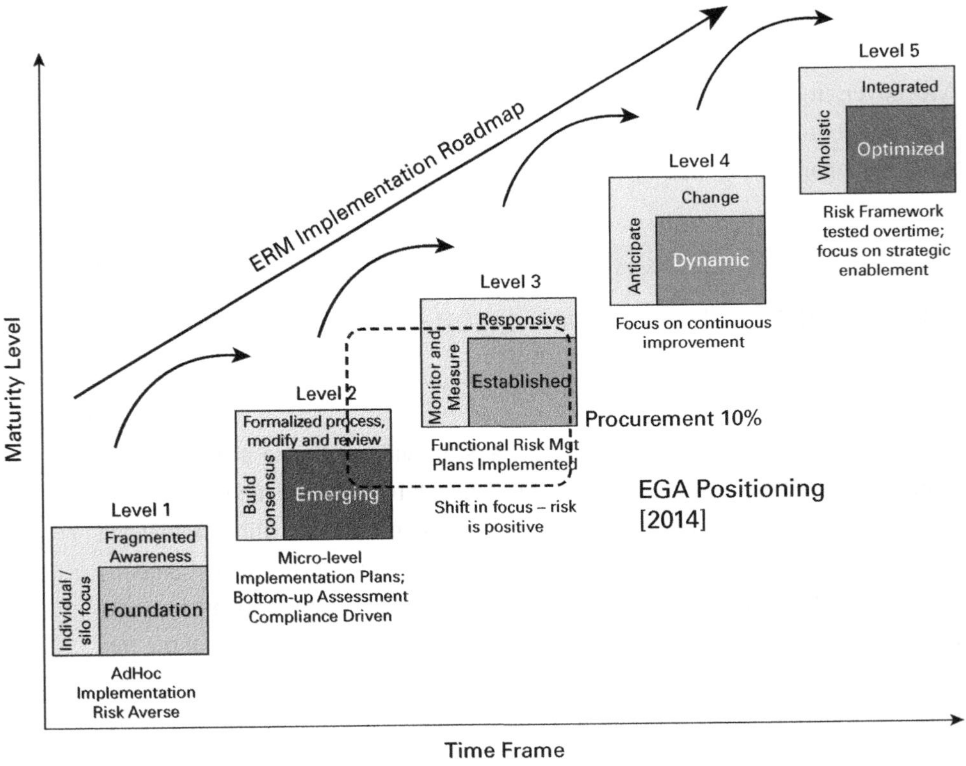

SOURCE: Adapted from Willis Group by EGA and reprinted with kind permission from EGA

FIGURE 5.7 EGA structured roll-out

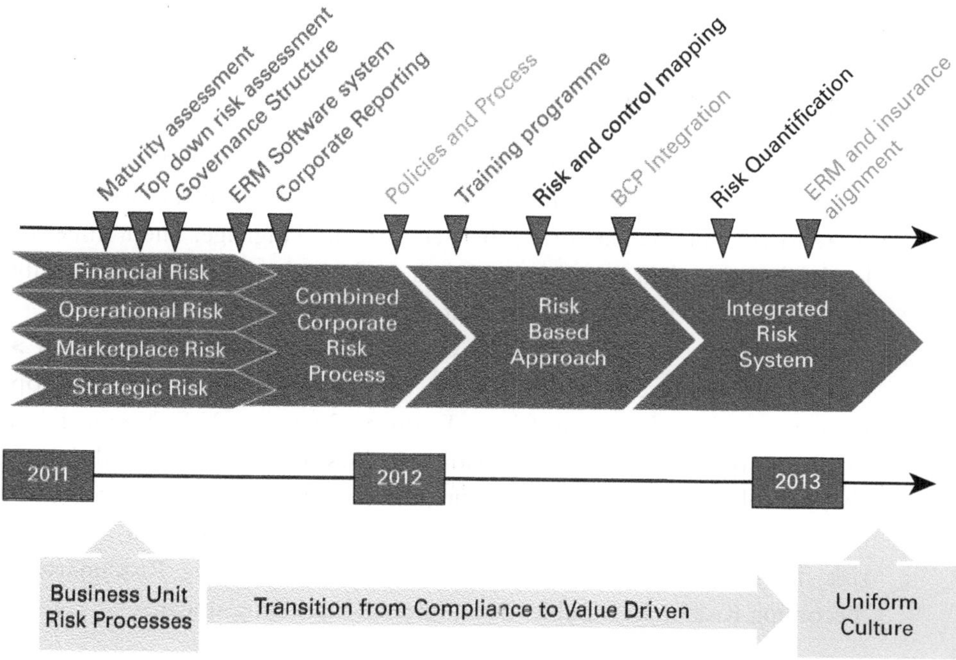

SOURCE: Reprinted with kind permission from EGA

Levels – choosing the right amount

The number of levels may not be as important as the type of label or name but it needs to be fit-to-organization. Three to four levels may have been typical of the 1990s but nowadays five to six are common, and even up to eight or more. Fewer levels, say four, may fit an early maturity organization where the need to KISS (keep it simple, stupid) is paramount. More than five levels may suit technical, sophisticated or mature organizations, or those wishing to add a 'world-class' top level (if supported by benchmarking evidence).

Some maxims do apply. If your preferred risk management model methodology is based on *self-improvement from a %-baseline rating* – then four or five levels are convenient. These make it easier to communicate to the lines of business as they allow for clean quartile or quintile grades, ie 1st quintile 0–20%, 2nd 21–40% etc. If it is based on *a 'top-down' non-detailed approach* – then the level titles are less important as they denote generalized evolved states more than true grades and are more suited to an 'intuitive' rating by the CRO or others. If it is based on *a 'bottom-up' detailed milestone approach* – then the level titles are more important as they denote real grades based on accurate, granular, specific or detailed rating criteria.

Levels – summary

In summary, choose progressive maturity level titles and descriptions tailored to your organization, avoiding absolutes. Maturity vocabulary has to make sense to your people, factoring their culture and language. The number of levels, the titles, their meanings and their evolved sequence should naturally flow and reflect evolved stages of maturity progression.

For example, I prefer to use [Novice > Immature > Maturing > Adult > RiskSmart] because it works for me with both line managers and top management/board (see near foot of Figure 5.12 on page 232). No one takes offence ('are you saying we are bad?'). It does not attract internal debate about absolutes and idealisms. Repeating the word *maturity* reinforces continual improvement on maturity capabilities to a moving goal-post of informed risk decision making and right risk taking (ie becoming RiskSmarter). 'Becoming RiskSmart' doubles as an internal marketing slogan.

Enhancements to the design of a maturity model

We now touch on four popular ways to enhance your risk maturity model: report types, targeting future improvements, weighting your capability assessments and employing a marketing slogan.

Enhancements by report types

There are many different ways to report your assessment or performance as generated from a risk maturity model. The pie chart, bar chart or spider chart reporting formats are probably the most popular ones in use. They are most often used to convey future as-is results versus to-be targets. The field is open, however, to the type of format your organization prefers.

As an example, the SCRLC model generates three styles of report, as shown in Figures 5.8–5.10 (SCRLC, 2014), which we reproduce with the kind permission of the Board of the Supply Chain Risk Leadership Council of the United States. Figure 5.8 is a candlestick chart, 5.9 is a bar-line chart and 5.10 is a radar chart.

FIGURE 5.8 SCRLC candlestick chart

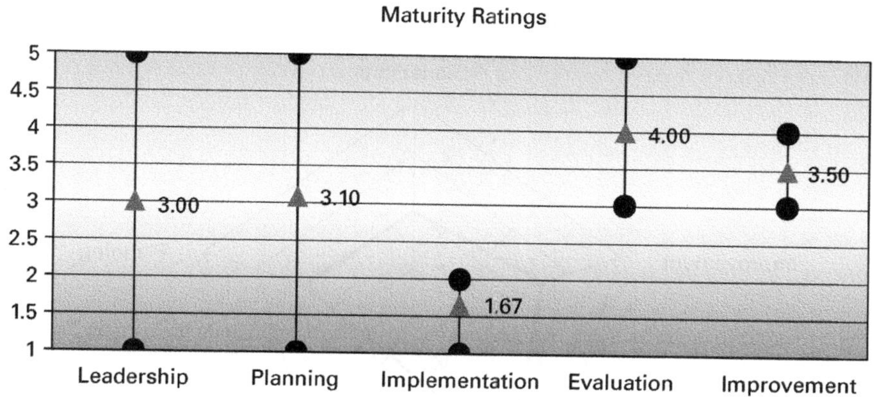

FIGURE 5.9 SCRLC report as bar-line chart

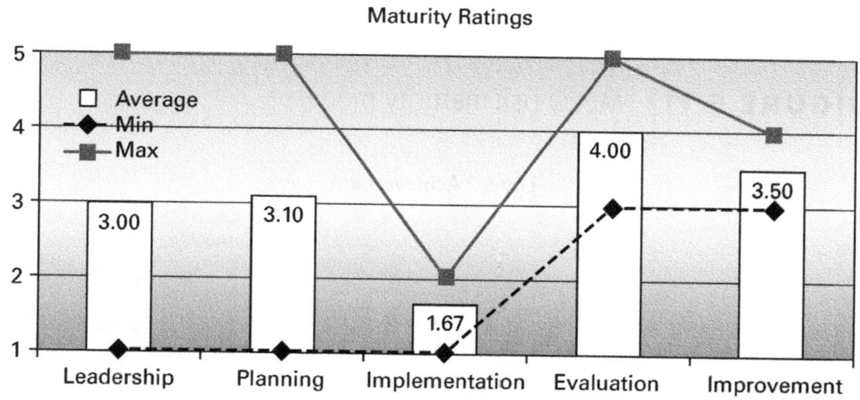

Another popular form of charting by Marsh and other firms is the 'slide-bar' chart. Figure 5.11 shows the MECO risk maturity model Level 2 Achievement on a bar chart. The MECO case study for a real-life Middle East oil company by Alexander Larsen is interesting (Fraser, Simkins and Narvaev, 2015). Larsen's team tailor-made their own risk maturity model specific to MECO and aligned to ISO 31000 over 2010–11. They used the same methodology not only to self-assess themselves but rate where 'leading' competitor and other oil and chemical businesses were on the maturity curve. They mapped this onto a five-maturity-tier graphic to back their case for an ERM programme to top management. They placed themselves at Formalized Maturity Level 2 Benchmark, way behind Statoil as the leader at the Optimized Maturity Level 5 ahead of a group at Embedded Level 4 (being Shell, Chevron,

FIGURE 5.10 SCRLC report as radar chart

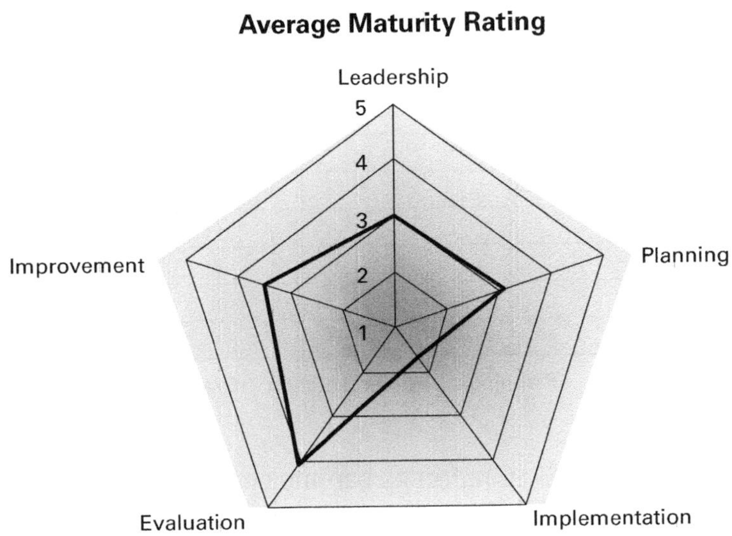

FIGURE 5.11 MECO risk maturity model

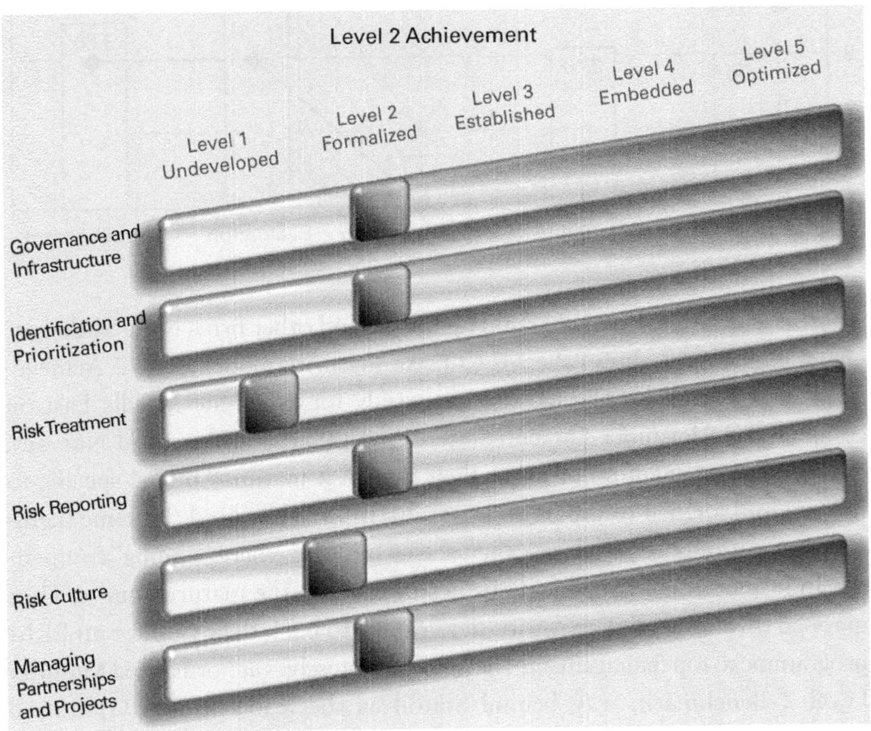

SOURCE: Reproduced with kind permission of Alexander Larsen formerly of MECO

GE Oil & Gas and SABIC). Figure 5.11 represents the type of report the risk officers at MECO presented to their executive committee. It presents where MECO risk maturity was starting from (baseline), being an average Level 2 Achievement on the 'risk maturity curve' within a range of Level 1 to 2. This figure was used in association with a similar five-tier graphic (not shown here) benchmarking MECO at Level 2 versus competitors at Levels 5 and 4 (Fraser, 2015).

One advantage of the 'slide-bar' style of graphic is that it reinforces to managers the several concepts underpinning risk maturity, in terms of its sensitivity to the change forces of progression, regression and stasis and that the maturity status across different capabilities will most likely be staggered rather than uniform at any point in time.

Enhancements by targeting future improvements

Risk maturity models are dynamic diagnostic tools. Most organizations will find themselves assessed at lower levels when starting out on the risk maturity journey. Rather than just rely on a one-off assessment it is better to think of that initial assessment as a starting point or 'baseline' for self-improvement of their capabilities staggered over time to realistic budgets, resources and schedules.

The idea is to realistically target self-improvements to future higher levels over target periods in a staggered way with a 'bottom-up' approach per capability. Self-improvements are usually measured over the long term in years (not months) and are refined, and fed into, an annual risk management plan. These higher levels need to avoid optimistic targets and represent realistic achievable targets over time with maybe some 'stretch' in the targets.

CASE STUDY INFRACO – example of long-term risk maturity reporting

This staggered future-targeted approach over time is demonstrated in Figure 5.12. This shows an example of multi-year targeting from a real company carrying the pseudonym INFRACO. The multi-year bar graph is produced from the Benchmarker™ risk maturity model. It depicts how the risk maturity model measures ERM effectiveness over time for INFRACO, including progression-stasis-regression levels staggered across various risk management system capability modules.

FIGURE 5.12 INFRACO Benchmarker™ multi-year bar chart

Measures ERM effectiveness improvement over time

Sample Risk Maturity Model for Organization	Pre	2012	2013	Re-org F2014	F2015
1. Sponsorship and Positioning: Board and Senior Management	11%	43%	47%	68%	81%
2. Managing the Risk Management Process: integrated	2%	21%	43%	21%	29%
3. Identification: to objectives and context	7%	21%	43%	60%	66%
4. Prioritization: focus time and resource	3%	21%	43%	31%	31%
5. Treatment: implement risk action	5%	21%	43%	29%	29%
6. Reporting: consistent, appropriate across silos	8%	21%	48%	36%	36%
7. Monitoring: continuous re effectiveness and efficiency	14%	25%	43%	14%	25%
8. Culture and Embedding: people capability and tools to embed	0%	18%	21%	13%	21%
9. Communication: continually consult and communicate	4%	10%	29%	15%	38%
10. Working with Counterparties: robust practices	0%	5%	18%	29%	56%
Rating Avg	6%	11%	40%	32%	40%

Desired Maturity Level and Rationale and Action:		*Score:*	*Rating:*
RiskSmart:	Embedded practice consistent with recommended practice. Monitoring and continuous improvement.	>79%	
Adult:	Observed practice consistent with recommended practice. Limited need for further development.	60-79%	
Maturing:	Good ability to demonstrate adherence to recommended practice. Opportunity for improvement.	40-59%	
Immature:	Material gap between current practice and recommended practice. Substantial opportunity for improvement.	20-39%	
Novice:	Starting off on the ERM journey. Ad hoc, intuitive, reactive, just do it, sporadic risk practices.	<20%	

How to Measure, evaluate and verify its ERM performance against STRATEGIC OBJECTIVES and compliance requirements in order to promote continuous improvement

CASE STUDY WCG – example of risk maturity reporting tailored to King III Code

Targeting future improvements can be combined with tailoring and benchmarking. This is evidenced in practice by this case study. Beulah Misrole, provincial risk officer for the Western Cape Government (WCG) of South Africa, presented to the G31000 conference in NYC in 2014. The topic was the WCG's targeted multi-year progress for ERM risk

FIGURE 5.13 WCG King III and Benchmarker™ case study

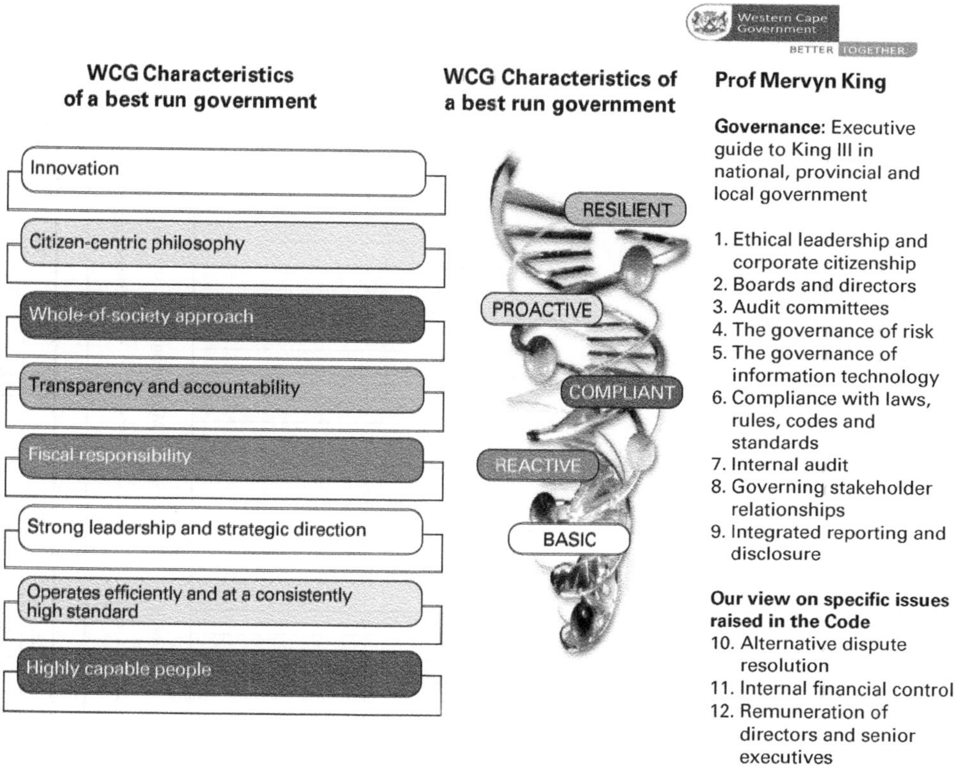

SOURCE: Reprinted with kind permission from Western Cape Government 2014

maturity aligned to ISO 31000. Their tailoring approach adapted an early version of the Benchmarker™ risk maturity model benchmarked by 'cross-walk' to ISO 31000:2009. See Figure 5.13 for how WCG further tailored their model by deleting profit-related capabilities then adding their own 'cross-walk' to the characteristics of a 'best run' government drawn from the King III corporate governance and other guidelines relevant to their organization (see Chapter 4 for more on King III).

The WCG also demonstrate how they prefer to report risk maturity improvement over time. Figure 5.14 is an example of a historical bar-chart tracking progress by one of the Western Cape Government major departments from a baseline on 2010–11 and over the next targeted two-year period for over 90 capabilities themed into 10 modules. Figure 5.15 shows the same data represented as a radar chart. Both Figures are reprinted with kind permission from Western Cape Government 2014.

FIGURE 5.14 Western Cape Government risk maturity over 10 modules as a bar chart

Pareto Principle Graph (20/80)

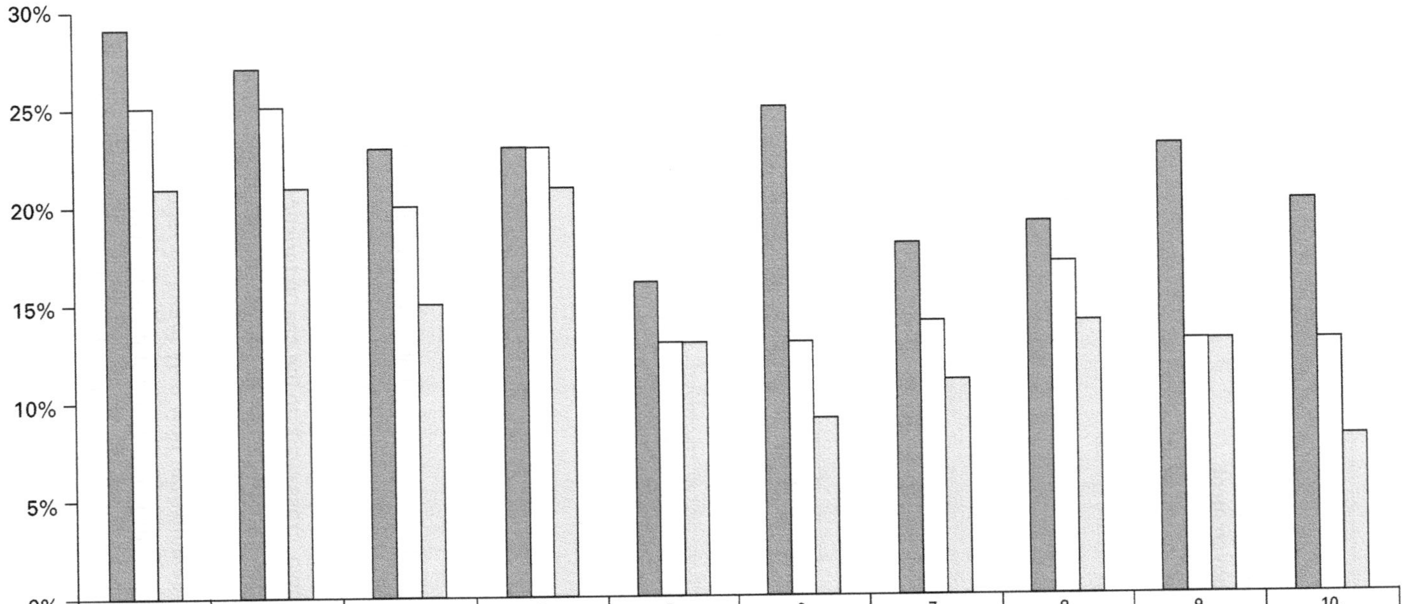

	1. Sponsorship and Positioning:	2. Managing the Risk Management Process:	3. Identification:	4. Prioritization:	5. Treatment:	6. Reporting:	7. Monitoring:	8. Culture and Embedding:	9. Communication:	10. Working with Counterparties:
FY 2014/2015										
FY 2012/2013	29%	27%	23%	23%	16%	25%	18%	19%	22%	20%
FY 2011/12	25%	25%	20%	23%	13%	13%	14%	17%	13%	13%
Sep 2010-Mar 2011	21%	21%	15%	21%	13%	9%	11%	14%	13%	8%

FIGURE 5.15 Western Cape Government risk maturity over 10 modules as a radar chart

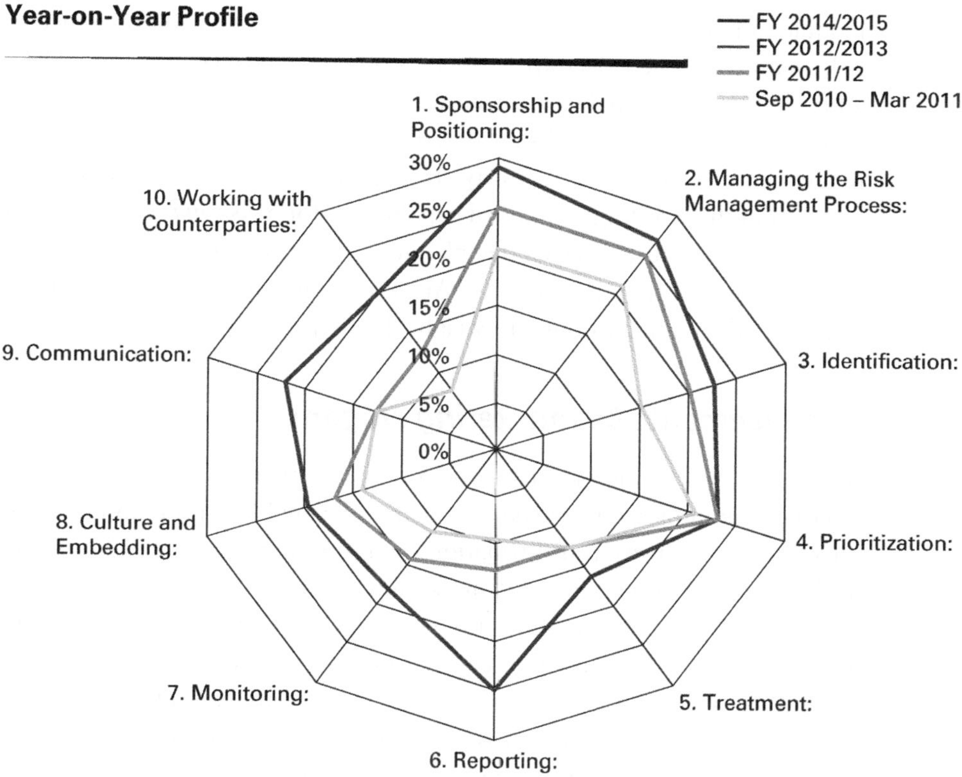

Enhancements by maturity score weighting

More advanced users and others may prefer to enhance their risk maturity model by up-weighting certain capabilities or modules over others. One way is to add more columns on the spreadsheet, recalculating the raw scores into weighted scores. The practical difficulty here is in the reporting because the past experience of many risk professionals is that this can invite thorny debate over the rationales for the weightings amongst managers, boards and auditors for no apparent gain over raw scoring.

Another way to add weighting, which may avoid the pitfalls of complicating your spreadsheet with weighting formulae and complexity, is to deliberately overlap some of your capabilities within the model. The end result is that the end score naturally gives a subtle enhanced weighting to those that are more important than others or more interdependent for your organization.

For example, take risk maturity as an overall capability in itself. You may design it in twice in your model questionnaire design by having one capability read 'A risk maturity *strategy* is in place' under a risk process module (aligned specifically with the only explicit ISO 31000 reference to risk maturity). Then overlap it under a separate governance module by adding a separate capability for a 'A risk maturity *model* is in place. It is tailored. It... etc' – with a fulsome description from this book of what a good model can deliver for the maturity strategy. To go further, you could then add within the wording for a third capability – for a *risk management plan* – that the plan must receive effective inputs from the maturity assessment and link the risk maturity strategy. All three elements are effectively made interdependent and naturally up-weight the subject of risk maturity.

Enhancements by marketing slogans

An internal marketing-oriented programme title theme may work well for internal communications purposes if there is a new ERM programme introduction or a maturity transformation/ramp-up programme. My *Becoming RiskSmart Programme* internal marketing slogan drove a CFO-led ERM launch and internal communications-plan programme for the Australian Red Cross in 2008. This initiated high internal awareness. It helped turn around the typical initial resistance retorts such as 'are you saying we're not doing risk management already or doing it badly' by answering 'no, we are saying we can make risk-smarter decisions about x'. '*RiskSmart* doubled as the label for the highest maturity level within the programme and was carefully chosen to position risk as part of what managers do every day – just a bit smarter. Deloitte use a similar 'risk intelligent' label with popular effect and relevance for their clients.

Optimizing objectivity, tailoring and reporting

10 techniques to improve objectivity in your risk maturity model

Reducing bias whilst improving objectivity – as well as tailoring – in the risk maturity models can be enhanced by certain techniques. The question 'but how objective is this risk maturity model?' often comes up during the model investment case and at model-produced presentations with board, management and auditors. Here we look at 10 techniques to improve objectivity and to answer these questions.

Option 1: using design principles to improve objectivity

Option 1 starts with the design of the risk maturity model as per Chapter 4 (designing). Choose capabilities that are tailored to your organization objectives and context. Choose a rating methodology that improves objective assessment by assessors during the very act of assessment. For example, optimism bias is increased if the assessor is asked to rate from a series of set answers or 'pick-a-box' that at the same time indicates the maturity level. This is partly why ascribing a maturity level to individual capability questions is not advised, as the responder is unduly influenced by the effects of the answers on the final level rating. The resulting inclination is to skew ratings upwards and to shortcut the evidence basis for the rating. This upweights the overall ratings. Such 'soft' ratings are to be avoided. We therefore tier the styles of risk maturity models that focus on this as 'intermediate'. Forcing the user to respond with no reference to the maturity level reduces this type of bias.

Option 2: using external surveys to improve objectivity

Practitioner Chris opts for cross-sector external benchmarking to boost objectivity

Chris knows his CFO boss likes *surveys* and Chris wishes he could use them more in his construction firm. His research when designing his risk maturity model found that a number of model-authoring organizations quoted the use of surveys with large numbers of clients across many sectors (see Chris's nine survey data sources previously listed in Chapter 4). As his own business clients operated across a number of quite diverse sectors, he thought a model backed by cross-sector usage was a good thing because it may boost the objectivity of what he was doing with his model and answer any auditor criticism that he was not objective enough.

Chris's research suggests that external surveys (Option 2 above) are fine but the constraint is that they date easily. He notes that the RIMS/Logic Manager risk maturity model made strong claims to be in use with many clients but he did not trust their content, as it originated from a workshop in 2006 led by a software developer and had not been content-updated since. He noticed that Marsh Risk Consulting had quoted using their model with n=2,000+ clients across many sectors but that the data dated back to around 2008. He found Deloitte claimed n=1,541 multiple-sector firms for their risk intelligent risk maturity model but that, as far as

Chris was aware, it was last surveyed in 2009. Whilst those sort of survey participant numbers were impressive, the outdatedness of the data did not impress Chris.

Worried that these models are too dated, Chris finds that the Aon-Wharton Risk Maturity Index online refreshes their data at least annually. Aon-Wharton claimed to have received responses from risk and finance leaders at more than 600 organizations representing more than 25 industries over 2013. Moreover, Aon-Wharton accumulates external benchmarking data each year and publish the results online by December. Chris opts to make a start with his own model by doing the online Aon-Wharton RMI assessment. As his firm has a directive culture, Chris is happy to start out with the one he thinks best. See Figure 5.16 for the type of benchmarking published by Aon-Wharton.

FIGURE 5.16 Aon-Wharton RMI bar chart 2013

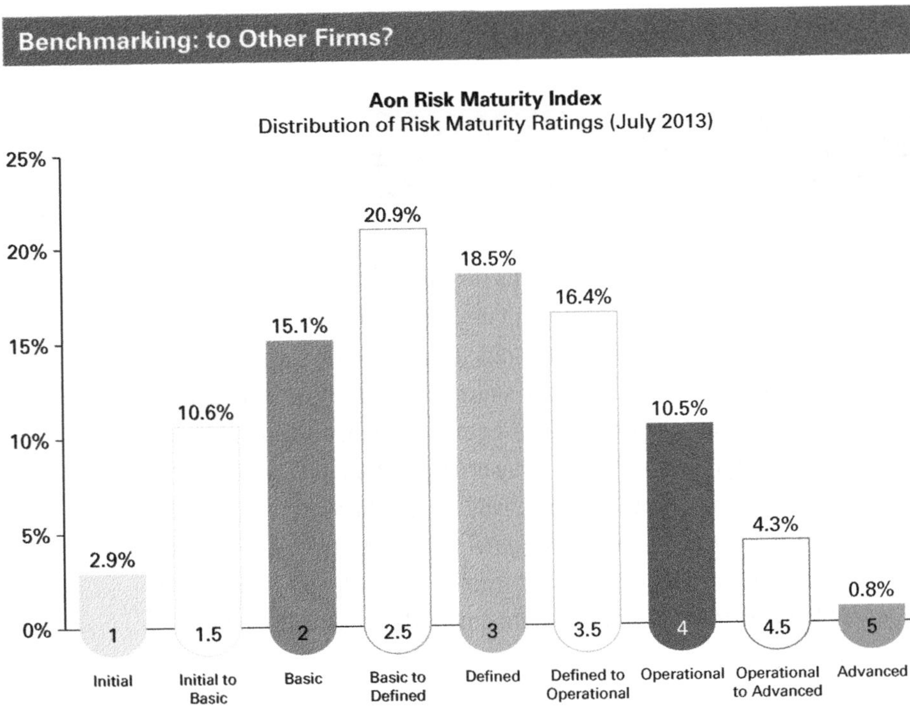

SOURCE: Reproduced with the kind permission of Aon-Wharton © Aon Risk Consultants, Inc. 2013

Other options

Increasing objectivity in the design and using an external survey-supported model are just two technique options. There are at least another eight options, which we number 3 to 10 below, most of which may be used in combination with each other:

- Option 3: use *internal* Delphi subject matter experts. (The Delphi method is a forecasting method based on the results of questionnaires sent to a panel of experts. Several rounds of questionnaires are sent out, and the anonymous responses are aggregated and shared with the group after each round. The experts are allowed to adjust their answers in subsequent rounds. The Delphi method seeks to reach the 'correct' response through consensus because multiple rounds of questions are asked and because each member of the panel is told what the group thinks as a whole.)
- Option 4: use *external* Delphi subject-matter experts.
- Option 5: accept a *range* rating from multiple internal or external sources.
- Option 6: reassess internally with internal audit and/or other functions.
- Option 7: reassess externally with paid external consultants.
- Option 8: use external reference standards and voluntary codes.
- Option 9: use multiple risk maturity models (as a hedging strategy).
- Option 10: continual improvement by referencing evolving industry knowledge over time – this will change your mix of maturity capabilities, levels and scale definitions and will increasingly refine your scales.

Options 3 and 4: using your own simple Delphi exercise to improve objectivity

A simplified Delphi exercise can run something like this. Send out a questionnaire to sector-specific subject-matter experts or experienced people who can contribute to this posed question: '*What does a good or leading <your sector/type of> organization look like in terms of inherent organization capabilities (do not think of your past or an actual company, think inherently)?*' Send the questionnaire to a reasonable number of subject-matter experts all around the world/region both inside and outside the company. Expect the Round 1 of raw responses to vary a lot (this seems to be in the nature of a subject-matter expert). Prepare centrally one synthesized report listing all inherent capabilities grouped under appropriate subheadings for each capability module (eg people, strategy, process, culture). If the responders include those affiliated or formerly affiliated with competitors then you may be able also to analyse preferred capability lists from three different sources: internal versus competitor versus non-competitor results.

Send another questionnaire back to the subject-matter experts as Round 2 with a simple request. The subject-matter experts must mark up an answer to this question: '*Now, think of who you regard as the LEADING <x> organization relative to other same organizations, what score would you give them for each capability listed? Name the company. Do not answer where you disagree with the capability but please send us a revised description or reason for the purposes of our continuous improvement.*' Now you may not only benchmark against the content of this risk maturity model but a new competitor/leader benchmark rating.

Options 4, 5, 7 and 10 combined to improve objectivity

Practitioner Asha uses external consultants for Delphi exercise

Asha starts off using external consultants (Option 7). These are carefully selected to act as subject-matter experts in order to reduce bias and improve objectivity in her maturity model (Option 4). Asha's recruitment firm prides itself on using the best people and expertise. If these cannot be found internally then the firm has no problem sourcing subject-matter expertise.

She selects a risk management-consulting firm after a selection process. She gets them to coordinate a Delphi method exercise tapping the best minds in the recruitment industry from around the world to form a second synthesized assessment based on their industry-tailored knowledge.

The independent external subject-matter experts arrive at a baseline maturity rating of 14% base index. She compares this to her own rating at 26%. Asha realizes it might take far more time and more consulting engagements to resolve the large rating difference and to work out the best set of tailored maturity capabilities. So, she starts off using the range rating 14–26% (Option 5).

Asha acts on some of the subject-matter-expert recommendations (Option 10). She adds six more capabilities new to her first-cut model. She tightens most of the descriptions so they give others in her organization a good picture of 'what good looks like' for each capability. She notes that there is a marked maturity gap to the competitor/leader most-named by the subject-matter experts on three of the 'new' capabilities.

This gave her ammunition to add more value to the organization. She converts this competitor-model finding into three new business-improvement opportunities on her risk register then agrees with the chief operating officer and the CEO how to optimize them to regain a competitive edge. She brings the three to the attention of the strategy head, who updates the following year's KPIs on the balanced scorecard performance management system. By doing the above, Asha has significantly increased the objectivity of her model and reduced the risk of her personal – and some other – biases.

Option 5 Using ranged score ratings to improve objectivity

Option 5 means accepting a range score or rating rather than a fixed one. Reality or politics sometimes dictates this can be a reasonable starting option. Below, we use a GULFCO case study and two practitioner perspectives to exemplify that shared scoring between the risk and audit functions has three advantages: first, in reducing potential bias and that stakeholder differences over point scores may be resolved with the acceptance of ranged score ratings (GULFCO); second, in leveraging independent and added-value internal audit collaboration (Alan); and third, in providing a useful alternative scoring approach for culturally immature organizations (Megan).

CASE STUDY GULFCO: resolving clashes in ratings with ranged score ratings

The newly appointed CRO of a real-life multinational Gulf company ('GULFCO') performs his first risk maturity model assessment. GULFCO has never had a dedicated risk function before. The CRO arrives at an organization risk maturity initial rating at 9% (ie the lowest Level 1) via desktop analysis during his orientation period of three months. A 9% score placed GULFCO overall at the lowest 'Naive' Level 1 of five levels.

The CEO suggests wisely to allow internal audit (IA) to have a turn by independent assessment using the same CRO model. IA rates the organization at 47%, representing a wide gap to the CRO score. Eventually mutual agreement is reached following two independent rounds of workshops and interviews to explore the differences. The first-ever risk maturity level assessment is agreed as a ranged score of 21–27% (an adjusted 21% by the CRO and 27% by IA). The CRO defers to the greater experience and the shared information from IA. IA defers to the CRO's greater understanding of ERM and the tool. The CEO is comfortable reporting to his board that a self-improvement road map has now kicked off.

Practitioner Alan encourages a range-scored maturity model for ERM function

Alan is lucky. As an internal auditor he can bring to the ERM manager's table some help as Alan is close to their people in the Strategy and Performance Management section of the Corporate Planning Department, whereas the ERM manager is not so close. So after the ERM manager completes the first risk maturity model assessment, Alan compares the IA's independent assessment (Option 6) then jointly assists the ERM manager to repeat the assessment and analysis process independently by another two methods.

First, he tees up the ERM manager to run a group workshop with their colleagues in the Strategy and Performance Management section. Second, he validates the self-paced individual questionnaires that the ERM manager designs then issues them to the risk specialists in Legal, Compliance, Health and Safety and Security. The latter functions say that they are 'too busy' to all get to one workshop and prefer a self-paced questionnaire. The three sets of scores come in at 19% by the ERM manager, 22% by IA and 29% maturity index averaged over the risk specialists.

Alan later that year completes his annual IA assessment of risk management effectiveness and the ERM function. He notes in the report that the risk maturity model is a constructive and powerful tool being put to satisfactory and improving use by the ERM and line functions. He also notes positively that the ERM manager role is still establishing their authority with senior management, and that the ERM manager is wise in respecting all three sets of different scores as a ranged rating (Option 5) rather than declaring one better than another. Alan likes the way the IA collaboration on the risk maturity model is also providing extra benefits for the IA function (in becoming more familiar with improving risk maturity, more forward-looking for their risk-based audit plan and thinking 'up the strategic curve', and improving the IA-risk functional relationship and combined assurance).

Practitioner Megan's work culture leads to range scoring

Megan has a difficult risk-averse culture to deal with. She believes after discussion with her HR department that it may take several years for her managers to arrive at any consensus on a single-score rating for maturity. She prefers to have the managers ease into becoming more familiar over the initial first couple of years of implementing the ERM programme and building the risk management system. She opts for range scoring (Option 5) by desktop analysis in this interim period. A precise rating at this early stage in the ERM programme for her NGO is impractical so the range-rating approach here provides a useful alternative scoring approach for this culturally immature organization.

Option 6: reassess internally with IA and/or other functions to improve objectivity

Another option is to collaborate and share the same risk maturity model methodology between internal functions to arrive at independent assessments that can be post-shared for further refinement and resolution of conflicting or contrary data and scores. This option reduces resistance to the model and improves awareness and 'education by doing' on top of the improved objectivity benefit it brings. Megan experienced these benefits, as below.

Practitioner Megan taps IA for combined assurance

Megan has followed our Chapter 3 design steps and built a simple spreadsheet-based risk maturity model based on 43 underlying maturity capabilities. She creates the 43 by using the Chapter 3 resources: using the SCRLC downloadable gratis spreadsheet (Table 3.72), adapting and building on the 22 capabilities from the Monda ERMi model (Table 3.60) with others she chose by researching the quality management-originated and not-for-profit maturity models such as Hillson, LTRC/EFQM, ALARM, Fraser Health and HM Treasury (Chapter 4, Table 4.4 'Sector origin of maturity models').

Megan is conscientious because she wants to 'grow into ERM' so she strives to be as 'objective' as possible and avoid any personal bias in the content of the risk maturity model. Megan considers Options 1 through 10 to reduce bias listed above and realizes she has already covered Options 1 and 2. She feels that options 5, 9 and 10 are not options for her as she was a new modeller. She could not afford external help (Options 4 and 7) as her NGO was quite cost-constrained. She thought it was too hard to identify then access internal subject-matter experts and run a two-round correct Delphi procedure with her organization's risk-averse culture (Option 3).

However, she found to her mild surprise that the IA team was not only accessible but also quite keen to independently assess using her new risk maturity model methodology she had tailored to her NGO (Option 6). They could then jointly compare the results with her and, in so doing, be more objective about what their initial benchmark is and the capability self-improvements required to move from this baseline that would then feed into her risk management planning. Megan heard from IA that this collaborative approach had the mutual benefit of providing the Audit and Risk Committee with *combined assurance*. In this way, Megan adroitly tapped the expertise of her IA team for combined assurance so as to improve how it helped them formally assess risk management effectiveness at least once a year.

Option 7: outsourcing to improve objectivity

You may outsource your risk maturity model to an external consultant or purchase a model directly, for example, online via online publishers such as Specialty & Technical Publishing (**www.stpub.com**). We saw earlier that practitioner Asha had used a management-consulting firm to coordinate a Delphi selection-and-implementation exercise. You may just outsource everything to do with your model, from design to assessment, reporting, monitoring and reassessment processes. Certainly there are consultant providers with international, regional or national experience who can do this but the cost and elapsed time may be a constraint. Our practitioner Megan finds an interesting solution to this cost constraint.

Practitioner Megan taps external insurance broker at no cost to improve her model

Megan finds in Year 2 that she wants to add more risk maturity objectivity, given that she is not a trained-up risk manager. She still appreciates the great help that IA has given since Year 1 but now discovers that her firm's existing insurance broker operates a risk-consulting arm. She explains to her internal insurance manager that whilst she has no budget for external consultants she has a need for advice on the robustness of the risk maturity model she is using. Her insurance manager makes use of a credit rebate with the insurance broker. The broker facilitates a free half-day workshop and 'educational' access to their bigger, more robust maturity model they use with clients. Megan is pleased with the result.

Option 8 and 9: using external reference standards and voluntary codes and using multiple risk maturity models (as a hedging strategy) to improve objectivity

If the above outsourcing is not feasible then readers should in-source and use Chapters 3 and 4 to research and compare models in the market and tailoring to standards, codes and other external reference sources.

Practitioner Chris adds codes and hedges Option 8 and 9 to improve objectivity

Chris decided for Year 2 of his risk maturity strategy implementation to improve objectivity in his maturity model. He prefers to do this by adding an external reference standard or set of standards and guidelines (Option 8) to augment the Aon-Wharton RMI model he had started using in Year One. His earthy construction firm CEO has also remarked caustically '*What can a bunch of academics at Wharton teach us anyway?*' Chris thinks he can achieve more 'objectivity' without using expensive consultants by tapping into the two 'leading' voluntary reference codes ISO 31000:2009 and COSO ERM and as these codes were developed by external technical committees and subject-matter experts (SMEs).

In Year 2, Chris designs his own tailored simple model using our steps 1 to 3 earlier in this chapter. He expands his own set of capabilities to ensure they cover the sets within ISO and COSO and 'cross-walks' those that have a specific reference from each capability if it has an ISO- or COSO-specific section reference. In this way, he can score three ways: comparing one score for ISO 31000 alignment, another for COSO ERM alignment and yet another for a total score, including capabilities not referenced by either ISO 31000 or COSO ERM. He still uses the RMI to cross-validate as a type of natural hedge (Option 9).

In Year 3 he uses his risk maturity model in spreadsheet format as an integrated and tailored risk maturity strategy and plan cross-walked to ISO 31000 and COSO ERM capabilities. He validated the results of his model with that from Aon. When his CFO also pointed out they had a large sensitivity to Standard & Poor's credit ratings, as well as heavy refinancing of the organization, Chris could easily cross-walk his model to S&P-preferred risk capabilities in the organization.

Option 9: using multiple models to improve objectivity and tailoring

One option is to choose only one proprietary risk maturity model exclusively over another. This will invariably carry a cost but offers the option of choosing 'nearest-fit' from a wide range and quality of models. There is currently not a 'one-model-fits-all' solution for ERM – at least, not one that allows the full flexibility to tailor to your own organization as well as enjoying acceptance by most recognized bodies or by popular market sales. Nevertheless, starting with one 'nearest-fit' model that lends itself as a ready 'off-the-rack' solution can be practical and effective, assuming appropriate factoring for fit-to-organization, bias and cost-to-benefit. This starting approach lends itself to low-maturity and/or smaller organizations at the lower cost end of risk maturity models who are feeling their way up the risk maturity curve. Alternatively, it may suit higher-maturity and/or larger organizations that may select a 'nearest-fit' model from the higher-cost range on offer.

A second option is to choose more than one risk maturity model non-exclusively and run them side by side at a lesser or no cost as compared to one proprietary model. This may combine a mix of proprietary and open approaches. CROs have been known to use a mix of up to five paid and gratis risk maturity model sources as their way of tailoring. A dashboard report may then average or range the scores.

A third option is to create your own proprietary-to-self risk maturity model and use it exclusively at no cost, as we have shown earlier in this chapter, with a simple spreadsheet format. This is a relatively simple solution for which a dashboard can be created then allowed to evolve over time using initial inputs from a range of sources, as noted in Chapters 3 and 4. These may all be gratis. You may start by 'cherry-picking' from any number of potential capabilities from open sources, which may include – to suggest a few – the ISO 31000 'enhanced attributes' (n=5), COSO components (n=8) and models from Monda (n=22), RIMS (n=68) and Aon (n=40). This example set may build a long-list of 200+ capabilities that can be tailored and culled down. Of course, these are suggestions not recommendations, which need to be informed by the unique context and objectives of your organization.

The technique of using multiple risk maturity models to naturally hedge the risk of bias is always available. It can repay such an investment many times over as there is such a wide and growing availability of options in the market, including much information accessible online for free, as we saw in our directory in Chapter 3. Our previous practitioner examples show how Megan moved to two risk maturity models and Chris to three or more.

One approach to tailoring is to use one or more of the specialty risk maturity models alongside or integrated with that for your ERM. For example, the BCCM® business continuity risk maturity model by VirtualCorp can be run and monitored separately by your business continuity management (BCM) manager/function for the initial years of your new ERM model. As your organization risk maturity and risk resourcing grows, you may add one capability devoted to BCM to your ERM model with a predetermined cross-scaling to track improvement over time. A 53% score on the Business Continuity Maturity Model BCCM®, say, may then be allocated a rating (see Table 3.10, BCMM® Business Continuity Maturity Model by VirtualCorp, 2003).

There are mutual advantages for ERM and specialty disciplines in the above approach. For the ERM model, it reduces objectivity bias, improves the robustness of certain ratings and validates its level of integration with existing management systems. For specialty disciplines, it improves the assurance of their risk maturity model ratings and their strategic and tactical value to existing management systems.

The ERM function should promote as many specialty risk maturity models as possible. In the absence of permanent specialty functions, the

ERM function should step in if organization objectives for a period are best served by adding, say, a project risk maturity model during a key 12-month ERP programme or a one-off key construction project. If specialty functions are unaware of the value of running their own risk maturity models, the ERM function should promote their purchase or use – even as a cost-effective simple spreadsheet-based matrix format. The detailed sub-capabilities do not have to clutter the ERM model, but an overall rating onto the ERM model based on robust data input at specialty level is of value.

How one CRO uses multi-models to improve objectivity

As a CRO, I currently deploy up to 15 different model sources at any time to inspire, compare, tailor and validate my own preferred tailored model in order to optimize objectivity and tailoring and reduce my personal or other biases. The number and type of models I use change with each organization objectives, context and risk profiles. The 15 are made up of cross-walks to the two most widely held reference codes (ISO 31000 and COSO ERM), comparison results from three other ERM models, cross-checks to six ERM/project risk maturity models and four specialized submodels as input domains (for culture, business continuity, supply chain and technology). Only one of the 15 is a paid service. I combine this with reassessments by internal auditors with plans to expand into reassessments to unit heads and others in the future. This technique doubles as a form of combined buy-in and training. See the map in Figure 5.17 for more detail on my approach, which readers are free to adopt or adapt to their own needs. When stakeholders challenge me as to bias in the model and why I call it 'tailored', I use Figure 5.17 to aid discussion.

At one point, for example, as CRO I had to accommodate the need to tailor my risk maturity model to suit at least seven stakeholders. The board and CEO preferred ISO 31000 as an umbrella global standard. The CFO preferred COSO ERM and respected Deloitte as the external auditor who, in turn, preferred the Deloitte model. Our Protiviti-assisted IA team preferred King III code and the Protiviti model. Our quality management and head of operations were keen on the EFQM framework. Our powerful PMO running a key or mega-project preferred PMI maturity. Our insurance team and their broker Aon preferred Aon's model. So my solution was to find an ISO-aligned risk maturity model tailored with cross-walk references to the salient capabilities preferred by COSO, Deloitte and the others for risk maturity feeding up to the ERM risk maturity model. It can be done.

FIGURE 5.17 Tailoring your model with multiple inputs to improve objectivity and tailoring

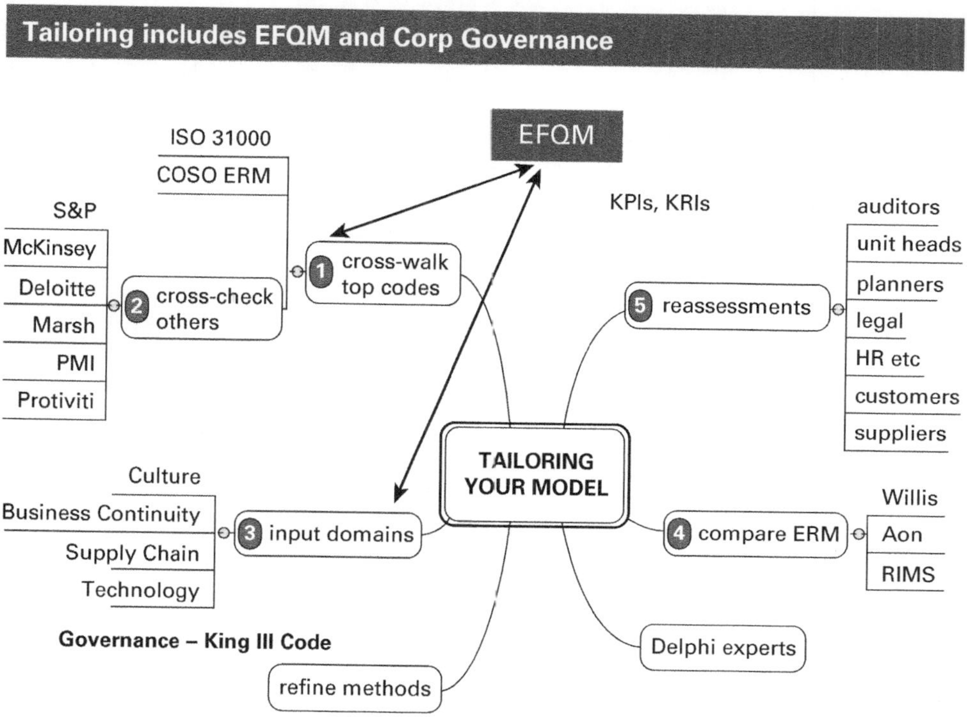

SOURCE: Copyright © Domenic Antonucci 2014

Figure 5.17 shows a real internal presentation slide to the audit and quality management teams to explain how it all works together.

If I only have one slide to present to board and management, I prefer to report the three most important communication elements together on the one slide. The changing profile of the *top risks* are heat-mapped but I join the heat map with a *treatment index* indicating the progress on completing the risk action plans by risk owners against these top risks. I then add the S-curve graphic representing the *overall index maturity* for the risk management system that is reporting those risks and their treatment progress. The multi-year actual and future-targeted improvement S-curve becomes a regular reminder of the level of reliability that can be attached to the two other report elements as well as the need by board and senior management to re-mandate and commit to risk maturity improvement over the long term. Figure 5.18 is a composite of actual data from two organizations as a sample of this one-slide approach (organization names are protected).

FIGURE 5.18 Risk report dashboard includes risk maturity

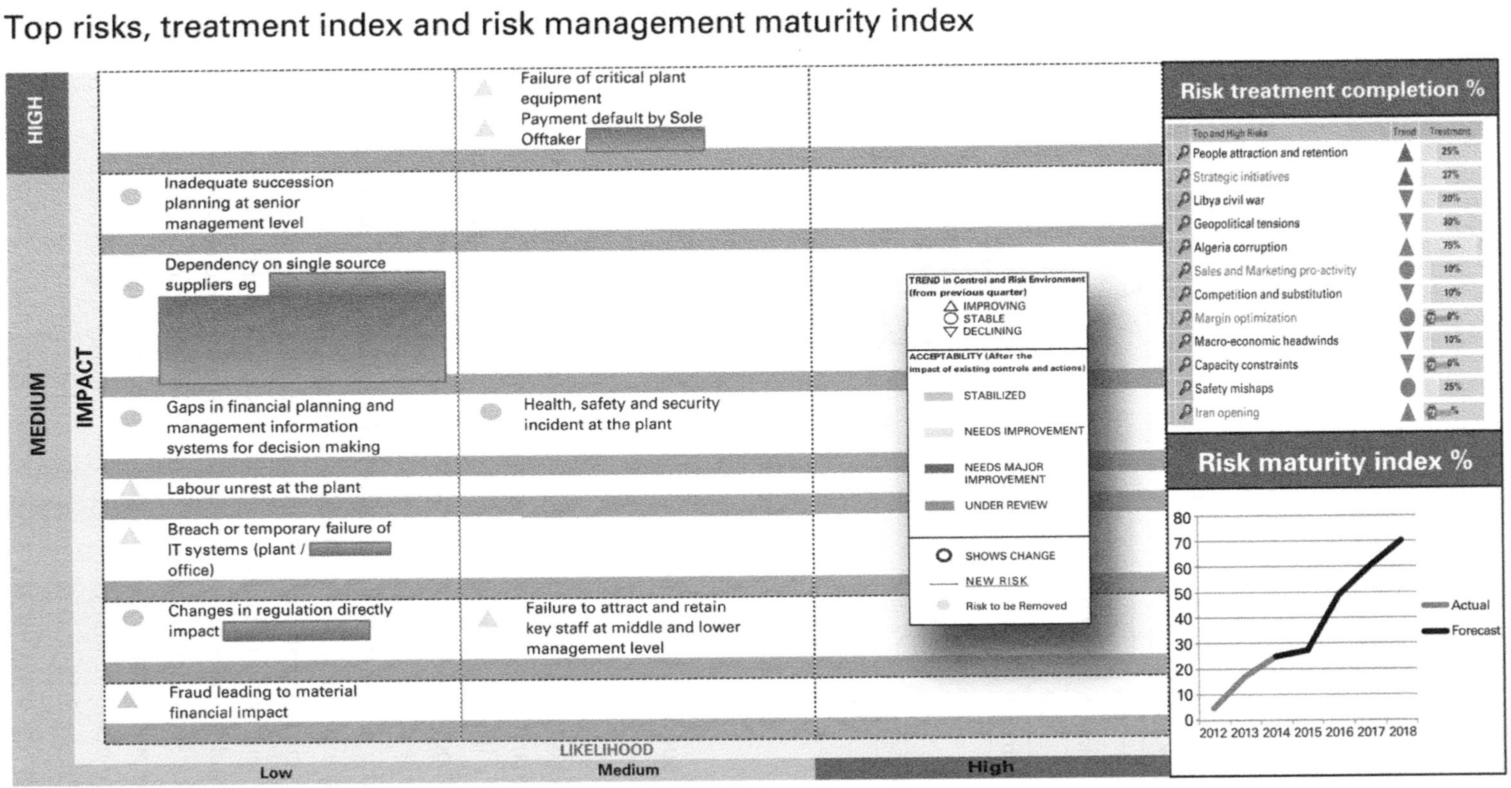

Summary

Using the understanding of risk maturity models and the resources made available from comparing models in the marketplace (Chapter 3) and a wealth of other reference sources (Chapter 4), you designed your own tailored risk maturity model.

Organization size, resources or budget should not deter any organization from getting started on designing their own simple risk maturity model. Expensive or external software is not required. You may begin with a simple spreadsheet matrix format and easy alternatives are also shown by way of a Word template or by adapting an open-source spreadsheet with ready-made dashboard reports (SCRLC model).

The highest purpose behind risk maturity models, amongst other uses, is to assess risk management effectiveness tailored to your unique organization and its integrated risk management system. The typical design components work in a basic sequence: Components = Domains + Capabilities + Levels + Scales. The three-step design process is simple: 1) enter your preferred ERM-domain capabilities on a matrix; 2) then rate them with preferred scales; 3) in order to arrive at your preferred maturity levels.

Novice or existing users may then access more technical guidance in this chapter to explore a wide range of alternative design formats, enhancements and 10 techniques to improve objectivity and tailoring. A range of practitioner perspectives, real organization case studies, tables, figures and reports support the guidance.

Readers will find some advantages and disadvantages in alternative design formats, levels and scales. The usefulness of one over another will depend on tailoring fit to your organization. I prefer a capability completeness format with a five-point rating scale together with a risk dashboard report showing a risk maturity S-curve.

You can also compare four popular ways to enhance your risk maturity model: report types, targeting future improvements, weighting your capability assessments and employing a marketing slogan.

Reducing bias whilst improving objectivity and tailoring can be enhanced by at least 10 techniques. This helps answer the typical question posed to modellers 'But how objective and tailored is this risk maturity model?'

06 How risk, audit and board functions benefit from risk maturity

This chapter covers:

- Risk function
- Internal audit function
- Board and CxO function
- Benefits for these functions
- Summary

Introduction

Megan now knew that using the risk maturity model was a powerful tool to assess risk management effectiveness. But she also knew that even the most powerful tool needs the right hands to guide its use. She was still unsure what risk maturity meant in terms of her job role as the unofficial addition of risk officer/manager duties to her official quality manager role. Also, she wanted to bolster the investment case by appealing to the self-interest of some key stakeholders. She wanted to understand the underlying 'what's in it for me' (WIFM) motive from the perspective of the key influencers – that will motivate them to rightly invest and support a successful risk maturity model implementation.

This chapter gives guidance on the combined roles of the risk officer, internal auditor and board/CxO functions as the key influencers on the success of a risk maturity model. It gives broad guidance as to how they should work separately and together to optimize this risk maturity tool in the RACI terms of responsibility, accountability, consultation and being informed (see 'Summary').

The risk function and risk maturity

Risk maturity role for risk officers as steward

The risk function and its risk officers/managers are broadly the stewards or *drivers* of the risk maturity model and risk maturity strategy. They are not the *enablers* in terms of an economic value chain (see Chapter 4). This is alongside the responsibility of all managers to manage risk, as well as other organization arrangements.

Risk function as steward for the risk maturity model

The risk officer function has the primary role for the risk maturity model as its steward. The top-five core risk maturity function responsibilities are as follows:

1. *Create and steward the risk maturity model* as the primary tool to assess risk management effectiveness by road-mapping gap-improvement over time to risk management system capabilities. These need to be tailored to the organization objectives, context and risk profile (ISO 31000:2009).
2. *Ensure appropriate risk management principles* applying to ERM are also applied to the risk maturity model. Refer to ISO 31000:2009 Principles, especially Principle (k) promoting the development of a risk maturity strategy, to which the risk maturity model gives effect.
3. *Balance all four components of the PDCA* as in the plan-do-check-act framework to continuously improve the risk maturity model (refer to ISO 31000:2009 Framework PDCA, later in this chapter).
4. *Manage the risk maturity model process* from the 'case for' to 'compare' to 'tailor' and 'benchmark', and the design steps as per Chapters 2 to 5. This includes initial selection or design if a risk maturity model does not exist, as well as redesign to continuously improve and upgrade the model.

5 *Ensure that the risk management plan and the risk-based IA plans* receive as inputs all the gap self-improvement outputs from regularly reassessed risk maturity model. If tailored, the risk maturity model can also serve as an integrated risk management plan aligned with the rolling annual organization plans (see later in this chapter for more detail).

The above can be reframed. The following points of responsibility for risk maturity may be incorporated into the terms of a generic risk officer job description:

- **stewards**, facilitates and champions risk maturity at a strategic and operational level;
- sets risk maturity **strategy** plans, policies and implementation goals;
- **integrates** risk maturity within ERM and with other business planning and management activities, particularly through the risk management plan and risk-based internal audit plan;
- road-maps and tracks the **risk management system** by identifying and measuring its maturity capabilities benchmarking current against future gap-improvements within a tailored risk maturity model so as to deliver the risk maturity strategy alongside other organization arrangements;
- builds a risk-aware **culture** within the organization, including appropriate education as to the implementation of a tailored risk maturity model via risk management committees and other team and individual ways of informed risk decision-making;
- designs and reviews a **programme** and **processes** for risk management system-capability improvement so as to optimize the regular assessment of risk management effectiveness (minimum annual assessment);
- ensures **international standards** are transparent within a risk maturity model through cross-walking references or similar mechanisms;
- coordinates the **various functional activities** relevant to risk maturity improvement and advises on issues impeding the latter;
- prepares **reports** and improves disclosure for the board and the stakeholders on the level of risk maturity, capability gap-improvements required and assessment of risk management effectiveness;

- is senior enough to attract the **mandate** and commitment from the top with the appropriate **resourcing** and manager **accountabilities** and **responsibilities** to effect risk maturity;
- continuously improves risk maturity by balancing all four components of the **PDCA** plan-do-check-act framework (see later in this chapter for more on this);
- includes risk maturity in **incentive systems**;
- defines a common risk maturity **language** integrated with the broader risk vocabulary;
- supports, coaches and facilitates to **line management** who carry primary responsibility and accountability for managing risk within their respective areas.

Risk maturity and the risk management plan are interrelated

The risk function is responsible for the risk management plan (the 'plan'). The plan and the risk maturity model are interrelated. The plan is typically the 'backbone' to implementing ERM as a programme of which risk maturity model is a part. Moreover, the plan itself and its attributes can be incorporated as one or more of the capabilities within the model itself.

ISO 31000:2009 describes attributes of a plan. It cites the need for a reiterative plan together with an external stakeholder communication plan. ISO 31000 describes the plan as a key 'organizational arrangement'-type of architecture component but effectively positions the reiterative plan as the 'backbone' to ERM implementation. It is difficult to understand how without a plan and a risk maturity model anyone can implement ISO 31000 Scope 1 ISO Principle (k). Principle (k) requires strategies to improve risk management maturity alongside all other organization aspects.

In ISO 31000 attribute terms, the plan explains how the ISO 31000 risk management system should be implemented. It is central to planning how the organization builds risk management into organization processes, activities and practice. That is, it explains how and what is needed for the framework to give effect to principles and implement the risk management process. It can be applied for all-organization, or part thereof for functions and levels, projects, processes and products. The plan includes any appropriate components of both types, being foundation or organizational arrangement types. It includes: component descriptions, approach, resources to manage risk, progress and deviations to the plan, reviews of whether the plan (and policy and framework) are still current given changing organization external and internal context or need improvements, especially to how it manages risk and the risk culture. The plan is key to monitoring, review and continuous improvement to ensure the ERM framework is effective and up to date.

Given the above, the plan is the perfect receiver of the outputs from the risk maturity model. That is, the risk maturity model target/future/to-be improvement activities are fed as inputs to the plan. This serves for embedding purposes into organization management systems, for rolling out further improvements, for training, for special-risk treatment such as business continuity planning and, of course, for tracking measurements and schedule/timelines. It can generate a numerical score that links to KPIs and performance management. It can link to insurance-premium distribution and create an incentive. The risk management information system can manage these model outputs. Overall, it can refocus on what matters for your organization and can raise the bar regularly.

In fact, for some CRO practitioners the risk maturity model is designed to be one and the same *as* the plan. The model design, in this case, can aggregate all the to-be gap-improvements into one report acting as the plan with associated resources and timelines added. At the time of assessment, the assessor just needs to record these improvements in the appropriate forward-looking detail to the plan requirements fit to the organization.

A dedicated or central risk-function role is critical for the risk management plan and risk maturity model. Neither the plan nor the model can be expected to be owned outside such a function. In practical terms, the business lines tend to look to the risk function to be the driver, although in theory the former could take or share this responsibility.

Risk maturity and the plan-do-check-act framework are interrelated

The risk function must continuously improve risk maturity by balancing all four components of the interrelated plan-do-check-act framework (PDCA) because ISO 31000 Scope 1 ISO Principle (k) Continuous Improvement requires strategies to improve risk management maturity. Risk management maturity is best put into effect by a tailored risk maturity model.

ISO 31000:2009 benefited in adapting the PDCA framework. The ISO 31000 risk management framework recommends a Mandate and Commitment (4.2) and the Design of Framework (4.3) steps driving a quality management cycle originating in the PDCA approach. ISO has re-badged

PDCA as Design of Framework 4.3 (plan), Implementing Risk Management 4.4 (do), Monitoring and Review of Framework 4.5 (check) and Continual Improvement 4.6 (act).

Summary of the risk function role

The risk function coordinates and inputs the improved risk maturity capabilities assessed by the risk maturity model into the plan. The risk function also sources inputs from: business plans, strategic performance reports, revised business plans/objectives, corporate communications statements and annual plans, project scope and schedules, organization personnel and other asset plans and context. The plan may include or deliver these elements: approach/road map, management components, resourcing and budgets, people competencies and talent building, activity calendar, schedules for reporting meetings/workshops, communications-plan milestones and key annual activities and governance presentations, and the risk-rating criteria to be approved by CEO and/or board before its use for risk assessment.

The internal audit function and risk maturity

Risk maturity role for internal audit for combined assurance

The central role of IA is to reasonably assure risk maturity and that the risk maturity model serves in the organization's best interests to improve the risk management system and to assess risk management effectiveness over the long term. They are not the *enablers* in terms of an economic value chain (see Chapter 4). In the absence of a dedicated risk function, IA must independently use a risk maturity model and assess risk management effectiveness, but maintain their objectivity by encouraging the board and management to mandate and commit to a shared risk maturity model.

The remainder of this section assumes a combined assurance approach. Combined assurance means the joint and aligned organization assurance processes by the management and internal audit functional lines to maximize risk management, governance oversight and control effectiveness, and to optimize overall assurance to the audit and risk committee (King III, 2009).

IA function as assurer for the risk maturity model

The IA function has the secondary role for the risk maturity model as its assurer. The top-five core risk-maturity function responsibilities are as follows:

1. *Promote, use and assure the risk maturity model* as the primary tool to assess risk management effectiveness by validating the design and use of a risk maturity model so that it gives IA a protocol to follow, and by sharing the results of the IA independently run risk maturity assessment using the same tool as the risk and line functions.
2. *Assure appropriate risk management principles* applying to ERM are also applied to the risk maturity model. Refer to ISO 31000:2009 Principles, especially Principle (k) promoting the development of a risk maturity strategy, to which the risk maturity model gives effect.
3. *Focus on two components of the PDCA*, being the *plan* (eg risk-based audit plan) and *check* (assure) components of the plan-do-check-act framework to continuously improve the risk maturity model.
4. *Assure the risk maturity model process* from the 'case for' to 'compare' to 'tailor' and 'benchmark', and the design steps as per Chapters 2 to 5.
5. *Ensure that the risk-based internal audit plan* (and risk management plan) receive adequate inputs as to all the gap self-improvement outputs from a regularly reassessed risk maturity model.

The board and CxO function and risk maturity

Risk maturity role for board and CEO for oversight

The central role of the board – including the CEO – is to provide *risk oversight* over risk maturity and to oversee that the risk maturity model serves in the organization's best interests to improve the risk management system and to assess risk management effectiveness over the long term. They are the critical *enablers* in terms of an economic value chain (see Chapter 4) and, without them, any risk maturity model is unlikely to succeed no matter the support of the risk and internal audit functions. The board *must give risk maturity development equal importance to the risks* themselves. They must demand and compare independent risk maturity assessments from the three lines of defence/offence. In the context of risk maturity, they should oversee that appropriate risk management principles are in-effect or not in-breach, how the risk and business functions do their risk managing and how IA coordinates combined assurance of the risk maturity model process.

In the absence of a dedicated risk function, the board and CEO ensure that IA must independently use a risk maturity model and assess risk management effectiveness but maintain their objectivity. However, the board and CEO should as soon as practicable give the mandate and commitment to at least nominate a line manager to use a risk maturity model, or create a part-time or full-time risk function to effect the same.

The board and CEO functions occupy the role for the risk maturity model as its overseers and strategists. The top four core risk maturity function responsibilities are as follows:

1. ***Mandate and commit*** to a risk maturity model as the primary tool to assess risk management effectiveness by promoting the use of a risk maturity model, demanding its reports be presented to the board, by overseeing risk maturity strategy and ensuring appropriate resourcing, accountability and responsibilities are maintained in the long term.
2. ***Oversee combined assurance*** by IA, risk and line functions to assure that appropriate risk maturity model principles, PDCA framework and processes are maintained.
3. ***Focus on two plan-do-check-act (PDCA) framework components***, being the ***plan*** (eg risk maturity strategy, risk model integration to the risk management plan) and ***check*** (via reporting and combined assurance) components to continuously improve the risk maturity model.
4. Add a board Risk Director as a Chief Risk Officer-level director on the board leveraging his/her ***competencies*** based in ERM and the risk maturity model (or an equivalent board executive with a dedicated focus on oversight of the risk maturity model). The emerging Board Risk Director role will be a growing source of mandate, commitment and support of risk maturity on the board. This is necessary given the multi-year planning over the long term required to nurture risk maturity and the technical nature of the risk management competencies as to why it improves board confidence in the assessment of risk management effectiveness.

Benefits for risk, IA and board functions

Those wanting to secure support to start a risk maturity model, and to sustain it over the years to enjoy the benefits from risk maturity modelling, should tap the underlying 'what's in it for me' (WIFM) motive from the perspective of the risk, internal audit and board functions. These three functions represent key influencer-functions for risk maturity. Tapping the WIFM motive within these three key influencer-functions will motivate these three and other functions to support successful risk maturity implementation.

Benefits for the risk function in risk maturity

The risk maturity model offers a risk function with seven solid benefits:

1. Its assessment results serve as a proxy for rating the level of confidence an organization has in its ability to manage and report risks, alongside the so-called 'top 10' and other significant risk and risk-profile reporting. This is the headline benefit.
2. It elevates the risk management discipline into a profession by shaping consensus on what the core and related risk management capabilities required are that can act as the foundation of recognition as a profession. This will help raise the seniority of risk officers within the organization and win that critical board and CxO-level mandate and commitment for investment and resourcing for risk maturity. This is a primary benefit.
3. It moves risk managers closer to the so-called 'top table' of risk decision-making such as the C-suite and board tables, and keeps them there sustainably over the many years required to build capability improvement.
4. It turbo-charges the risk management plan (recommended by ISO 31000:2009) with the detail and benchmarking needed to serve as a KPI to justify personal job-performance reward and recognition.
5. To the so-called first line of defence/offence – it proves to them that the risk function can schedule, budget, scope baseline and track in the same language as the business lines (eg baseline, to-be improvement) and it makes ERM more tangible to them as a programme containing multiple 'projects'.
6. To the so-called second line – it demonstrates risk director-level competencies.

7 To the so-called third line – it offers a partnering bridge to the risk function; it makes the shared assurance role easier; it helps the third line become more forward looking and it opens up an opportunity for the third line to move judiciously into a consulting role in order to assist the first and second lines with combined assurance (ie not '*you Audit guys just get in the way*').

Benefits for the IA function in risk maturity

The risk maturity model offers an IA function several benefits. In Chapter 2 we dealt with why the model is the most potent tool for assessing risk management effectiveness in answer to the mandate to do so imposed on all internal auditors by the Institute for Internal Audit (IIA). This is the paramount benefit for IA in investing in a risk maturity model. IA can conduct their own objective risk maturity assessment and share the results independently or jointly with the risk and line functions. These results can serve as a proxy for rating the level of confidence the organization has in its ability to manage and report risks.

There are other benefits as well for the IA function. It offers a valuable input to the risk-based audit plan. It provides a partnering bridge to the risk and first-line functions and makes combined assurance easier. It helps IA to become more forward looking and it opens up an opportunity for IA to move judiciously into a consulting role in order to assist the risk and first line with combined assurance. It helps IA to assure many aspects of risk management, not the least of which is the risk management plan and risk function competencies to deliver the maturity capability improvements.

Benefits for the board function in risk maturity

The risk maturity model drives the risk management system gap-improvements and integrates the risk management plan with the detail and benchmarking metrics needed by the board and CxOs to integrate these with organization planning with implementation and resourcing. The shared model reported by the risk and audit functions can serve as a proxy for rating the level of confidence that the board and CxOs have in the ability of the organization to manage the system that is reporting risks.

There are also other benefits for the board and CxO functions. The risk maturity model clarifies what the risk management function does and what the risk management profession is defined as, by shaping consensus on what the core and related risk management capabilities required for risk management actually are. Using the model moves the board and senior management table *closer* to what is really happening with the so-called three lines of defence/offence. The strategic nature and longevity of the risk maturity model can demonstrate the competencies in the risk function and CRO role.

Summary

Supporting a risk maturity model has a range of benefits for the three key influencer-functions on the success of the model. For the risk function, it boosts their – and the organization's – level of confidence in its ability to manage and report risks; it helps elevate the risk management discipline into a profession; it can boost their job competencies performance, reward and recognition as well a range of other role-enhancing benefits. The risk maturity model is the most potent tool for assessing risk management effectiveness in answer to the mandate to do so imposed on all internal auditors by the Institute for Internal Audit (IIA) and serves other secondary benefits to their profession. For the board and CxOs, the benefits revolve around increased confidence in the risk management system behind the risks being reported.

These three key influencers should work separately and together to optimize this risk maturity tool. A summary of how their roles are combined takes the form of a RACI analysis, as set out in Table 6.1.

TABLE 6.1 RACI matrix summarizing risk maturity model functional roles

	Risk Function	Internal Audit Function	Board and CXO Functions
Oversight			R
Mandate and commitment			R
Steward	R		A
Assurance by first line	C	I	A
Assurance by third line		R	A
Risk-based audit plan input	C	R	A

TABLE 6.1 *Continued*

	Risk Function	Internal Audit Function	Board and CXO Functions
Creation of risk function		C	R
Principles put into effect, including risk maturity strategy (ISO 31000 Principle k)	R	I	A
Incentive and rewards	C		R
Plan (PDCA)	R	R	R
Do (PDCA)	R		
Check (PDCA)	R	R	R
Act (PDCA)	R		A
Risk maturity model process	R		A
Risk management plan integrated with risk maturity model	R		A
Integrates with ERM and organization	R		A
Coordinates functional activities	R		A
Risk management system capabilities	R		A
Risk mature culture	R		A
International standards aligned	R		A
Reporting	R	I	A

RESPONSIBLE: who is assigned to do the work

ACCOUNTABLE: final decision-maker with ultimate ownership

CONSULTED: who must be consulted *before* a decision or action

INFORMED: who must be informed that a decision or action *has* been taken

Summary of risk maturity models from practitioner perspectives

Each of our risk maturity modeller practitioners mapped out a different route on their respective journeys to creating their new risk maturity model or improving an existing one. Each was following a continuous journey of tailoring, benchmarking and redesigning the model to their organization, in order to achieve the highest purpose (amongst others) of such a model, being the assessment of risk management effectiveness.

Practitioner Megan learns to leverage resources to move up the curve

Practitioner Megan was the quality manager for an NGO running diverse welfare, mental health and education programmes with no existing risk maturity model. Megan demonstrated that having no dedicated risk function or training, no budgets and resources and even a 'risk-averse' work culture are all not a bar to developing an effective risk maturity model. Megan took an exploratory, low-cost and learn-as-you-go approach to successfully build her risk maturity model. She understood from the BP Gulf of Mexico case study that risk maturity is not only about taking time and managing progression, but regression and stasis states as well.

Megan researched well from all our preceding chapters before following our three design steps. She used Chapter 3 resources to build a simple spreadsheet-based risk maturity model based on 43 underlying maturity capabilities. She used the SCRLC downloadable gratis spreadsheet; then adapted and built on the 22 capabilities from the Monda ERMi model with other capabilities she chose (by researching the quality management-originated and not-for-profit maturity models such as Hillson, LTRC/EFQM, ALARM, Fraser Health and HM Treasury). She used Chapter 4 to survey the large field of guidance standards and codes. She preferred the European Foundation for Quality Movement (EFQM) and the leading King III code because King III had the clearest, specific and most numerous guidance for capabilities in a risk management system compared to any other global corporate governance code.

Despite her lack of ERM experience and resources, Megan had no difficulties following our three-step design process (Chapter 5). She preferred the technical robustness of the capability completion format over the text-in-box format and tailored her model's range scoring to fit her work culture. After year one, she adroitly tapped the expertise of her internal audit team for combined assurance so as to improve the model. This helped them formally to assess risk management effectiveness at least once a year. After year 2, she cleverly tapped her external insurance broker to also improve her model, at no cost.

Practitioner Chris learns to keep it simple moving up the curve

Practitioner Chris started with no existing risk maturity model as a young risk and insurance manager for a 'small/lean/mean' construction outfit. He maintained a 'keep it simple' approach to creating his own risk maturity model through our three-step design process. This started with a simple spreadsheet made up of components working in a basic sequence: Components = Domains + Capabilities + Levels + Scales.

In year one, he compared the maturity-model field from our directory resources for the simpler basic and conceptual tier models (Chapter 3). He learnt to separate effective from efficient risk management systems. He liked external benchmarking and tailoring and used external Aon benchmarking to help build his model and entered his preferred ERM domain-capabilities on a matrix. He considered scored ratings bias before opting for the four-point scale method as better fit to his firm and used it to arrive at a first-time 'baseline' maturity level rating.

In year 2 and beyond, Chris continued to improve on his maturity model. He opted for cross-sector external benchmarking to boost objectivity in his model. He took content bias into consideration and found a technique called 'cross-walking' to stay neutral and, in so doing, he aligned his model's capabilities to both the two leading codes of ISO 31000 and COSO ERM (whilst adding Standard & Poor's requirements). In effect, Chris learnt to adopt a mix of techniques to add guidance codes. He thus benefited from natural hedging by using Chapter 5's 10 techniques to improve objectivity in his maturity model.

Practitioner Asha learns advanced external benchmarking

Practitioner Asha was the experienced head of ERM for a large multinational listed recruitment firm and started her journey with no existing risk maturity model. Asha was proud of the proven array of risk maturity ERM and success metrics that are available and made use of them to justify an investment case in risk maturity models and her use of external consultants (Chapter 2).

Asha wanted the 'best' available model. She compared the model directory (Chapter 3) and took an interest in the models in the benchmark-able, intermediate and specialist tiers. She researched a selection from the array of guidance codes (Chapter 4) and found King III and ISO 31000 the most useful to build the mix of capabilities she wanted to design into her spreadsheet model. Asha was adroit at learning from Chapter 4 how to align her risk function operating model to her organization operating model (OpMod); then leveraging certain missing capabilities exposed by these techniques to focus and tailor her three-step designed risk maturity model. Contrary to Chris and Alan, Asha favoured five-point rating scales and even created her own detailed scale descriptions in order to reduce rating biases such as optimism bias (adapted from HB158 standards).

Over the ensuing years, Asha continued to refine and improve the ability of her risk maturity model to assess risk management effectiveness. She invested in external consultants using a Delphi method exercise with subject matter experts and found ways to improve the objectivity and tailored content of her risk maturity model with improvements such as ranged scoring and new capabilities to be rated.

Asha found that the model also gave her ammunition to add more value to the organization. She converted a competitor finding into three new business-improvement opportunities on her risk register then agreed with the chief operating officer and the CEO how to optimize them to regain a competitive edge. She brings the three opportunities to the attention of the strategy head, who updates the following year's KPIs on the balanced-scorecard performance management system.

Practitioner Alan learns advanced self-benchmarking

Practitioner Alan was an internal auditor for a medium-sized government-owned power utility. Alan assured and acted as an independent assessor for an existing risk maturity model that the ERM manager stewarded. Alan happily maintained the risk maturity model – alongside the risk function – as a productive shared tool to meet the Institute for Internal Audit (IIA) mandatory requirement to assess risk management effectiveness at least annually.

Alan took a collaborative and relatively advanced technical approach to monitoring and reviewing their existing risk maturity model. Alan was aware of its origins and supportive of its evolution away from the single-to-one-process capability model approach to the modern risk maturity model approach of rating an expanded set of multi-capabilities. The latter took in not just process but people, technology, culture, decision-making practices and many other multi-capabilities. Alan recommended using a certifiable business continuity submodel to carry its score up to the ERM maturity model thereby tailoring the ERM level more to the continuity risk profile of the utility. Alan preferred four-point but added weighted scales to arrive at a range-scored maturity model.

Alan preferred, like Chris, *not* to be solely aligned with the two leading guidance codes (ISO 31000 and COSO ERM) as they were too limiting for his organization. He preferred to focus on using the inherent self-benchmarking strength of a risk maturity model to self-improve the organization by gap-filling from current to targeted improvements in risk management system capabilities. Alan adapted the templates provided in Chapter 4 to conduct internal and joint-functional organization OpMod and economic value chain reviews. The results not only updated the shared risk maturity model but the risk maturity strategy, as executed through the risk management plan as well as the risk-based audit plan. Alan wondered why every organization did not use a risk maturity model in these ways.

Summary and future moving up the risk maturity curve

All organizations should develop strategies to improve their risk management maturity alongside all other aspects of their organization. All organizations should assess risk management effectiveness as mandated within the IA profession. Risk maturity models in their various and still-emerging forms are the most powerful tools available today to effect such a strategy and assessment together.

All our realistic fictional practitioners – regardless of their different journeys and model design tactics – overcame organization restraints. They anticipate a bright future for their respective risk maturity models as the most powerful tool to assess risk management effectiveness and to provide other benefits. They understand that any single tool cannot guarantee organization success and that capability improvement means a probabilistic solution. They are confident that future redefinitions of the alternatives or outputs/outcomes required to assess risk management effectiveness will only strengthen risk maturity models. Risk maturity models have it in their DNA to absorb such redefinitions and changes.

Risk maturity models will continue to evolve and grow from the relative 'teenagers' they are today. Ironically, they will move themselves further up their own maturity curve of development and application. There are no size, time, budget and resource constraints stopping models being put to use. They will spread across the developing world at the same time as the developed world learns to more fully utilize their as-yet unrealized potential in the right management hands. That future will see risk maturity absorb more cross-disciplinary learning from other disciples and sciences such as neuroscience and heuristics.

Even the most powerful tool such as a risk maturity model needs the right hands to guide the tool and support the investment case to implement and sustain it. The combined roles of the risk officer, internal auditor and board/CxO functions are the key influencers on the success of a risk maturity model. The risk function may steward it and the IA function assure it but the board/CxO functions must provide risk oversight and ongoing mandate and commitment. The future will see boards and CxOs increasingly ask for the risk maturity progress of their organization as naturally as they now ask for reasonable assurance that an organization is taking the right risks to achieve objectives.

The higher the level of risk management system maturity, the higher the level of confidence stakeholders enjoy that the organization is managing its risks effectively – and the higher the chance of organization success. Higher-maturity organizations benefit by outperforming their peers when it comes to revenue growth, firm value and by a variety of both 'hard' and 'soft' measures.

So Megan, Chris, Alan and Asha want to ask you: *what is stopping your organization moving up the risk maturity curve?*

GLOSSARY

(*Italics* represent cross-defined words)

assessing risk management effectiveness To evaluate or diagnose how well an *organization risk management system* is doing the right things (*effectiveness*) to manage *risk*. For internal audit/board: an objective written assessment of the effectiveness of the system of risk management and the internal control framework to the board (King III, 2009).

benchmarking The use of internal or external points of reference or standards against which *risk management system* and *effectiveness* may be compared, checked or assessed.

board The board of directors responsible for *organization* risk oversight and their equivalents in public agencies and not-for-profits.

board risk director Emerging role as a risk specialist individual or chief risk officer-level director sitting on the *board* leveraging their competencies in *enterprise risk management* and *risk maturity models*.

capabilities Specific abilities, faculties or powers of an *organization* enabling it to collectively deliver organization objectives in the face of threats and to leverage opportunities.

capability level An indicator, position or stage on a scale of quantity, extent, rank or quality of organization *capability*.

capability maturity model (CMM) A model based on the maturation of one specific *organization process capability* such as software development.

capacity A maximum amount that can be contained or produced; typically expressed in metric terms for the use or build-up of resources to a desired or measured level, optimum or maximum.

combined assurance The joint and aligned organization assurance processes by the management and internal audit functional lines to maximize *risk management*, governance oversight and control effectiveness, and optimize overall assurance to the audit and risk committee and board (King III, 2009); also the *three lines of defence/offence* concept (IIA).

competency An underlying ability of an individual to perform a job or task properly or excel at it; by combining a set of observable knowledge, skills, attitude that often result in work behaviours.

components Parts or units, as in the interlinked parts that make up a *risk maturity model*; typically in a sequence of *domains*, *capabilities*, *levels* and *scales*.

corporate governance A framework of rules and practices by which a board of directors ensures accountability, fairness and transparency in a company's relationship with all its stakeholders (BusinessDictionary.com) (King III).

COSO Committee of Sponsoring Organizations of the Treadway Commission (2004) comprised of five bodies: the American Accounting Association; the American Institute of Public Accountants; Financial Executives International; the Association of Accountants and Financial Professionals in Business; and the Institute of Internal Auditors.

decision-analysis A science and *organization* discipline comprising the philosophy, theory, methodology and professional practice necessary to address important decisions in a formal manner and structured way.

domain A sphere of activity or knowledge; a subject area or content theme such as business continuity or corporate strategy, which themes or modularizes the *capabilities* within a *risk maturity model.*

effective decision-making A cognitive and managerial *process* alongside an integrated *risk management system* for making the right decisions when faced with choice(s) to achieve and optimize organization objectives or outcomes.

effectiveness To produce a desired or intended result and a focus or mantra on 'doing the right things' within *organizations.*

efficiency Commonly, the ratio of the useful work performed by a machine or in a *process* to the total energy expended or heat taken in (COED) and a focus or mantra on 'doing things right' in terms of achieving organization objectives faster, better or cheaper.

enterprise Synonymous with *organization.*

enterprise risk management (ERM) typically synonymous with *risk management* for all sectors; also used to emphasize an integrated and holistic 'umbrella' approach delivering objectives by managing *risk* across an *organization,* its silos, its risk specialist and other subfunctions and *processes.*

format As in the design arrangement of the *risk maturity model* used to arrive at a *maturity* level or assessment, eg text-in-box or capability-based format.

governance, risk and compliance (GRC) An emerging cross-discipline and information systems domain to bring together corporate governance, *risk management* and compliance disciplines.

key performance indicators (KPIs) Performance metrics specific to an *organization* that measure progress against its objectives and key success factors; may include a risk maturity model assessment index rating or measure.

key risk indicators (KRIs) Thresholds specific to an organization, which if crossed, indicate levels of risk that may be outside the organization's risk tolerance, that is, levels of risk aversion (Caralli, Allen and White, 2011); may be represented by part or whole of *risk maturity model* assessment index rating(s) or measure(s).

King III Code: 2009 Leading corporate governance code for universal application in terms of quantity and quality of *risk management* guidance with detailed, specific and clear requirements for risk management by board, internal audit, risk and other functions.

levels The steps, classes or tiers of overall *risk management* capability or *capabilities* often themed into modules as a *component* within a *risk maturity model.*

Likert scales A statistical method of ascribing quantitative value to qualitative data to make it amenable to statistical analysis. Commonly used in questionnaires as a five- or seven-point scale (scoring step). Sometimes stepped with negative and positive values to a neutral mid-point. Sometimes stepped in ascending sophistication, quality or other measure.

matrix Data or information sorted into boxes for ease of analysis, typically by two sets of criteria, eg 'number' times 'year' on an x and y axis.

maturity Concept relating to the current or future state, fact, or period of evolving development, quality, sophistication and *effectiveness* (not necessarily age-dependent).

maturity model A simplified system that 'road maps' improving, desired, anticipated, typical or logical evolutionary paths of organization actions. The ascending direction implies progression and increased organization effectiveness over time (albeit subject to stasis and regression).

measurement A quantitatively expressed reduction of uncertainty based on one or more observations. For risk maturity models, may be expressed as an overall index score to 100% within which certain percentiles equate to ascending *maturity* levels; and/or, as *Likert scales* to assess the *capabilities* being assessed to arrive at the overall score.

organization Synonymous with enterprise as in ERM; an administrative structure in which people collectively manage one or more services/activities as a whole, share senior management and operate under a set of policies (Caralli, Allen and White, 2011).

process A series of discrete steps, activities, actions or tasks towards achieving a particular end (COED) or that contribute to the fulfillment of a service or product mission (Caralli, Allen and White, 2011).

reasonable assurance To check for correctness and truthfulness; achieved when the *risk* is at an acceptable level according to common sense and logic; whilst: 1) acknowledging that it is not possible to assert absolutely and certainly that an event will (or will not) occur; and 2) qualifying that while a standard conforms to known limits, it is not excessive in any way (**http://www.businessdictionary.com/definition/reasonable-assurance.html**).

risk The effect of uncertainty on objectives where the effect is a deviation from the expected – either positive and/or negative (ISO Guide 73:2009 1.1).

risk management Coordinated activities that direct and control an *organization* in pursuit of its objectives and with regard to *risk* (ISO 31000:2009 and its associated vocabulary Guide 73:2009 2.1).

risk management plan A scheme within the *risk management* framework specifying the approach, the management components, accountabilities and resources to be applied to the management of *risk* and how to implement *risk maturity strategy* (ISO 31000); and, how to implement the improvement outputs 'road-mapped' by a *risk maturity model.*

risk management system The interconnected mechanisms and initiatives organizing the right *organization capabilities* to deliver *risk management effectiveness*; inputs and desired risk management outputs-to-outcomes; may include risk management information systems.

risk manager Typically, a risk officer/functionary within a full- or part-time dedicated *risk management* function to technically support line managers who remain the *risk* owners and managers. Sometimes extended to mean all board, executive and staff members who all share risk management accountably.

risk maturity model An abbreviation for a *capability maturity model* specialized to an expanded set of *risk management system capabilities.* It represents a diagnostic tool using levels of *maturity* to track gap-improvement of the right organization capabilities designed to deliver risk management effectiveness. More correctly and in full: a *risk management system capability maturity model.*

risk maturity strategies To develop and implement schemes to *improve risk management maturity* alongside all other aspects of their organization (ISO 31000:2009 Principle k).

risk specialty or subdisciplines A group label for sub-ERM disciplines such as safety and health and related organization functions such as legal.

scales See Likert scale.

silo factor A state where department-based management of organization activity and/or compartmentalized risk management activities may result in a narrow, parochial view of risk that prevents management from understanding risks facing the entire enterprise (adapted from IRMi, 2015).

standard Commonly, a level of quality or attainment or a required or agreed level of quality or attainment; formally, the most commonly agreed standard by accredited technical bodies for risk management representing nations ie ISO 31000:2009.

tailoring To align the *risk management* approach to the unique-to-organization objectives, internal and external context and risk profile(s) (ISO 31000:2009). For *risk maturity models*, tailoring is driven primarily by choice and quality of the *capabilities* content and *scales* and influenced by external and internal *benchmarking*, model design of *components*, and other techniques and methods.

three lines of defence/offence An assurance approach relying on *risk management* cooperation between the organization front-line managers and operating functions, support functions and internal audit function. 'Defence/offence' relates to risk management functions combining *capabilities* to create as well as protect organization value and/or to deal with *risk* sources with either/both or alternating negative or positive consequences. Source: the IIA, which adapted it from ECIIA/FERMA Guidance on the 8th EU Company Law Directive, article 41 [Online] **https://na.theiia.org/standards guidance/Public%20Documents/PP%20The%20Three%20Lines%20of%20Defense%20in%20Effective%20Risk%20Management%20and%20Control.pdf**.

REFERENCES

Aberdeen Group Inc (2014) Operational Risk Management: Building a framework to identify, assess and remediate, Analyst Insight Primary Research, February 2014 [Online] www.aberdeen.com/_aberdeen/Operational%20Risk%20Management%5Bc%5D%20Building%20a%20Framework/-/-/-/search.aspx [accessed 23.9.15]

Accenture (2011) Report on the Accenture 2011 Global Risk Management Study: Risk management as a source of competitive advantage and high performance, United States [Online] https://www.rims.org/resources/ERM/Documents/Accenture_Global_ %202011.pdf [accessed 23.9.15]

ALARM (2015) The ALARM National Performance Model for Risk Management in the Public Services Booklet, UK [Online] http://www.alarm-uk.org/asset.ashx?assetid=bd5d3887-be73-4dfa-ab86-70b0f01f7ff0 [accessed 23.9.15]

Althonayan, A and Killackey, H (2012) ERM Culture Alignment to Enhance Competitive Advantage, 2012 ERM Symposium, 18–20 April 2012, Washington DC [Online] www.ermsymposium.org/2012/research-papers.php [accessed 23.9.15]

Andrews, KR (1986) *The Concept of Corporate Strategy*, Irwin, United States

Antonucci, D (2014a) Tales from the east: behind the ERM curve part 1, *Risk Management Today*, **32**, pp 212–15

Antonucci, D (2014b) Tales from the east: behind the ERM curve part 2, *Risk Management Today*, **32** (24) February, pp 12–16

Antonucci, D (2014c) Moving boards up the risk maturity curve, Board Management Report edition, *StrategicRISK*, January, p 9

Antonucci, D (2015) Benchmarker™ enterprise risk maturity software synopsis [Online] http://www.stpub.com/Radar-Enterprise-Risk-Management-ERM-BenchMarkerTM_p_302.html [accessed 10.10.15]

Aon (2015) *RMI Risk Maturity Index Insight Report*, November 2015, United States

Aon-Wharton (2013) Risk Maturity Index, *Aon Centre for Innovation and Analytics Limited and Wharton Business School, University of Pennsylvania*, first released Feb 2013 [Online] http://www.aon.com/rmi/ [accessed 25.9.15]

Arguden, Yilmaz (2010) Measuring the Effectiveness of Corporate Governance, INSEAD Business School Knowledge 16 April 2010 [Online] http://knowledge.insead.edu/leadership-organisations/measuring-the-effectiveness-of-corporate-governance-1149 [accessed 25.9.15]

ASX (2015) Corporate Governance Council [Online] http://www.asx.com.au/regulation/corporate-governance-council.htm [accessed 25.9.15]

Bain & Co (2012) Winning Operating Models, 14 September 2012 [Online] http://www.bain.com/publications/articles/winning-operating-models.aspx. [accessed 25.9.15]

Baroudi, R (2010) *KPI Mega Library: 17,000 key performance indicators*, self-published, Charleston, United States

BD Institute (2005) Capability Maturity Model® for Business Development, Version 1.0 – Staged Representation – Sustainable Results in a Competitive World, *Business Development Institute International BD-CMM Development Team and Steering Committee*, Phoenix, United States, August 2005 (with updates through April 2007) pp 101–04 [Online] http://www.bd-institute.org/pdf/BD-CMM_2013_0524_Download.pdf [accessed 28.9.15]

Beasley, MS, Branson, B and Hancock, B (2015) Report on the Current State of Enterprise Risk Oversight: Update on trends and opportunities, Deloitte and ERM Initiative at North Carolina State University on behalf of AICPA American Institute of CPAs Business Industry and Government Team, 6th edition, February 2015 [Online] www.ncsu.edu [accessed 4.5.2015]

Box, GEP (1976), Science and statistics, *Journal of the American Statistical Association*, 71 (356), pp 791–99

Caralli, RA, Allen, JH and White, DW (2011) *CERT Resilience Management Model (RMM): A maturity model for managing operational resilience*, Version 1.1 SEI Series, Pearson, United States

CEB (2016) ERM Maturity Diagnostic, *CEB Risk Management Leadership Council of the Corporate Executive Board Company* [Online] https://www.cebglobal.com/exbd/risk-audit/risk-management/index.page? [accessed 4/3/16]

Chapman, R (2006) *Simple Tools and Techniques for Enterprise Risk Management*, John Wiley and Sons Ltd, UK

CIPSA (2012) Six Building Blocks to Bolster Procurement Capability, white paper written by Peter Morichovitis, *Chartered Institute for Purchasing and Supply for Australia (CIPSA)*, August 2012 [Online] http://www.cips.org/Documents/Resources/White%20papers/Six%20Building%20Blocks%20to%20Bolster%20Procurement%20Capability.pdf [accessed 21.3.16]

Clayton, Dan (2011) Risk Maturity [Blog] Marks On Governance, comment on post 29 March 2011 [Online] https://normanmarks.wordpress.com/ [accessed 3.9.15]

Clayton, D (2012) Dan Clayton – Response to COSO Update – 29 March 2012 [Online] http://www.coso.org/documents/IC_COSO_COMMENTS/PREVIOUS/50-f388bcd0-5c43-4af7-8986-55ffed6c7095_Dan%20Clayton%20COSO%20Response%203-29-12.pdf [accessed 6.10.15]

COED *Concise Oxford English Dictionary* (2011), Oxford University Press, UK

COSO Committee of Sponsoring Organizations of the Treadway Commission (2004) Enterprise Risk Management—Integrated Framework, United States [Online] http://www.erm.coso.org/Coso/cosem.nsf/vvWebResources?PDF_Manuscript?$file/COSO_Manuscript.pdf. [accessed 19.12.14]

COSO Committee of Sponsoring Organizations of the Treadway Commission (2015) Guidance on Enterprise Risk Management [Online] http://www.coso.org/-ERM.htm [accessed 3.10.15]

DCRO Directors and Chief Risk Officers Group and Governance Council, Qualified Risk Director Guidelines, 5 June 2013 [Online] http://www.thegovernancefund.com/DCRO/PDF/Qualified_Risk_Director_Guidelines.pdf. [accessed 27.9.15]

Deloitte (2006) *The Risk Intelligent Enterprise: ERM done right*, Deloitte Touche, UK

Deloitte (2008) *Designing a Successful ERM Function*, Deloitte Touche, UK

Deloitte (2010) Risk Intelligent Enterprise Management: Running the Risk Intelligent Enterprise™ [Online] http://www2.deloitte.com/content/dam/Deloitte/lu/Documents/risk/lu-en-riskintelligentmanagement-05012012.pdf [accessed 30.9.15]

Deloitte (2012a) Cultivating a Risk Intelligent Culture: Understand, measure, strengthen and report, *Deloitte Touche* [Online] https://www.politesi.polimi.it/bitstream/10589/91722/3/2014_04_Ravasi.pdf p150 [accessed 16.10.15]

Deloitte (2012b) Risk Intelligent Governance: A Profile-of-Maturity, 30 September 2015 [Online] http://deloitte.wsj.com/cio/2012/05/07/risk-intelligent-governance-a-profile-of-maturity/ [accessed 30.9.15]

Deloitte (2013a) *Global Risk Management Survey*, Deloitte Touche, UK p 14

Deloitte (2013b) Creating a Risk Intelligent Infrastructure: Getting risk intelligence done [Online] http://www2.deloitte.com/content/dam/Deloitte/global/Documents/Governance-Risk-Compliance/dttl-grc-creatingriskintelligentinfrastructure-gettingriskintelligencedone.pdf [accessed 5.10.15]

Deloitte (2015) Putting Risk in the Comfort Zone: Nine principles for building the Risk Intelligent Enterprise [Online] http://www2.deloitte.com/content/dam/Deloitte/global/Documents/Governance-Risk-Compliance/dttl-grc-puttingriskinthecomfortzone.pdf. [accessed 26.9.15]

Ernst & Young (2012) *Turning Risk into Results: How leading companies use risk management to fuel better performance*, EYGM Limited no. AU1082 [Online] Available at: http://www.ey.com/Publication/vwLUAssets/Turning_risk_into_results/$FILE/Turning%20risk%20into%20results_AU1082_1%20Feb%202012.pdf [last accessed 14/5/16]

Farrell, M and Gallagher, R (2014) The Valuation Implications of ERM, *Journal of Risk & Insurance*, Doi 10.1111/jori.12305

FERMA (2012) FERMA Risk Management Benchmarking Survey 2012, *Federation of European Risk Management Associations in partnership with Ernst & Young and AXA*, 6th edn, 30 October 2012 [Online] http://www.ferma.eu/blog/2012/10/ferma-risk-management-benchmarking-survey-2012-the-results/ [accessed 3.10.15]

FERMA (2015) Risk Management Standard [Online] http://www.ferma.eu/blog/2012/10/ferma-risk-management-benchmarking-survey-2012-the-results/ [accessed 3.10.15]

Fraser, J, Simkins, B and Narvaev, K (2015) *Implementing Risk Management: Case studies and best practices*, Wiley & Sons, United States

Gallagher, R and Farell, M (2013) The Valuation Implications of Enterprise Risk Management, 2013, abstract [Online] http://onlinelibrary.wiley.com/doi/10.1111/jori.12035/abstracts [accessed 23.4.14]

Genius Methods Software (2014) Risk Culture Building – The Future of Risk Management [Online] author Horst Simon, http://community.mile.org/index.php/downloads/file/162-risk-culture-building-the-future-of-risk-management#.U55tKS-DzDt [accessed 10.6.14]

G31000 (2013) *C31000 ISO 31000 Certificate Training Handbook*, The Global Institute for Risk Management Standards, Masterclass Version 1.4, November 2013, author Alex Dali, November 2013, self-published, Belgium

Gladwell, M (2009) *What the Dog Saw: And other adventures*, Penguin, United States

Grant Thornton, Risk Maturity Assessment [Online] http://www.grantthornton.co.uk/en/services/advisory/business-risk-services/risk-maturity-assessment/ [accessed 8.11.15]

Halliday, SW (2013a) The Great Debate: ERM and internal audit, presentation to Enterprise Risk Management conference in Dubai, 23 September 2013

Halliday, SW (2013b) *The Structure of Risk Management in Leading Australian Companies*, unpublished doctoral dissertation, Charles Sturt University, Bathurst, NSW, Australia

Hancock, D (2014) The case for risk leadership: focus on soft skills, *RMProfessional*, Autumn 2014, pp 34–37

Hillson, D (1997) Towards a risk maturity model, *International Journal of Project and Business Risk Management*, **1** (1), January pp 35–45

Hillson, D and Simon, P (2013) Practical Project Risk Management: The ATOM methodology [Online] http://www.atom-risk.com/templates.html [accessed 8.11.15]

HM Treasury (2004) *The Orange Book Management of Risk: Principles and concepts*, October, UK

HM Treasury (2009) Orange Book Self-Assessment Tool: Risk Management Assessment Framework (RMAF), revised edn July 2009 [Online] https://www.gov.uk/government/uploads/system/uploads/attachment_data/file/191516/Risk_management_assessment_framework.pdf UK [accessed 02.10.2015]

Hopkinson, M (2011) *The Project Risk Maturity Model: Measuring & improving risk management capability*, Gower, UK

Humphrey, WS (1988) *Managing the Software Process*, Addison-Wesley, United States

IIA IPPF (2010) Mandatory practice guidelines, assessing the adequacy of risk management using ISO 31000, *Institute for Internal Audit IIA*, United States, December

IIARF (2012) The Institute of Internal Auditors Research Foundation, Sobel, PJ and Reding, KF, *Enterprise Risk Management: Achieving and sustaining success*, Institute for Internal Audit Research Foundation IIARF, United States

IIARF (2013) CRMA Exam 1st Edition Study Guide Domain 111 Assurance Role of the Internal Auditor sub-section 111.D, Provide Assurance on Risk Management Processes, pp 151–64, *Institute for Internal Audit Research Foundation IIARF*, United States

IRM (2015) Decisions, Decisions, *RMProfessional*, Spring, pp 32–33

IRMi (2015) Dictionary [Online] http://www.irmi.com/online/insurance-glossary/terms/s/silo-factor.aspx [accessed 10.10.15]

ISACA (2003) [Online] http://www.isaca.org/Journal/Past-Issues/2003/Volume-3/Pages/The-COBIT-Maturity-Model-in-a-Vendor-Evaluation-Case.aspx

ISACA (2009) *RiskIT based on COBIT: The RiskIT practitioner guide*, ISACA, United States

ISO International Organization for Standardization (1993) ISO/IEC 15504 Information Technology – Process Assessment, also known as Software Process Improvement and Capability Determination (SPICE), Switzerland

ISO International Organization for Standardization ISO/IEC (2009a) ISO/IEC 31000:2009 Risk Management – Principles and Guidelines on Implementation, Switzerland

ISO International Organization for Standardization (2009b) Guide 73: Risk management – Vocabulary, 2nd edn, Switzerland

ISO International Organization for Standardization (2009c) ISO/IEC 31010:2009 – Risk Management – Risk Assessment Techniques

ISO International Organization for Standardization ISO/IEC 33001:2015 Information technology – Process assessment standard, Switzerland

Kerzner, H (2005) *Using the Project Management Maturity Model (PMMM): Strategic planning for project management*, 2nd edn, Wiley, United States

King III (2009) King Report on Governance for South Africa, and the King Code of Governance Principles, by Institute of Directors in Southern Africa (IoDSA), came into effect on 1 March 2010 [Online] http://www.iodsa.co.za/?kingIII [accessed 12.10.15]

Knight, KW (2009) Transitioning to the new risk management standard AS/NZS/ISO 31000:2009, slide presentation as chairman of the ISO Working group – risk management standard and technical committee, Australia, August [Online] http://ddata.over-blog.com/xxxyyy/0/32/13/25/Risques/2009_IRMCAUG_ISO31000.pdf [accessed 21.3.16]

Knight, RF and Pretty, DJ (2000) The Impact of Catastrophes on Shareholder Value: A research report, *The Oxford Executive Research Briefings, Templeton College, University of Oxford* [Online] http://www.b-c-training.com/user_uploaded/files/The-Impact-of-Catastrophes-on-Shareholder-Value.pdf [accessed 20.3.16]

KPMG (2008) Enterprise Risk Management Complacency is No Longer an Option, but a Practical Start Is, *KPMG*, Hong Kong [Online] https://www.kpmg.com/CN/en/IssuesAndInsights/ArticlesPublications/Documents/erm-0803.pdf [accessed 9.11.15]

Lau, W (2013) [Blog] 4 April 2013 [Online] [accessed 9.11.14]

Lawrence, RQ (2005) ERM: Embracing a total risk model, *Financial Executives Internationals*, **21** (1), pp 32

Leech, T (2012) Complying with IIA Standard 2120: How to assess and report on the effectiveness of risk management processes, conference presentation paper [Online] http://riskoversight.ca [accessed 9.11.14]

Leech, T (2013) Risk Oversight [Blog] 3 April 2013 [Online] http://riskoversight.ca [accessed 9.11.15]

Luyckx, F (2009a) Maturity level & ROI: Enterprise BPM framework [Online] http://www.ariscommunity.com/users/frlu/2009-03-09-enterprise-bpm-framework-maturity-level-roi [accessed 9.11.15]

Marks, N (2011) Measuring the Maturity of Risk Management [Blog] Marks On Governance, 29 March 2011 [Online] https://iaonline.theiia.org/measuring-maturity-of-risk-management [accessed 28.9.15]

Marks, N (2012) Respected Risk Thought Leaders Opine on the Future Role of Internal Audit [Blog] Marks On Governance, 11 May 2012 [Online] file:///Users/Domenic/Documents/Benchmarker%20Project%20RMM%20library%20/Marks%20Future%20Role%20of%20IA%20Schanfield%20Purcy%20Fraser%20Shortreed%203100%20COSO%2020512.webarchive [accessed 28.9.15]

Marks, N (2014) What Are the Characteristics of a World-Class Risk Management Function? [Blog] Marks On Governance, 8 March 2014 [Online] https://iaonline.theiia.org/what-are-the-characteristics-of-a-world-class-risk-management-function [accessed 28.9.15]

Marks, N (2015) *World-Class Risk Management*, CPSIA self-published, United States

Marsh (2008) Shareholder Value: Impact of risk events and relevance of intangible assets, public presentation slide bar-chart (2009), courtesy of the author

Marsh McLellan (2013) Insurance Maturity Model [Online] http://www.worldinsurance-network.com/news/marsh-launches-new-insurance-maturity-model-060313/ [accessed 9.11.15]

Marx, F (2011) *Development of a Maturity Model for IT Support of Business Management*, dissertation 3970, Universität St Gallen, Bamberg, Germany

Mayer, J and Fagundes, LL (2009) A Model to Assess the Maturity Level of the Risk Management Process in Information Security, 4rd IFIP/IEEE International Workshop on BDIM [Online] https://www.researchgate.net/publication/251892864_A_Model_to_Assess_the_Maturity_Level_of_the_Risk_Management_Process_in_Information_Security [accessed 9.11.15]

Monda, B and Giorgino, M (2013) An ERM Maturity Model, paper to ERM Symposium 22–24 April 2013 in Chicago, Ill, United States [Online] http://www.ermsymposium.org/2013/pdf/erm-2013-paper-monda.pdf. Italy [accessed 9.11.15]

Morichovitis, P (2012) Six Building Blocks to Bolster Procurement Capability, *Chartered Institute of Purchasing and Supply (CIPS) Australasia Pty Ltd*, white paper [Online] https://www.cips.org/Documents/Resources/White%20papers/Six%20Building%20Blocks%20to%20Bolster%20Procurement%20Capability.pdf [accessed 03.10.15]

Murphy, RJ (2009) The 4 Levers of Success: Introducing the 4E Model, paper presented at the RiskSIG & PMI, Rome Chapter, International Risk Management Conference, 5–6 November 2009 [Online] https://pmiromechapter.files.wordpress.com/2011/05/rome_risksig_conference_ronan_murphy_2009.pdf [accessed 9.11.15]

NSW Treasury (2012) Risk Management Toolkit for NSW Public Sector Agencies: Volume 2 [Online] http://www.treasury.nsw.gov.au/__data/assets/pdf_file/0020/22565/TPP12-03C_Risk_Management_Toolkit_Vol2-Templates_dnd.pdf [accessed 3.10.15]

OECD (2010) Corporate Governance and the Financial Crisis: Conclusions and emerging good practices to enhance the implementation of the principles, white paper for steering group on corporate governance to the OECD Directorate for Financial and Enterprise Affairs, by Richard Anderson, 17 February [Online] http://www.oecd.org/corporate/ca/corporategovernanceprinciples/44679170.pdf [accessed 10.10.15]

Parkins, S (2010) ERM Readiness Assessment Tool, Fraser Health presentation to ORMIS Conference, Toronto Canada, 21 April 2010, unpublished presentation, Canada

PatelMiller (2015) How To Design the Operating Model to Support Your Business Strategy and Get Everyone Lined Up to Deliver It [Online] http://patelmiller.com/what-we-think/insights/operating-model-design/ [accessed 26.9.15]

Peldzius, S and Ragaisis, S (2011) Investigation Correspondence between CMMI-DEV and ISO/IEC 15504, *International Journal of Education and Information Technologies*, 4 (5), pp 361–68

Pergler, M (2012) Enterprise Risk Management: What's different in the corporate world and why?, McKinsey Working Papers on Risk, No 40, United States, *McKinsey & Company*, December [Online] https://www.google.ae/search?client=safari&rls=en&q=190.+Pergler,+Martin+(2012)+%E2%80%98Enterprise+Risk+Management:+What%E2%80%99s+Different+in+the+Corporate+World+and+Why%3F%E2%80%99&ie=UTF-8&oe=UTF-8&gfe_rd=cr&ei=CyCBVqf3NMuq-wbZgKDgBg [accessed 28.12.15]

Peshawaria, R (2012) The Other Duty of Corporate Governance [Online] http://www.forbes.com/sites/rajeevpeshawaria/2012/12/01/the-other-duty-of-corporate-governance/ [accessed 4.1.16]

RIMS (2008) State of ERM Report 2008 and RIMS Risk Maturity Model for ERM, published by RIMS and produced by LogicManager and authored by Steven Minsky, with contributions by members of the RIMS ERM Development Committee [Online] https://www.rims.org/ERM/Pages/RiskMaturityModel.aspx [accessed 4.1.16]

RIMS (2013a) RIMS 2013 Enterprise Risk Management (ERM) Survey, Risk and Insurance Management Society & Advisen Ltd Insurance Intelligence, United States [Online] www.rims.org or https://web.actuaries.ie/sites/default/files/erm-resources/rims_erm_survey_2013_09.pdf [accessed 21.11.14]

RIMS (2013b) RIMS Risk Maturity Model (RMM) for Enterprise Risk Management, Risk and Insurance Management Society, United States [Online] www.rims.org/erm/pages/riskmaturitymodel.aspx, 2013 [accessed 9.11.15]

RIMS (2014) Risk Management and Organization Alignment: A strategic focus, released in the Excellence in Risk Management X1 Report by Risk and Insurance Management Society & Marsh, United States, RIMS Denver Conference, April 2014, reports cited in *Commercial Risk Europe*, 5 (4), May, p 1

RIMS (2015a) RIMS Risk Maturity Model (RMM) for Enterprise Risk Management: Executive summary, *Risk and Insurance Management Society* [Online] www.rims.org/erm/pages/riskmaturitymodel.aspx [accessed 20.3.16]

RIMS (2015b) About the RIMS Risk Maturity Model: RIMS executive report, *LogicManager* [Online] www.rims.org/erm/pages/riskmaturitymodel.aspx [accessed 25.11.15]

Riskconnect (2012) Practical Tools to Support Your Growing ERM Program, Presentation to RIMS Conference, Philadelphia, United States, 16–18 April, unpublished

Röglinger, M, Pöppelbuß, J and Becker, J (2012) Maturity models in business process management, *Business Process Management Journal*, 18 (2), p 3

Rosemann, M, de Bruin, T, Freeze, R and Kulkarni (2005) Understanding the Main Phases of Developing a Maturity Assessment Model, Australasian Conference on Information Systems (ACIS), Sydney [Online] [accessed 9.11.15]

S&P (2012) Ratings Direct Methodology: Management and governance credit factors for corporate entities and insurers, Standard & Poor's, 13 November, p 10 [Online] http://www.nietzer.info/wp-content/uploads/2012/11/02-Commentary-on-MG-Criteria.pdf [accessed 6.10.15]

SCRLC (2014) Supply Chain Risk Maturity Model, *Supply Chain Risk Leadership Council USA* [Online] http://www.scrlc.com/ [accessed 28.9.15]

Simpson, JA and Weiner, ES (1989) *The Oxford English Dictionary*, Oxford University Press, UK

Taylor, L (2014) *Practical Enterprise Risk Management: How to optimize business strategies through managed risk taking*, Kogan Page, UK

Treasury Board of Canada (2015) Risk Management Capability Model, *Treasury Board of Canada*, 11 July 2011 [Online] http://www.tbs-sct.gc.ca/tbs-sct/rm-gr/guides/rmcm-mcmgr-eng.asp [accessed 3.10.15]

Western Cape Government South Africa (2014) The Value of Risk Management in the Public Sector, presentation to G31000 Conference, 14 July 2014, by author Beulah Misrole, United States

FURTHER READING

Accenture (2015) Risk Management Capability Framework Diagram [Online] www.google.com/search?q=Accenture,+Risk+Management+Capability+Framework+Diagram&client=safari&rls=en&prmd=ivns&tbm=isch&tbo=u&source=univ&sa=X&ved=0CBQQsARqFQoTCNSaktGsjcgCFYUmHgodVBcOgw [accessed 23.9.15]

Aho, M (2009) A Capability Maturity Model for Corporate Performance Management: An empirical study in large Finnish manufacturing companies, slide presentation [Online] http://www.ebrf.fi/_file/26562/; and http://www.drmika.com/download/Aho_-_A_Capability_Maturity_Model_for_Corporate_Performance_Management.pdf [accessed 23.9.15]

ALARM (2015) The Risk Success Story: improving performance in risk management [Online) http://www.alarm-uk.org/news/risk-success-story; and http://www.alarm-uk.org/member-services/benchmarking [accessed 23.9.15]

ANOA (2014) Public Sector Governance Strengthening Performance Through Good Governance, *Australian National Audit Office Canberra* [Online] http://www.anao.gov.au/~/media/Files/Better%20Practice%20Guides/2013%202014/ANAO%20-%20BPG%20Public%20Sector%20Governance.pdf [accessed 3.9.14]

Arguden, Y (2010) A Corporate Governance Model: Building responsible boards and sustainable businesses, *IFC World Bank Group Global Corporate Governance Forum Private Sector Opinion Issue 17* [Online] http://www.gcgf.org/wps/wcm/connect/1ff2c18048a7e72daa5fef6060ad5911/GCGF%2BPSO%2Bissue%2B17%2B3-4-10.pdf?MOD=AJPERES [accessed 25.9.15]

Arthur J Gallagher & Co (2013) Collaborative Risk Management: 'Risk Management' vs. 'Managing Risk', *Gallagher Higher Education Practice* [Online] http://www.ajgrms.com/portal/server.pt/gateway/PTARGS_0_28406_584576_0_0_18/AJG%20HEP%20Collaborative%20RM%20White%20Paper%202013.pdf [accessed 9.10.15]

AS:NZ HBR 436:2014 Standards Australia/Standards New Zealand Committee OB-007–Draft for Public Comment Risk Management Australian/New Zealand Handbook Risk management guidelines Companion to AS/NZS ISO 31000:2009 (Revision of HB 436:2004)

ASX Corporate Governance Council (2014) Principles of Good Corporate Governance and Best Practice Recommendations [Online] http://www.asx.com.au/documents/asx-compliance/cgc-principles-and-recommendations-3rd-edn.pdf [accessed 25.9.15]

BD-Institute (2015) Capability Maturity Model® for Business Development [Online] http://bd-institute.org/wordpress/?download=the-capability-maturity-model-for-business-development [accessed 28.12.15]

Beasley MS and Frigo, ML (2008) Strategic Risk Management: Creating and protecting value, *Journal of Corporate Accounting and Finance*, 1, pp 81–88

Beasley, MS, Branson, B and Hancock, B (2010) Report on ERM: current state of enterprise risk oversight and market perceptions of COSO's ERM framework, Deloitte and ERM Initiative at North Carolina State University on behalf of AICPA American Institute of CPAs Business Industry & Government Team, 2nd edn [Online] http://www.coso.org/documents/COSOSurveyReportFULL-Web-R6FINALforWEBPOSTING111710.pdf [accessed 17.10.15]

Beasley, MS, Branson, B and Hancock, B (2012) Report on the Current State of Enterprise Risk Oversight: Update on trends and opportunities, Deloitte and ERM Initiative at North Carolina State University on behalf of AICPA American Institute of CPAs Business Industry and Government Team, 3rd edn [Online] www.ncsu.edu [accessed 4.5.2015]

Beasley, MS (2013) Strengthening the Role of the Chief Risk Officer in an Organization [Online] https://erm.ncsu.edu/library/article/strengthening-the-role-of-the-chief-risk-officer-in-an-organization/ [accessed 5.11.15]

Berssaneti, FT, Fernando, T, de Carvalho, MM, Muscat, N and Namur, A (2012) Impact of reference model for project management and project management maturity models on performance: an exploratory study in information technology projects, *Production*, 22 (3), pp 421–35, May/Aug [Online] http://www.scielo.br/pdf/prod/v22n3/en_aop_t6_0002_0497 [accessed 25.9.15]

BIS (2014) Guidelines: Corporate governance principles for banks July 2015 global guidance for banks only by Bank for International Settlements [Online] http://www.bis.org/bcbs/publ/d328.pdf [accessed 3.11.15]

Calandro, J and Lane, L (2006) Insights from the Balanced Scorecard: An introduction to the enterprise risk scorecard, *Measuring Business Excellence*, pp 31–40

Capgemini (2015) Sigma Map™ and Framework: Multi-dimensional analytics for the risk management maturity model [Online] https://www.capgemini.com/sigma-maptm-framework [accessed 27.09.2015]

CEB (2013) ERM Maturity Diagnostic, *CEB Risk Management Leadership Council of the Corporate Executive Board Company* [Online] http://www.executiveboard.com/exbd-resources/pdf/legal-risk-compliance/risk/CEB%20Risk%20Maturity%20Diagnostic.pdf [accessed 31.12.15]

Chapman, R (2014) *The Rules of Project Management*, Gower, UK

Chartered Institute of Internal Auditors (2014) Governance and Risk Report 2014: Internal audit's perspective on the management of risk, 2014 survey of internal audit leaders by the UK affiliate of the IIA [Online] https://www.iia.org.uk/media/1023003/0819-iia-gov-risk-summary-24-10-14-final.pdf [accessed 8.11.15]

Clayton, Dan (2010) Building the Case for ERM [Blog] Marks on Governance 29 October [Online] https://normanmarks.wordpress.com/2010/10/28/building-the-case-for-erm/ [accessed 3.9.15]

COSO Committee of Sponsoring Organizations of the Treadway Commission (2014) Enterprise Risk Management – Integrated Framework, Update Project

Frequently Asked Questions (FAQ) [Online] http://www.coso.org/documents/COSO%20ERM%20FAQs%2011%205%2014.pdf [accessed 3.10.15]

CSA Q31001:2011 Implementation Guide To CAN/CSA-ISO 31000, Risk Management – Principles And Guidelines, Canadian Standards Association

Davies, M (2012) Operational Risk and Credit Maturity Map [Online] http://causalcapital.blogspot.sg/2014/04/risk-based-audit.html [accessed 24.10.15]

Davies, M (2014) Risk Based Audits: 31000 Risk Frameworks: A working case study [Online] http://causalcapital.blogspot.sg/2014/04/risk-based-audit.html. [accessed 24.10.15]

Deloitte (2012) *Risk Angles*, Deloitte Touche, UK

Deloitte (2014a) Aligning Risk and the Pursuit of Effectiveness, Efficiency and Accountability: Risk transformation [Online] www2.deloitte.com/content/dam/Deloitte/au/Documents/risk/deloitte-au-risk-aligning-risk-pursuit-effectiveness-efficiency-aountablity-0614.pdf [accessed 30.9.15]

Deloitte (2014b) Exploring Strategic Risk [Online] http://www2.deloitte.com/content/dam/Deloitte/global/Documents/Governance-Risk-Compliance/dttl-grc-exploring-strategic-risk.pdf

Eadie, R, Perera, S and Heaney, G (2011) Key process area mapping in the production of an e-capability maturity model for UK construction organisations, *Journal of Financial Management of Property and Construction*, **16** (3), pp 197–210

Elmaallam, M and Kriouile, A (2011) Towards a Model of Maturity for IS Risk Management, *International Journal of Computer Science & Information Technology* (IJCSIT), **3** (4) August, pp 171–81

Ernst & Young (2009) Risk Management Framework Review of a Maturity Model, Briefing Paper, United States

Ernst & Young EY (2015) Rethinking Risk Management: 2015 risk management survey of major financial institutions, sixth annual study of risk management practices conducted by EY in cooperation with the Institute of International Finance (IIF) [Online] http://www.ey.com/Publication/vwLUAssets/EY-rethinking-risk-management/$FILE/EY-rethinking-risk-management.pdf [accessed 18.10.15]

FAA (2009) Safety Management System: Flight standards pilot project process, 12 November [Online] http://www.faa.gov/about/initiatives/sms/pilot_projects/afs_process/ [accessed 11.11.15]

FAA (2002) Federal Aviation Administration (FAA)-integrated Capability Maturity Model, (FAA-iCMM) [Online] http://www.asq0511.org/Presentations/0702/index.htm [accessed 11.11.15]

Farrell, M and Hoon, A (2009) What's Your Company's Risk Culture? *Directorship*, 12 May, p 118 and [Online] http://www.businessweek.com/managing/content/may2009/ca20090512_720476.htm [accessed 11.11.15]

Ferrando, A and Parra, C (2008) Operational Risk Management Maturity Model for Mutual Insurer Control Systems, *BDO Audiberia Portugal* [Online] https://provisoes.files.wordpress.com/2008/09/i2.pdf [accessed 25.9.15]

Financial Times (2010) Emerging Risks: Steering the course, seizing the opportunity, in association with Oliver Wyman survey August 2010 [Online] www.commerce.depaul.edu/sev/docs.Risks_Roundtable_Materials/OW_EN_CR_PUBL_2010_Emerging_Risks.pdf [accessed 4.11.14]

Fraser, J, Simkins, B and Narvaev, K (2010) *Enterprise Risk Management: Today's leading research and best practices for tomorrow's executives*, Wiley & Sons, United States

FRC (2014) UK Corporate Governance Code, Review of the Combined Code: Final Report, *Financial Reporting Council Limited* [Online] https://www.frc.org.uk/Our-Work/Publications/Corporate-Governance/UK-Corporate-Governance-Code-2014.pdf [accessed 3.11.15]

Frigo, ML (2009) Strategic Risk Management: The new core competency, balanced scorecard report, Boston, *Harvard Business Review*, January–February, pp 7–10

Frigo, ML and Anderson, RJ (2009) Strategic Risk Assessment: A first step for improving risk management and governance, *Strategic Finance*, December, pp. 24–33

Frigo, ML and Anderson, RJ (2011) Embracing Enterprise Risk Management: Practical approaches for getting started, COSO – The Committee of Sponsoring Organisations of the Treadway Commission

Frigo, ML and Anderson, R (2014) Risk Management Frameworks: Adapt, don't adopt, *Strategic Finance*, January, pp 48–53

FSB (2014) Guidance on the Supervisory Interaction with Financial Institutions on Risk Culture: A framework for assessing risk culture, *Financial Stability Board* [Online] http://www.financialstabilityboard.org/wp-content/uploads/140407.pdf?page_moved=1 [accessed 9.11.15]

Gartner (2013) Gartner IAM Program Maturity Model [Online] http://www.slideshare.net/smooregartner/the-gartner-iam-program-maturity-model [accessed 8.11.15]

Happy Manager, The (2015) 7 Step Decision Making Process Infographic [Online] http://www.the-happy-manager.com/tips/7-step-decision-making-process-infographic/ [accessed 4.11.15]

Herrinton, M (2012) How Mature is Your Risk Management? *Harvard Business Review* 29 June [Online] http://blogs.hbr.org/2012/06/how-mature-is-your-risk-manage/ [accessed 28.9.15]

Hindson, A (2010) Developing a Risk Culture, *Risk Management Professional*, December, pp 28–29

Hindson, A (2011) Embedding Risk Management and Creating a Risk Culture, *The Institute of Risk Management UK*, 25 November [Online] http://www.iiag.org.uk/events/documents/Alex_HindsonIAAG_Presentation_25111_embedding_risk.pdf [accessed 9.11.15]

Hogan, T (2008) The adaptive leadership maturity model, *Organisation Development Journal*, **26** (1) Spring p 55

Hüffner, T (2007) The BPM Maturity Model: Towards a framework for assessing the business process management maturity of organizations, thesis paper with Patrick Hammer, Tanja Hammer, Matthias Knoop, Julius Mittenzwei, Georg Steinbach u. Michael Teltscher, GRIN Verlag GbR, 2007.l [Online] http://www.grin.com/en/e-book/33497/the-bpm-maturity-model-towards-a-framework-for-assessing-the-business [accessed 8.11.15]

Humphrey WS (1988) Characterizing the Software Process: A maturity framework, *IEEE Software*, 5 (2), March 1988, pp 73–79

ICCA (2013) *Concise Guide to Treasury Risk Management*, The Institute of Chartered Accountants of Australia, Australia

IBM (2012) Combating Risk with Predictive Intelligence: An analytical approach to enterprise risk management, *Global Services Institute for Business Value Executive Report* [Online] ftp://public.dhe.ibm.com/software/au/201301/Anticipate_9Combating_risk_with_predictive_intelligence_Executive_Summary.PDF [accessed 9.10.15]

IIA (2010) Standard Practice Advisory 2120–1, *Institute for Internal Audit*

IIA (2012) Global Internal Audit Competency Framework, *Institute for Internal Audit*

IIA (2013) Three Lines of Defense; Standards Over Guidelines Over Tools & Techniques, *Institute for Internal Audit* [Online] https://na.theiia.org/standards-guidance/Public%20Documents/PP%20The%20Three%20Lines%20of%20Defense%20in%20Effective%20Risk%20Management%20and%20Control.pdf [accessed 8.11.15]

INCOSE (2002) Risk Management Maturity Level Development: Processes and methods, developed jointly by International Council on Systems Engineering Formal Collaboration between INCOSE Risk Management Working Group; Project Management Institute Risk Management Specific Interest Group; UK Association For Project Management Risk Specific Interest Group, UK [Online] https://acc.dau.mil/CommunityBrowser.aspx?id=17748 [accessed 8.11.15]

IRM (2015) Risk Management Standards [Online] https://www.theirm.org/knowledge-and-resources/risk-management-standards.aspx [accessed 26.9.15]

IRM (2012) Risk Culture: Under the microscope guidance for boards, *Institute of Risk Management UK and Protiviti* [Online] https://www.theirm.org/media/885907/Risk_Culture_A5_WEB15_Oct_2012.pdf [accessed 19.10.15]

IRM/Alarm/AIRMIC (2002) A Risk Management Standard, joint publication [Online] http://www.oat.ethz.ch/education/Autumn_term_09/Material_on_Psychological_Aspects/AIRMIC_Risk-Management-Standard_1_.pdf [accessed 19.10.15]

ITGI (2006) IT Governance Institute, *Enterprise Value: Governance of IT investments – the VAL IT* framework, IT Governance Institute, Rolling Meadows, United States

ITGI (2014) IT Reliability Process Maturity Model RPMM, *International TechneGroup Incorporated, USA* [Online] http://www.iti-global.com/solutions/reliability/index_rpmm.php [accessed 8.11.15]

Janis, I (1972) *Victims of Groupthink*, Houghton Mifflin, United States

Kahneman, D (2011) *Thinking Fast and Slow*, Farrar Straus & Giroux, United States

Kahneman, D, Slovic, P and Tversky, A (1982) *Judgement Under Uncertainty: Heuristics and biases*, Cambridge University Press, UK

Kenny, J (2006) Strategy and the learning organization: a maturity model for the formation of strategy, *The Learning Organization*, 13 (4), pp 353–68

Kloman, FH (1999) *Risk Management Reports, Seawrack Press* [Online] www.riskinfo.com/rmr/rmrdec99.htm [accessed 8.11.15]

Kloman, FH (2008) *The Fantods of Risk: Essays on risk management*, Xlibris, United States

KPMG (2013) Expectations of Risk Management Outpacing Capabilities – It's Time For Action, ERM survey jointly with Economist Intelligence Unit, May 2013 [Online] https://www.kpmg.com/Global/en/IssuesAndInsights/ArticlesPublications/risk-management-outpacing-capabilities/Documents/expectations-risk-management-survey-v2.pdf [accessed 9.11.15]

Kraus, M (2008) Risk Management: Roadmap to 'maturity, directors and boards' [Online] www.directorsandboards.com/html/4thQtr2008depts.html [Online] [accessed 9.11.14]

Lai, FW and Samad, FA (2010) Enterprise Risk Management Framework and the Empirical Determinants of its Implementation, International Conference on Business and Economic Research [Online] http://www.ipedr.com/vol1/73-G10003.pdf [accessed 17.10.15]

Lam, J & Associates (2008) Emerging Best Practices in Developing Key Risk Indicators and ERM Reporting, executive white paper sponsored by Cognos, January [Online] ftp://service.boulder.ibm.com/software/data/sw-library/cognos/pdfs/whitepapers/wp_best_pract_in_dev_key_risk_indicators_erm_rep.pdf [accessed 9.11.15]

Lederman, PF (2012) Getting buy-in for your information governance program, *Information Management*, July/August, pp 34–37

Lin, Y, Wen, MM and Yu, J (2011) Enterprise Risk Management: Strategic antecedents, risk integration and performance, working paper [Online] http://www.researchgate.net/profile/Yijia_Lin/publication/228232031_Enterprise_Risk_Management_Strategic_Antecedents_Risk_Integration_and_Performance/links/02e7e5298aab1dfa2c000000.pdf [accessed 9.11.15]

LogicManager (2006) Risk Maturity Model Launch [Online] http://www.logicmanager.com/erm-software/knowledge-center/news/rims-launches-risk-maturity-model-for-enterprise-risk-management/ [accessed 9.11.15]

Luyckx, F (2009b) Enterprise BPM Framework [Online] http://www.ariscommunity.com/users/frlu/2009-03-02-enterprise-bpm-framework [accessed 9.11.15]

Luyckx, F (2012) Enterprise BPM Roadmap Assessments [Online] http://www.lulu.com/shop/frank-luyckx/enterprise-bpm-roadmap-assessments/paperback/product-20265487.html [accessed 10.10.15]

Malaysia Securities Commission (2012) Code on Corporate Governance, update for listed companies [Online] http://www.sc.com.my/wp-content/uploads/eng/html/cg/cg2012.pdf [accessed 3.11.15]

Managenable.com (2015) Risk Maturity Model [Online] https://www.managenable.com/risk-template/ [accessed 9.11.15]

Marcellis-Warin, N de and Teodoresco, S (2012) Corporate Reputation: Is your most strategic asset at risk? Burgundy Report synthesis document for Centre for Interuniversity Research and Analysis on Organizations Knowledge Into Action (CIRANO) of Quebec Canada and Preventa Inc [Online] http://www.cirano.qc.ca/pdf/publication/2012RB-01.pdf [accessed 3.9.15]

Marks, N (2010) Assessing the Risk Management Program [Blog] Marks on Governance 22 November [Online] file:///Users/Domenic/Documents/Benchmarker%20Project%20RMM%20library%20/Marks%20Assessing%20the%20Risk%20Management%20Program%20221110.webarchive [accessed 28.9.15]

Marsh McLellan, Insurance Maturity Model [Online] http://www.worldinsurance-network.com/news/marsh-launches-new-insurance-maturity-model-060313/ [accessed 9.11.15]

McKinsey (2012) – see Pergler, Martin (2012) in References section

McShane, MK, Nair, A and Rustambekov, E (2010) Does Enterprise Risk Management Increase Firm Value? *Journal of Accounting, Auditing and Finance*, **26** (4), pp 641–58

Mitchell, R (2011) Ascending the Maturity Curve: Effective management of enterprise risk and compliance, *Economist Intelligence Unit* [Online] http://digitalresearch.eiu.com/enterpriseriskandcompliance/report [accessed 3.4.15]

Monahan, G (2008) *Enterprise Risk Management: A methodology for achieving strategic objectives*, Wiley & Sons, United States

Myerson, M (1996) *Risk Management Processes for Software Engineering Models*, Artech House Publishers, United States

NACD (2009) Risk Governance: Balancing risk and reward, *National Association of Corporate Directors Blue Ribbon Commission*, report also known as the Blue Ribbon Report [Online] http://www.wlrk.com/docs/1605831_1.pdf [accessed 5.11.15]

OCEG (2015) Red Book 2.0: 2009: A governance, risk and compliance capability model [Online] http://www.oceg.org/ [accessed 03.10.15]

OGC (2009) Managing Successful Projects with PRINCE2, *Office of Government Commerce UK* [Online] https://www.gov.uk/government/publications/best-management-practice-portfolio/about-the-office-of-government-commerce [accessed 9.11.15]

OGC (2013) Management of Risk: Guidance for practitioners and the international standard on risk management, ISO 31000:2009, white paper, Office of Government Commerce UK, by Michael Dallas, Director of certifiers APM Group Ltd, UK: The Stationery Office, April

OGC Office of Government Commerce Portfolio, Programme and Project Management Maturity Model (P3M3), Version 2.1 (2006) [Online] https://www.axelos.com/best-practice-solutions/p3m3 [accessed 9.11.15]

Paape, L and Speklé, R (2012) The adoption and design of enterprise risk management practices: an empirical study, *European Accounting Review* **21** (3), pp. 533–64

Parkins, S (2009) ERM Readiness Assessment Tool, presentation on behalf of Fraser Health to Healthcare Enterprise Management Conference, Meeting the ERM Integration Challenge, Canada, unpublished

PMI Global Operations Centre (2003) *Organizational Project Management Maturity Model (OPM3®)*, Project Management Institute (PMI), Newtown Square, Pennsylvania, United States

Porter, ME (1985) *Competitive Advantage*, Free Press, United States

Porter, ME (1996) *What is strategy? The Value Chain*, Harvard Business Review, United States

Power, M, Ashby, S and Palermo, T (2013a) Risk Culture in Financial Organisations: Final report, *Financial Services Knowledge Transfer Network* [Online] www.lse.ac.uk/researchAndExpertise/units/CARR/pdf/Final-Risk-Culture-Report.pdf [accessed 01.12.15]

Power, M, Ashby, S and Palermo,T (2013b) Guidance on Supervisory Interaction with Financial Institutions on Risk Culture: Feedback on the FSB's consultative document [Online] http://www.financialstabilityboard.org/wp-content/uploads/c_140206c.pdf [accessed 12.11.15]

PMI (2008) *A Guide to the Project Management Body of Knowledge*, 4th edn, Newton Square, Project Management Institute, United States

Praxiom Research Group (2010) ISO 31000 Introduction [Online] http://www.praxiom.com/iso-31000-intro.htm [accessed 9.11.15]

Protiviti (2006) Guide to ERM: Frequently asked questions [Online] http://www.knowledgeleader.com/KnowledgeLeader/content.nsf/Web+Content/WhitePapersArticlesGuidetoEnterpriseRiskManagementFrequentlyAskedQuestions!OpenDocument [accessed 14.9.14]

Protiviti (2014) Establishing and Nurturing an Effective Risk Culture: Enabling the chief risk officer's success, series white paper [Online] http://www.protiviti.com/en-US/Documents/White-Papers/Risk-Solutions/CRO-Series4-Establishing-and-Nurturing-an-Effective-Risk-Culture-Protiviti.pdf [accessed 9.11.15]

Purdy, G (2008) Executive Workshop: Implementing risk management in 2008, *Institute of Risk Research University of Waterloo* [Online] http://www.irr-neram.ca/pdf_files/May9-2008/report.pdf [accessed 27.9.15]

PwC (2013) Risk Survey 2013 [Online] http://www.pwc.com/gx/en/services/audit-assurance/publications/risk-in-review.html [accessed 9.11.15]

PwC (2015) The Alignment Challenge: How strategic is your ERM program? *How To Achieve Excellent Enterprise Risk Management Series*, Article 2, April 2015

[Online] https://www.pwc.ie/media-centre/assets/publications/2015-pwc-ireland-enterprise-risk-management-erm-strategies.pdf [accessed 9.11.15]

Rasmussen, M (2013) 20/20 Research GRC Enterprise Architecture CMM [Online] http://thriveonrisk.com/conversations/watch/18/The-Future-of-Enterprise-GRC-Architecture, Posted 22 Mar 2013 [accessed 9.11.15]

Rosemann M and Brocke J vom (eds) (2010) *Handbook on Business Process Management 1*, 107 International Handbooks on Information Systems, Springer-Verlag, Berlin Heidelberg

Ryan, T (2011) Business-IT alignment maturity: The correlation of performance indicators and alignment maturity within the commercial airline industry, ProQuest, UMI Dissertation Publishing, BiblioBazaar

Salz, A (2013) An Independent Review of Barclays Business Practices, *Barclays PLC* [Online] http://online.wsj.com/public/resources/documents/SalzReview04032013.pdf [accessed 9.11.15]

Sagacious Consulting (2009) Product Team Maturity Model [Online] http://blog.sagaciousconsulting.com/2009/09/product-team-maturity-model/ [accessed 9.11.15]

Shortbreed, J, Fraser, J, Purdy, G and Schanfield, A (2011) The Future Role of Internal Audit in (Enterprise) Risk Management [Online] https://annex.mville.edu/images/stories/Graduate_Academics/GPSCenterForRiskManagement/ResourceLibrary_Articles/TheFutureRoleofInternalAuditinEnterprise_RiskManagement.pdf [accessed 9.11.15]

Schuh, R (2004) A Maturity Model for Measuring Nonprofit Organizational Development, doctoral dissertation [Online] http://d-scholarship.pitt.edu/8301/ [accessed 9.11.15]

SEC (2009) Rule 33-9089 and 404 [Online] https://www.sec.gov/rules/final/2009/33-9089.pdf [accessed 9.11.15]

SEI (2001) People Capability Maturity Model® (P–CMM®) Version 2.0., *Software Engineering Institute at Carnegie Mellon University* [Online] http://pdf world.net/pdf/71115/People-Capability-Maturity-Model-pdf.php [accessed 9.11.15]

Shore, T (2013a) Enterprise Risk Management At Dubal, unpublished slide presentation, Dubai, UAE

Shore, T (2013b) A Case Study on Enterprise Risk Management Program in the Middle East [Online] https://www.youtube.com/watch?v=AThaJcvFn1c [accessed 9.11.15]

Singapore Corporate Governance Council (2012) Risk Governance Guidance for Listed Board [Online] http://www.mas.gov.sg/~/media/resource/fin_development/corporate_governance/RiskGovernanceGuidanceforListedBoards.ashx [accessed 3.11.15]

Snohomish County (2012) Electricity Subsector Cyber Security CMM PUD [Online] http://www.slideshare.net/EnergySec/john-fry-2012-09251128-esc2-m2-case-study (DA excellent on use for planning) [accessed 9.11.15]

Sturman, M (2013) Transgrid NSW Government Enterprise Risk Management Journey in TransGrid, Transgrid NSW Government TMF Conference paper, p 16 [Online] http://www.google.com/search?client=safari&rls=en&q=NSW+Government+Treasury+ERM+Risk+Maturity+Model+of+2013&ie=UTF-8&oe=UTF-8 [accessed 19.10.15]

Taylor, L (2010) Using the LTRC Risk Management Performance Ladder [Online] http://www.slideshare.net/liztaylor/ltrc-performance-ladder [accessed 10.11.12]

Teil, B (2013) Inductive Design of Maturity Models: Applying the Rasch algorithm for design science research [Online] http://www.abstract.xlibx.com/a-economy/132906-16-vorgelegt-von-david-raber-aus-deutschland-genehmigt-auf-antrag.php [accessed 9.11.15]

Thomson Reuters Survey (2013) The Evolving State of Enterprise Risk Management [Online] https://risk.thomsonreuters.com/whitepaper/evolving-state-enterprise-risk-management [accessed 9.11.15]

UMass Dartmouth (2015) Decision-making process [Online] http://www.umassd.edu/fycm/decisionmaking/process/ [accessed 4.11.15]

Ulrich, D (2012) What's next for HR? The six competencies HR needs for today's challenges [Online] http://www.personneltoday.com/articles/13/11/2012/58988/whats-next-for-hr-the-six-competencies-hr-needs-for-todays-challenges.htm [accessed 9.11.15]

Vergopia, C (2011) Project Review Maturity and Project Performance: An empirical case study, ProQuest, UMI Dissertation Publishing, BiblioBazaar, United States

Versace, M (2011) Enterprise Risk Management – Proof or Still Promise: An ERM maturity model paper, IDC 25 February [Online] https://idc-insights-community.com/financial/financial-services-technology/enterprise-risk-management-proof-or-still-promise [accessed 9.11.15]

Virtual Corp (2015) Business Continuity Maturity Model® (BCMM®) [Online] http://www.virtual-corp.net/Home/Services/BusinessContinuityMaturityModel.aspx [accessed 9.10.15]

Wendler, R (2012) The Maturity of Maturity Model Research: A systematic mapping study, Technische Universität Dresden, Faculty of Business Management and Economics, Helmholtzstraße 10, 01062 Dresden, Germany, *Information and Software Technology*, 54 (12), December, pp 1317–39 [Online] http://www.sciencedirect.com/science/article/pii/S0950584912001334 [accessed 9.11.15]

Wessman, WL (2006) *The Nature of Thought: Maturity of mind*, University Press of America, United States

Witkin, BR and Altschuld, JW (1995) *Planning and Conducting Needs Assessment: A practical guide*, Sage Publications, United States

Yang W (2012) Three-Dimensional Complex Construction Project Management Maturity Model: Case study of 2010 Shanghai Expo [Online] http://www.scientific.net/AMM.209-211.1363 [accessed 9.11.15]

Zurich Insurance (2012) Risk Management in a Time of Global Uncertainty, *Harvard Business Review Analytic Services* [Online] https://hbr.org/2012/03/risk-management-in-a-time-of-g.html [accessed 9.11.15]

INDEX

Note: The index is filed in alphabetical, word-by-word order. Within main headings, numbers are filed as spelt out in full, acronyms are filed as presented, ISO and ISO/IEC codes are filed in numerical order. Page locators in *italics* denote information contained within a Figure or Table.

Printed and bound by CPI Group (UK) Ltd, Croydon, CR0 4YY

16/09/2026

14963407-0002